VITAL SIGNS

2001

Other Norton/Worldwatch Books

VITAL SIGNS

2001

The Trends That Are Shaping Our Future

WORLDWATCH INSTITUTE

Janet N. Abramovitz
Lester R. Brown
Seth Dunn
Christopher Flavin
Hilary French
Gary Gardner
Brian Halweil
Ann Hwang
Janet Larsen
Nicholas Lenssen

Lisa Mastny
Ashley Mattoon
Anne Platt McGinn
Danielle Nierenberg
Michael Renner
David M. Roodman
Payal Sampat
Molly O. Sheehan
John E. Young
Linda Starke, *Editor*

In cooperation with the United Nations Environment Programme
UNEP

W.W. Norton & Company
New York   London

VITAL SIGNS and WORLDWATCH INSTITUTE trademarks are registered in the U.S. Patent and
Trademark Office.

The views expressed are those of the authors and do not necessarily represent those of the
Worldwatch Institute; of its directors, officers, or staff; of the United Nations Environment
Programme; or of any funders.

The text of this book is composed in ITC Berkeley Oldstyle with the display set in Optima

Composition by the Worldwatch Institute; manufacturing by the Haddon Craftsmen, Inc.
Book design by Elizabeth Doherty.

ISBN 0-393-32176-2 (pbk)

W.W. Norton & Company, Inc.
500 Fifth Avenue, New York, NY 10110
W.W. Norton & Company Ltd.
10 Coptic Street, London WC1A 1PU

1 2 3 4 5 6 7 8 9 0

♻ This book is printed on recycled paper.

New This Year: Worldwatch CD-ROM

Worldwatch offers the data from all graphs and tables contained in this book, as well as all other Worldwatch publications, on CD-ROM for use with PC or Macintosh computers. This includes data from the *State of the World* and *Vital Signs* series of books, Worldwatch Papers, and *World Watch* magazine in an easy to use, searchable format. In addition, the complete text of this year's editions of *State of the World* and *Vital Signs* are included in Adobe PDF format. For more information or to order, please see our website (www.worldwatch.org), or call (800) 555-2028 or (301) 567-9522; e-mail wwpub@worldwatch.org.

Visit our website at www.worldwatch.org

TABLE OF CONTENTS

PART ONE: KEY INDICATORS

PART TWO: SPECIAL FEATURES

ACKNOWLEDGMENTS

Each year, *Vital Signs* draws on the analytical and writing efforts of the entire research staff of Worldwatch Institute. Throughout the year, our researchers are busy following key trends, even while researching and writing papers and articles in their varied areas of expertise. Our full-time staff is joined in this tenth anniversary edition by two former senior researchers, Nicholas Lenssen and John Young, as well as by former interns Ann Hwang and Danielle Nierenberg, who has now joined Worldwatch as an adjunct researcher.

Independent editor Linda Starke once again brought a steady hand and years of experience to bear in unifying 49 manuscripts produced by 19 different authors scattered in a half-dozen locations to ensure consistency and readability throughout the book. Other members of the Institute's staff also play a vital role. Lori Brown and Jonathan Guzman run our library and ensure that researchers have access to the latest books, reports, and magazine articles and stay abreast of important studies and Web resources. Reah Janise Kauffman served as an invaluable liaison with the foreign publishers of *Vital Signs*.

Names not found in the individual bylines but nonetheless critical to this book our operations team of Barbara Fallin, Suzanne Clift, and Sharon Lapier; our development team of Mary Redfern and Millicent Johnson; our communications team of Dick Bell, Leanne Mitchell, and Niki Clark; and Joseph Gravely, who is responsible for shipping out publications.

Over the last year we redesigned the cover and several of the internal elements of *Vital Signs* to enhance its visual attractiveness and highlight its interdisciplinary nature. Many "vital signs," for example, now include a small box to alert readers to related pieces they might find of interest. Ed Ayres, Dick Bell, Hilary French, Brian Halweil, Millicent Johnson, Michael Renner, Molly O'Meara Sheehan, Linda Starke, Christine Stearn, and Denise Warden volunteered their time to accomplish the redesign. But Art Director Elizabeth Doherty played the most crucial role, on top of her already considerable responsibilities in connection with desktop production of *Vital Signs* and other Worldwatch publications. Three photos Liz chose to use are from Photoshare, the online photo database of the Media/Materials Clearinghouse at the JHU/Population Information Program at <www.jhuccp.org/mmc>.

All contributions to this book were reviewed by in-house staff as well as by a number of outside experts. For particular help with data requests, advice, or feedback on drafts, the authors wish to thank Claudine Aholou Putz, Wasantha Bandarage, Ed Benjamin, Greg Bischak, Ed Bos, Colin Couchman, Martin Dasek, Satoshi Fujino, Frank Jamerson, Clive James, Paul Jenner, Ken Kassem, Katrina Kulp, Rich Liroff, Birger Madsen, Paul Maycock, Gerhard Metschies, Donald Mitchell, Martin Palmer, John Pilgrim, Pat Plunkert, Sandra Postel, Matthew Quinlan, Annette Renner, Robert Rice, Jose Santamarta, Wolfgang Schreiber, Joseph Sheehan, Vladimir Slivyak, Carrie Smith, Ron Srnka, Alison Stattersfield,

Guy Taylor, Arnella Trent, Andreas Wagner, and Timothy Whorf.

At W.W. Norton & Company, our U.S. publisher, we are grateful to Lucinda Bartley, Amy Cherry, Andrew Marasia, and their colleagues for expediting our manuscript through the printing and publishing process. We thank them for their steady support over the years.

We also want to thank our new partner in *Vital Signs*, the United Nations Environment Programme. As described in the Foreword, we are now working together to provide the information and analysis needed to guide solid decisionmaking on environmental matters around the world. We thank Executive Director Klaus Töpfer and his entire staff in Nairobi and around the world for their dedication to the issues that we and they are so concerned about.

We are grateful to the W. Alton Jones Foundation for its funding of *Vital Signs 2001* and *Vital Signs 2002*, marking the tenth year of such support. The Jones Foundation's support of *Vital Signs* since its inception is central to allowing us to produce this volume each year. We thank Pete Myers, Charlie Moore, and the Board of the Jones Foundation for their dedication to a sustainable world and for their excellent work in nearly all of the fields that Worldwatch Institute focuses on, from climate change to biological diversity.

Some of the data we present in this book are outgrowths of our general research, conducted in the course of putting together *State of the World*, Worldwatch Papers, and *World Watch* magazine. We would therefore also like to thank the foundations that have supported this work during the past year: the Geraldine R. Dodge Foundation, the Ford Foundation, the Richard & Rhoda Goldman Fund, the William and Flora Hewlett Foundation, the John D. and Catherine T. MacArthur Foundation, the Charles Stewart Mott Foundation, the David and Lucile Packard Foundation, the Summit Foundation, the Turner Foundation, the Wallace Global Fund, the Weeden Foundation, and the Winslow Foundation.

In addition, we would like to acknowledge the support of the more than 2,000 individuals who provided financial support through the Friends of Worldwatch program last year. Our special appreciation goes to the members of the Institute's Council of Sponsors—Tom and Cathy Crain, James and Deanna Dehlsen, Roger and Vicki Sant, Robert Wallace and Raisa Scriabine, and Eckart Wintzen—and to the group of Benefactors: Adam and Rachel Albright, Junko Edahiro, Sara and Ed Groark, Hunter Lewis, and Izaak van Melle.

This year, we also want to note with pain the passing of one of the leading thinkers in the sustainable development field, a person whose ideas have helped inspire and guide our publications. Donella H. Meadows, one of the co-authors of *Limits to Growth* in 1972, died this winter after a brief illness. Dana, as she was known, who taught at Dartmouth College, was one of the first scientists to develop the field of global trend analysis, and we are thankful for both her intellectual and her moral support over the last quarter-century. Her commitment and humanity inspired scores of young people to work in the field of global sustainability.

* * *

New this year, all the data in the tables and figures in *Vital Signs* are available on CD-ROM (see page 6 for ordering information). And individual *Vital Signs* indicators can be downloaded in Adobe PDF format from our Web site, <secure.worldwatch.org/cgi-bin/wwinst/titles/vs>. Please send us your ideas for future *Vital Signs* indicators. You can reach us by e-mail (worldwatch@worldwatch.org), fax (202-296-7365), or regular mail.

Michael Renner, Project Director
March 2001

Worldwatch Institute
1776 Massachusetts Ave., N.W.
Washington DC 20036

FOREWORD

This year, for the first time, Worldwatch Institute and the United Nations Environment Programme (UNEP) have joined forces on *Vital Signs*. These two organizations, with a common dedication to achieving a healthy global environment, have worked together on this tenth volume of the series that Worldwatch launched in 1992. We believe that *Vital Signs 2001* provides decisionmakers and the public the latest and most complete picture of the health of the planet and its people.

UNEP is the principal United Nations body in the field of the environment. It plays a lead role in shaping the global environmental agenda, and in forging and implementing important environmental agreements. In recent years, UNEP has stepped up its efforts to analyze the state of the global environment and to assess global and regional trends, providing early warning of environmental threats.

This new collaboration is intended to maximize the synergy between an official United Nations body and a private, nonprofit research institute—drawing on our combined analytical strengths and our complementary abilities to reach key audiences around the world. At this time of rapid and confusing change, we are particularly keen on providing the information and insights the world will need as it approaches the World Summit on Sustainable Development in Johannesburg next year.

With this tenth edition of *Vital Signs*, we reach an important milestone. In *Vital Signs 2001*, we now have data for the year 2000. This has given us a full half-century perspective on many of the trends we follow, since most of our data sets begin in 1950, when global record-keeping became much more comprehensive and systematic.

For decades, analysts have been using the year 2000 as the end point for their long-term forecasts and projections. Now that this year has become a vantage point for looking backward, the view is breathtaking. The last half-century has been a period of sweeping, unprecedented change: change in the economy, change in society, and change in the very biosphere of the planet. Indeed, very few projections for the year 2000 have come anywhere close to the mark. Today we live in a world that is economically richer than could have been hoped for a half-century ago, but one that is ecologically poorer than hardly anyone could have imagined. Here are some of the trends of the last 50 years that are chronicled in this volume:

- There are now just over 6 billion people on the planet, up 3.5 billion since 1950, which means more than a doubling in just 50 years. Most of the growth has come in developing countries, many of them already overcrowded. The number of city residents has grown even faster—up fourfold since the middle of the twentieth century.
- The world economy has grown even more dramatically: up almost sevenfold in 50 years. This added wealth translates into

vast improvements in living standards—from nutrition to housing, health care, and transportation. But 1.2 billion people still live in severe poverty, and an estimated 1.1 billion do not have clean, safe water to drink.

- The world grain harvest has nearly tripled since 1950, allowing billions of people to enrich their diets. But the abundance of food has come at a price: falling freshwater aquifers and severe water pollution from massive use of fertilizers and pesticides. Despite the increase in production, over a billion people are still undernourished, while another billion are actually overnourished, which has created a global epidemic of obesity that is now spreading to the developing world.

- Emissions of carbon dioxide, the leading greenhouse gas, have risen by nearly 300 percent since 1950, boosting its concentration in the atmosphere to its highest level in at least 420,000 years. New scientific studies project dramatic changes in the climate in the current century, leading to increased storm intensity, agricultural losses, and economic disruptions due to accelerated global warming from the additional greenhouse gases.

- The world has lost more than half its wetlands and over one quarter of its coral reefs—losses that continue to accelerate. And the species that depend on these natural habitats are also in decline. Of the approximately 9,900 bird species that have been identified, 12 percent are threatened with extinction.

If there is one lesson of this extraordinary half-century, it is that most trends defy prediction by experts. The most important changes have generally come abruptly, with little warning. We never seem to know where the latest economic crisis or ecological catastrophe will come from, but we do know that the projections of smooth, gradual change that computer models churn out are almost always wrong. Until the 1970s, for example, oil forecasters were projecting exponential growth in demand

and steady, low prices through the end of the century—until severe oil shocks forced a wholesale revision in this sanguine outlook. The forecasters then moved as a herd to the conclusion that an era of permanent shortages would drive oil prices over $100 per barrel in 2000—just in time for the collapse of oil prices to $10 per barrel in the mid-1980s.

As the world becomes ever more complex, predicting the future becomes an ever less productive enterprise. But planning for the future can minimize the risks and maximize the opportunities presented by a fast-changing world. From this perspective, the challenge of the twenty-first century is to extend the economic progress of the last 50 years while halting the ecological decline and social misery that have sometimes marred this remarkable period. The first step is to understand the clear message that emerges from the welter of statistics in *Vital Signs 2001*: despite all the wonders of the modern information age, the human economy emerged from Earth's biosphere and remains dependent on it. A sick planet will, sooner or later, lead to a faltering economy.

The last year brought vivid reminders of that dependence. Just as the information economy fell to Earth, soaring oil and natural gas prices showed the economy's reliance on fuels contained in that earth. And the impressive proliferation of high-tech drugs and medical treatments was unable to prevent catastrophic new epidemics of human and animal diseases—or the social and economic chaos that have come with them. At the same time, computer-based weather forecasts have become remarkably sophisticated—but failed to prevent the economic toll of natural disasters from reaching $608 billion in the 1990s, more than 15 times the total for the 1950s.

The dramatic spread of democracy and open markets in the last decade, together with explosions in technology and communications, could lead to revolutionary change that would make the world a better place. But this will only happen if humanity acknowledges—and acts on the knowledge—that we remain dependent on a healthy natural world. Global integration provides the opportunity to raise living standards around the world, but also forces us to confront the fact that AIDS and foot-and-mouth disease can be efficiently carried halfway round the world in a matter of hours on the same aircraft that move people and goods so efficiently.

The new century has begun with many surprises, most of them unwelcome. But one thing is virtually certain: the next half-century will not see a repeat of the trends of the one just past. Earth simply will not support it. The question is whether humanity will forge a healthier, sustainable future or risk the downward spiral that would be the result of failing to understand the ecological and economic threshold on which we now stand. We hope that the statistical snapshot contained in *Vital Signs 2001* will help provide that understanding.

Christopher Flavin
President
Worldwatch Institute

Klaus Töpfer
Executive Director
United Nations Environment Programme

VITAL SIGNS

2001

TECHNICAL NOTE

Units of measure throughout this book are metric unless common usage dictates otherwise. Historical population data used in per capita calculations are from the Center for International Research at the U.S. Bureau of the Census. Historical data series in *Vital Signs* are updated each year, incorporating any revisions by originating organizations.

Data expressed in U.S. dollars have for the most part been deflated to 1999 terms. In some cases, the original data source provided the numbers in deflated terms or supplied an appropriate deflator, as with gross world product data. Where this did not happen, the U.S. implicit gross national product (GNP) deflator from the U.S. Department of Commerce was used to represent price trends in real terms.

OVERVIEW

The Triple Health Challenge

Michael Renner

This edition of *Vital Signs* presents a three-dimensional, integrated picture of Earth's health—environmental, human, and economic. Today's economy—thriving on massive resource use, generating large amounts of pollutants, and disrupting natural cycles—imposes increasingly unsustainable burdens on the environment. And the deterioration of critical ecosystems like wetlands and coral reefs can boomerang: communities have less protection against extreme weather events, and disease vectors are able to spread more easily, compromising human health and well-being. Measures taken in the name of furthering public health, on the other hand, can sometimes throw natural balances out of kilter: the escalating use of antibiotics, for instance, helps produce more virulent infectious disease strains. Environmental crises and health epidemics translate into rising economic costs—in the form of property losses from natural disasters and skyrocketing health care bills.

The health of human societies and the natural environment is strongly related to how robust they are in the face of adverse developments. Resilience derives in large part from diversity. Yet modern societies and economies have pursued specialization to the point where much of our rich biological and cultural diversity has vanished. This is true for livestock and birds as well as for coffee plantations and languages. The 49 trends documented in *Vital Signs 2001* provide some measure of that disappearing diversity, and of recent attempts to bolster our resilience.

ECOSYSTEM HEALTH

Decimating forests, damming rivers, draining wetlands, spreading copious amounts of toxic and long-lived materials, and destabilizing the climate have all contributed to an unraveling of Earth's complex ecological safety net.

More than half the world's wetlands vanished during the past century, for example—primarily in the northern hemisphere during the first half and mostly in the South during the second half. (See Figure 1 and pages 96–97.) Half of the remaining coastal wetlands are likely to be lost by 2080 to agriculture, urban sprawl, and rising sea levels as a consequence of climate change. These marshes, bogs, swamps, and peatlands provide a range of vital services: regulating water flow, recharging groundwater supplies, providing flood control, retaining essential nutrients, buffering other ecosystems against contaminants, and offering habitat for diverse biological communities.

The health of coral reefs worldwide is also deteriorating rapidly. (See Figure 2 and pages 92–93.) The share of reefs severely damaged rose from 10 percent as recently as 1992 to 27 percent in late 2000. Reefs provide a range of crucial ecological services and goods. They shelter coastlines from storm damage, erosion, and flooding, serving as protection for an estimated half-billion people, and they provide habitat for as many as 1 million different species. But they are also important feeding and breeding grounds for commercial fisheries, producing one tenth the global fish catch.

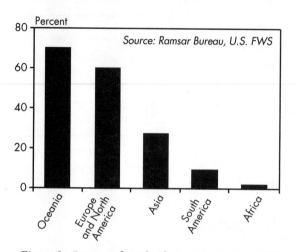

Figure 1: Percent of Wetlands Lost, by Region, 2000

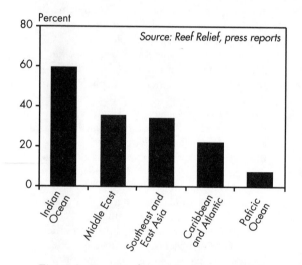

Figure 2: Percent of Coral Reefs Destroyed, by Region, 2000

The decay of ecosystems sets the stage for more frequent and more devastating "un-natural" disasters—natural disturbances made worse by human actions. (See pages 116–17.) And human vulnerability has increased due to the migration of people to coastal areas and urban centers and the expansion of the built environment. More than one third of humanity dwells within 100 kilometers of a coastline.

Climate change threatens to intensify many of the problems. Coral reefs, for instance, live at the upper edge of their temperature tolerance, and rising ocean temperatures spell greater stress for reefs. Impaired coral reefs are in turn less able to provide shelter against the rising storms associated with climate change. Climate change also expands the geographic reach of the *Anopheles* mosquito that transmits malaria. (See pages 134–35.)

Fossil fuel combustion has been a major driver of climate change. Although the use of oil, coal, and natural gas has declined slightly—down 0.3 percent from 1998—it is still extremely close to recent peak levels. (See pages 40–41.) One of the main factors is the unabated growth in the number of cars on the world's roads and the distances driven in them, along with inadequate progress in boosting fuel economy to offset these increases. Global automobile production rose 4 percent in 2000 to reach a record 40.9 million vehicles, and the total fleet grew to 532 million. (See pages 68–69.)

With annual carbon emissions from fossil-fuel combustion quadrupling over the past half-century to about 6.3 billion tons in 2000, a total of almost 220 billion tons of carbon have been released into the atmosphere. (See pages 52–53.) Carbon dioxide is only one of several greenhouse gases; chlorofluorocarbons, methane, and nitrous oxide play important additional roles. So do perfluorocarbons, released in the process of aluminum smelting—an energy-intensive and polluting process that has expanded 16-fold since 1950. (See pages 64–65.)

In order to stave off full-blown climate change, large-scale reductions in carbon emissions far beyond the 0.6-percent decline achieved in 2000 are needed. Unless drastic action is taken, however, annual emissions are actually expected to grow to 9–12 billion tons by

2020 and possibly to twice that number by 2050. In a new assessment in January 2001, the Intergovernmental Panel on Climate Change revised upward its projections for temperature increases during this century, which would make more frequent weather events—both droughts and storms—more likely. (See pages 50–51.)

Modern agriculture, too, is imposing significant environmental burdens. Livestock populations have almost tripled since 1961 and currently contribute 16 percent of total emissions of methane, a greenhouse gas far more potent than carbon dioxide. (See pages 100–01.) Traditional mixed farming systems, in which farm animals are kept in close proximity to crop production, allow for animal wastes to be returned to the soil—a practice that has helped maintain soil fertility and limited the need for synthetic fertilizers. Today this approach is often giving way to input-intensive methods. North America and Europe pioneered this industrial production system, but it is now spreading to countries like Brazil, China, and India.

Under the so-called feedlot system, accumulated animal wastes present a major threat to soil, air, and water quality. Groundwater resources are threatened by contamination from the excess nutrients in livestock manure and from agricultural runoff. Water quality worldwide is imperiled by these and a range of other sources that dump nitrates, pesticides, petrochemicals, arsenic, chlorinated solvents, and radioactive wastes into aquifers.

PUBLIC HEALTH

Societies across the planet confront a resurgence of infectious diseases, some well-known and some previously unknown. AIDS and malaria are among the biggest killers, causing the deaths of several million people each year. The spread of microbes that cause these diseases is facilitated by international travel, agricultural trade, and human population movements—all of which are on the upswing. (See pages 62–63 and 142–43.)

Environmental factors also play an impor-tant role in human susceptibility to and transmission of diseases, particularly malaria, diarrheal diseases, and acute respiratory infections. Worldwide, close to one fourth of all disabilities can be traced back to such factors as polluted air and water and unsafe food. More than 3 million people die each year worldwide from water-related diseases, mostly in developing countries. (See pages 94–95.)

The AIDS crisis marches on. To date, some 58 million people have been infected with HIV, the virus that causes AIDS; of these, 22 million have succumbed to the disease. (See pages 78–79.) And each year, nearly 6 million additional people are newly infected. Sub-Saharan Africa faces the most severe challenge: it is home to two thirds of the world's HIV-positive population. There, as elsewhere, people living in poverty, minorities, and women are hardest hit by the disease.

Malaria has staged a lethal comeback. (See pages 134–35.) It has been riding the coattails of environmental degradation (logging, dam- and road-building, and the warmer temperatures and increased precipitation associated with climate change) and the social upheaval caused by wars and refugee flows. Malaria remains one of the world's deadliest diseases, each year infecting nearly a half-billion people and claiming more than a million lives. Although close to 40 percent of the world's population is at risk, again inhabitants of sub-Saharan Africa are most affected. Among Africans, the death rate from malaria is nine times higher than the global average (see Figure 3), a consequence of higher exposure to disease vectors, the emergence of drug-resistant strains, and the sad fact of grossly inadequate health services.

Increasing drug resistance among microbes that cause a range of deadly illnesses makes many of these diseases harder and more expensive to control and threatens to reverse public health achievements of the past half-century. (See pages 132–33.) A key factor in making microbes more immune to drug treatment is the skyrocketing use of antibiotics and other antimicrobial drugs. At least half of all anti-

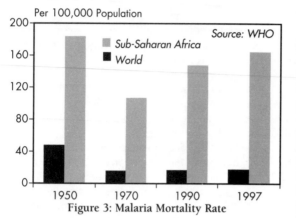

Figure 3: Malaria Mortality Rate

biotics used worldwide are believed to be prescribed unnecessarily, partly because of patient demand, but often also as a result of pressure from pharmaceutical companies and health management groups.

Another reason for rising drug resistance is the surging use in agriculture, horticulture, and animal husbandry of many of the same antibiotics used in human medicine. The ever-present threat of disease outbreaks in feedlots, where livestock are kept in intensive confinement, is strong incentive for massive applications of antibiotics. But farmers also know they can boost livestock growth by mixing antibiotics into animal feed. The practice of intensive feeding of grain, antibiotics, and hormones dramatically cuts the time required for cattle to reach market weight. (See pages 100–01.)

Industrial methods in animal husbandry have come into heavy disrepute in Europe with the outbreak of "mad cow" and foot-and-mouth disease in the United Kingdom and several other nations. Millions of people now question the once routine consumption of meat and meat products and consider industrial livestock production a prime threat to maintaining public health.

The pervasive use of synthetic materials has also triggered concern about health and environmental impacts. One example is polyvinyl chloride (PVC), the second most common plastic in the world. (See pages 110–11.) Some 250 million tons are in use today in building mate-

rials, packaging, electrical wiring, and many consumer goods, and 100 million tons have already been discarded. Production continues to grow rapidly—rising 39 percent between 1992 and 1999. But both PVC production and disposal generate highly toxic waste products. Dioxins, furans, and other compounds pollute the air, can leach into the soil and bodies of water, or can be ingested by plants, fish, and people. Consumers, governments, and private companies are increasingly questioning the use of PVCs, particularly since alternatives exist for most applications.

Illnesses induced by lifestyle choices are another key public health concern. Each year, 4 million people die prematurely from tobacco-related illnesses. World cigarette production remains near record levels, though per capita supplies are down more than 10 percent over the past decade. (See pages 76–77.) Although growing numbers of people in industrial nations reject smoking, cigarette sales in developing countries are on a strong upward trajectory. China is the world's leading consumer of cigarettes. But the increase in smoking is especially pronounced in Africa—if current growth rates continue over the next two decades, more Africans could die from tobacco-related illnesses than from AIDS, malaria, and childbirth complications combined.

Increasingly sedentary lifestyles are a key factor behind a new global epidemic: over-weight and obesity, its more extreme form. (See pages 136–37.) Obesity closely correlates with trends in television viewing and car ownership, both of which indicate a lack of adequate physical activity. Inadequate exercise, together with high consumption of sugar and fat, explains why one out of six people worldwide is now considered overweight. This is a major factor behind chronic diseases such as stroke, heart disease, cancer, and diabetes, which exert strong upward pressure on health care costs. Although these diseases of affluence are found predominantly in industrial countries, developing countries are increasingly affected: the

World Health Organization predicts that chronic diseases will surpass infectious ones as a burden on developing countries over the next quarter-century.

Health care expenditures have grown rapidly over the past 50 years, outpacing the growth of the overall economy and becoming one of its largest sectors. (See pages 138–39.) Skyrocketing health care outlays are in part driven by rising costs for prescription drugs. At the same time, health expenditures are heavily skewed toward the wealthier parts of humanity; hundreds of millions of poor people have no access to basic and affordable care.

The best-selling drugs are designed to treat First World illnesses, including heart disease, high blood pressure, and indigestion. Seeing a market without much purchasing power, pharmaceutical companies have tended to neglect the health needs of large chunks of the planet, including research on malaria vaccines. (See pages 106–07.) Only 1 percent of 1,233 new drugs that reached the market between 1975 and 1997 were approved specifically for tropical diseases. Roughly one third of humanity lacks regular access to essential drugs; one fourth of all children do not receive routine immunization with the six basic vaccines against polio, diphtheria, whooping cough, tetanus, measles, and tuberculosis.

ECONOMIC HEALTH

Ecosystem breakdown and a rising disease burden are increasingly taxing economic health, particularly that of poorer countries and of the poor within all societies. In the worst cases, environmental and health deterioration could trigger economic decay and social fragmentation, and perhaps even political upheaval.

The past 50 years have seen a dramatic increase in great disasters, which as noted earlier have increasingly been helped along by the human hand. At more than $600 billion, the economic toll of natural disasters during the 1990s alone was more than that of the previous four decades combined. (See pages 116–17.) More than 2 billion people worldwide were

affected by disasters in the 1990s.

Untreated yet treatable diseases not only cause unnecessary illness, suffering, and premature death, they also represent an economic burden. For example, African economies have lost an estimated $100 billion over the past 35 years due to malaria alone—losses that many of these struggling economies can ill afford. (See pages 134–35.) Resistant infections are costlier to treat than regular ones, and translate into prohibitive costs in poorer countries. The cost differential between highly resistant and regular strains of tuberculosis, for instance, can be as high as 100. (See pages 132–33.) As infectious diseases spread and more drug-resistant strains emerge, the prospect is one of escalating costs.

AIDS is killing the most economically productive people—the young, a cornerstone of any country's work force. The disease also has a devastating impact on education prospects in many countries. It is responsible for 70 percent of the deaths of teachers in Côte d'Ivoire, for instance. (See pages 148–49.) This epidemic, in concert with other diseases, threatens to overwhelm the feeble health systems of many developing countries. In just two decades, AIDS has erased a half-century's gains in life expectancy in many African nations. The impacts are severe enough to threaten social stability in nations that are already reeling economically and hard hit by violent conflicts raging on their territories. (See pages 82–83.)

The explosive rise in drug costs is affecting health care systems worldwide, making the profits (and great profitability) of the drug industry an increasingly controversial political issue. (See pages 106–07.) Reducing the cost of pharmaceuticals is a life-and-death issue for the poor. The need to make treatment affordable is particularly urgent for the millions of people living with HIV/AIDS. But this has turned into a high-stakes battle for markets and public opinion. Although a few pharmaceutical companies have agreed to reduce prices, many others—focused on their bottom lines—have opposed cheaper generic drugs offered by companies in Brazil and India.

The specter of unaffordable drugs would

appear to be a paradox in a world that ostensibly grows richer year after year. The world economy has expanded sevenfold since 1950, from $6 trillion to $43 trillion in 2000 (in 1999 dollars). (See pages 56–57.) But gross national product is clearly not a good indicator of how sound an economy is, how well people's current needs are being met, and how people will fare in the future. In fact, the economy is growing in part because the rising expenditures to deal with environmental and social calamities are counted as if they contributed to, rather than subtracted from, human well-being.

Economic health depends not just on a sufficiently large economic pie, but also on how that pie is sliced. The rewards and amenities that the economy provides continue to be divided up in extremely unequal fashion. In recent years, stock markets became increasingly prominent, with their capitalization rising to rival the size of the world economy by the late 1990s, driving a consumption boom in the United States and other western economies. (See pages 112–13.) But highly unequal stock ownership has contributed to a widening of wealth disparities not seen in many decades. And the volatility of equities markets that has been seen in recent months can potentially wreak havoc in an economy and distort social and economic development.

Even as the global economy continued on its upward trajectory, many developing countries were hard pressed to cover the basics. Following the largest single-year increase in 1998, the foreign debt of these nations remained high in 1999—$2.6 trillion. (See Figure 4 and pages 58–59.) While Latin American countries have managed to reduce their debt burden in recent years, other developing and former Eastern bloc nations have not. And sub-Saharan Africa confronts the specter of debt eating away at an ever growing share of its economy.

Many developing countries are struggling with an endless slide in the prices that their

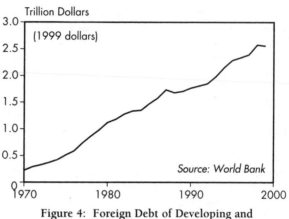

Figure 4: Foreign Debt of Developing and Former Eastern Bloc Nations, 1970–99

raw materials fetch in the world market; 65 nations rely on a single commodity for 40 percent or more of their foreign-exchange income. (See pages 122–23.) On average, nonfuel commodity prices are at less than half their mid-1970s level, and at only one third their 1900 level. Consequently, exporting countries have had to sell ever larger amounts of raw materials to make up for the decline in prices; in fact, so many have pursued the same export-oriented strategy that prices have been weakened even more. In the quest for export revenues—needed to pay off ballooning foreign debts—the environment has become a casualty of stepped-up mining, logging, and other resource extraction operations.

World coffee production, for instance, hit an all-time record in 2000. (See pages 36–37.) The higher yields that powered much of this growth have largely come from a shift from traditional mixed-use plots shaded by trees to larger areas of land where coffee is grown in monoculture fashion in the full sun. This has contributed to deforestation, to loss of biodiversity, and, because of heavier use of fertilizers and pesticides, to water pollution and the poisoning of farmland.

Food trade has grown particularly fast, quadrupling in volume and nearly tripling in dollar value since 1961. (See pages 62–63.) But falling world market prices for agricultural products have thrown many farmers in developing and industrial nations into rising debt, even as local food markets are increasingly embattled by cheap imports frequently controlled by a handful of transnational corporations.

SOLUTIONS

Even as the challenges to environmental, public, and economic health are rising, it is becoming clear what some of the solutions might look like. *Vital Signs 2001* discusses a number of these.

The rise in the prominence of stock markets and the growing influence of private corporations has motivated efforts to promote socially and environmentally responsible investing. (See pages 114–15.) This has taken a number of forms, including the channeling of money into investment funds that screen companies according to a variety of criteria, such as labor standards, environmental protection, and human rights. Many of these funds attempt to screen out the tobacco and military industries in particular. In the United States, money invested according to social and environmental criteria grew to about $2 trillion in 1999, or about one eighth of the total funds under professional management in the nation. Using a different approach, shareholder activists have tried to steer corporate policy toward more sustainable practices, introducing shareholder resolutions on issues like climate change, old-growth forests, genetically engineered organisms, and tobacco.

Whereas efforts to promote more responsible investment paths aim at the realms of high finance, microcredit initiatives try to help the poor overcome poverty and health problems. (See pages 110–11.) Microcredit, the provision of small-scale financial services to those not served by commercial banks and other lenders, is expanding rapidly. Almost 24 million people found assistance through such programs in 1999 (see Table 1),

and the aim is to reach 100 million by 2005. Some of the most effective programs combine income-generating activities with educational efforts, covering such topics as immunization against infectious diseases, diarrhea prevention, and HIV/AIDS counseling. Microcredit programs offer particular hope to women, who account for a disproportionate share of the recipients of small-scale loans. Although such loans hold considerable promise, it is also clear that they alone cannot serve the needs of the extremely poor; improved social security programs are still essential. (See pages 150–51.)

Besides socially responsible investment endeavors, there are also "ethical" consumer initiatives. Support for organically grown and "fair trade" coffee (produced under fair price and working conditions), though a small share of global coffee sales, is expanding rapidly. Such efforts are crucial to support coffee-growing that does not damage the environment irreparably or cause grave harm to the health of millions of coffee growers and workers. (See pages 36–37.)

Modern chemistry is no longer regarded as

Table 1: Growth and Composition of Microfinance Institution Clients, 1999

Region	Number of Clients	Increase over 1998	Poorest as Share of Clients[1]
	(thousand)	(percent)	
Africa	3,834	29	68
Asia	18,427	10	57
Latin America and the Caribbean	1,110	12	48
Middle East	47	6	61
North America	47	16	61
Europe and Countries in Transition	44	8	42
World	23,556	12	58

[1] The bottom 50 percent of a country's population living below the poverty line.
Source: Microcredit Summit, "Empowering Women with Microcredit: 2000 Microcredit Summit Campaign Report," <www.microcredit summit.org/campaigns/report00.html>, viewed 26 February 2001.

an unblemished blessing. Now efforts are directed at limiting or stopping the use of compounds that have proved to be highly toxic. In December 2000, officials from 122 nations signed a treaty to phase out a dozen of the most dangerous chemicals ever created, which are part of a group called persistent organic pollutants. The pesticide DDT is to be eliminated under this agreement. But since it has been used in malaria control efforts, some temporary exemptions were granted until alternatives can be phased in. The 1998 Roll Back Malaria Program, initiated by the World Bank and others, combines safer chemicals and nonchemical tools with efforts to strengthen public health systems. (See pages 134–35.)

A number of products and materials that carry high health risks or whose impacts are uncertain are attracting increasing scrutiny, and sometimes rejection, by consumers. This has been the case for PVC plastics, cigarettes, meat (following highly publicized outbreaks of mad cow disease and growing concern over the use of antibiotics in feed), and genetically modified crops.

In previous editions of *Vital Signs*, we have noted the promise that emerging wind power and solar electricity technologies hold for shifting away from our heavy reliance on fossil fuels. Though still contributing only a small share of the world's energy, both continued to surge in 2000. (See pages 44–47.) Ten times as much electricity is generated through wind power now as in 1990, and production of photovoltaic or solar cells is 10 times larger than in 1987. For now, applications of these innovative energy sources are concentrated in industrial countries.

Efficiency improvements are as crucial as developing renewable sources of energy. In *Vital Signs 2001*, we report on energy use in aluminum production, one of the most energy-intensive industries on Earth. (See pages 64–65.) Producing aluminum from recycled materials takes only 5 percent as much energy as producing it from bauxite ore. Recycled aluminum now accounts for 26 percent of total aluminum production, up just slightly from 21 percent in 1950 (and much of this is from alu-

minum scrap rather than "post-consumer" materials). A major expansion of post-consumer recycling is both possible and necessary in order to rein in the industry's large energy consumption.

Reducing the extreme reliance on cars in modern transportation could also save substantial amounts of energy. Recovering from a three-year decline, global bicycle production in 2000 rose by 22 percent, buoyed by rising purchases in China, Europe, and the United States. (See pages 70–71.) Bicycling also has important health benefits for people who need to lose weight. Another alternative to the automobile, urban light rail, is becoming increasingly popular. (See pages 126–27.) In Western Europe, a decades-long decline in this form of transportation has been reversed, and in the United States, light-rail riders are the fastest-growing segment of public transit riders. In combination, light rail systems and bicycling offer an attractive alternative to cars in many urban settings, provided that population densities are sufficiently high.

Finally, meeting the triple health challenge and achieving sustainability is not only about better technologies. Awareness and spiritual commitment to saving the planet and its inhabitants are critical. Religious communities of all different faiths are becoming a significant force for environmental change. (See pages 146–47.) Activities range from advocating sustainable resource use to supporting efforts to protect Earth's biological heritage, improving the stewardship of the estimated 5 percent of the world's land directly owned or controlled by religious groups, spurring green markets, and promoting energy alternatives. Many of these efforts derive from a desire to restore balance to the relationship of humans and their natural environment in a world that all too often worships at the altar of unbridled consumerism. The holistic nature of religious teachings helps reinforce the understanding that solutions will be most effective if they address environmental, human, and economic health together.

PART ONE

Key Indicators

Food and Agriculture Trends

World Grain Harvest Drops

Soybean Harvest Sets Record

Fertilizer Use Rises

Milk Production Maintains Momentum

Coffee Production Hits New High

Lester R. Brown

The world grain harvest dropped from 1,869 million tons in 1999 to 1,840 million tons in 2000.[1] (See Figure 1.) This decline of more than 1 percent marked the third consecutive decline in the world harvest.[2] The year 2000 harvest, the first in the new century, was down more than 2 percent from the historical high of 1,881 million tons harvested in 1997.[3]

The principal reason for the world grain harvest decline was the fall in China's grain harvest from 391 million tons in 1999 to 353 million in 2000—a drop of 10 percent.[4] This was due to low prices that discouraged planting nationally, combined with drought and tightening water supplies in the northern half of the country.[5]

Links: pp. 62, 120, 122

Grain output in the United States, the world's second ranking grain producer, climbed from 332 million to 343 million tons.[6] This increase of 3 percent was accounted for almost entirely by an improvement in the corn yield per hectare of nearly 3 percent over the preceding year.[7]

The world grain area in 2000 totaled 668 million hectares, down from the 674 million hectares in 1999.[8] The drop of nearly 1 percent was due largely to the shrinkage in China's grain area.[9]

The world grain yield of 2.75 tons per hectare in 2000 was down slightly from the 2.77 tons per hectare of 1999, the historical high.[10] Over the last four years, the world grain yield has changed little, fluctuating narrowly around 2.75 tons per hectare.[11]

Grain harvest per person declined again last year, dropping to 303 kilograms, the lowest since 1995.[12] (See Figure 2.) The 2000 harvest per person was down 13 percent from the all-time high of 342 kilograms per person in 1984.[13] Much of the long-term decline has been concentrated in Eastern Europe, the former Soviet Union, and Africa.[14]

In 2000, the world corn harvest of 588 million tons edged out the wheat harvest of 580 million tons, marking the third year in a row that corn has eclipsed wheat.[15] (See Figure 3.) The wheat harvest exceeded the 401-million-ton harvest of rice, the other major food grain,

by 179 million tons.[16] Although more than 100 million tons of the wheat harvest is fed to live-stock and poultry, far more wheat than rice is consumed as food.[17]

In India, where rice has traditionally been the dominant staple, wheat consumption is expanding much faster.[18] For the year 2000, rice consumption in India was estimated at 84 million tons, while wheat was expected to reach 72 million tons.[19] If the more rapid growth in wheat continues for another decade or so, wheat will supplant rice as India's principal food staple.

Production of corn, the main source of feed for the world's livestock, poultry, and farmed fish, was concentrated in the United States, which accounted for 43 percent of the world harvest.[20] The leading world producer of wheat today is China.[21] India is second, having overtaken the United States several years ago.[22] China also dominates production of rice, leading India by a wide margin.[23]

World grain trade is dominated by wheat and corn.[24] For corn, the United States accounts for over three quarters of all exports.[25] The United States is also the leader for wheat, followed by France, Canada, and Australia.[26] Rice exports, which are quite small compared with those of wheat and corn, are rather evenly distributed among China, Thailand, the United States, and Viet Nam.[27]

World wheat imports, until recently dominated by Japan, are now beginning to shift.[28] In recent years, Brazil has become the world's leading wheat importer.[29] Iran and Egypt, countries where imports are driven by shortages of irrigation water, have moved into second and third place, dropping Japan to fourth.[30]

In 2001, world carryover stocks of grain, the amount in the bin when the new harvest begins, are estimated at 60 days of world consumption—the lowest level in several years.[31] If this year's grain harvest is average or better, grain prices will likely remain stable. But if the 2001 harvest is below average, grain prices could become highly volatile, as they have in the past when stocks have dropped to 60 days or less.[32]

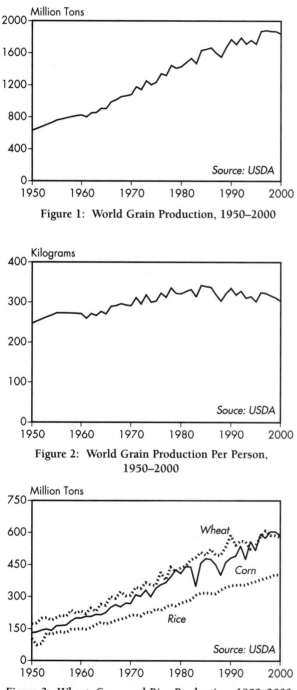

Figure 1: World Grain Production, 1950–2000

Figure 2: World Grain Production Per Person, 1950–2000

Figure 3: Wheat, Corn, and Rice Production, 1950–2000

World Grain Production, 1950–2000

Year	Total (mill. tons)	Per Person (kilograms)
1950	631	247
1955	759	273
1960	824	271
1965	905	270
1970	1,079	291
1971	1,177	311
1972	1,141	295
1973	1,253	318
1974	1,204	300
1975	1,237	303
1976	1,342	323
1977	1,319	312
1978	1,445	336
1979	1,411	322
1980	1,430	321
1981	1,482	327
1982	1,533	332
1983	1,469	313
1984	1,632	342
1985	1,647	339
1986	1,665	337
1987	1,598	318
1988	1,549	303
1989	1,671	322
1990	1,769	335
1991	1,708	318
1992	1,790	328
1993	1,713	310
1994	1,760	314
1995	1,713	301
1996	1,872	324
1997	1,881	322
1998	1,872	316
1999	1,869	311
2000 (prel)	1,840	303

Source: USDA, *Production, Supply, and Distribution*, electronic database, December 2000.

Soybean Harvest Sets Record

Lester R. Brown

The world soybean harvest in 2000 reached a new record of 167 million tons, up from 158 million tons in 1999.[1] (See Figures 1 and 2.) This 5-percent jump starts the new century with a continuation of the rapid growth that marked the last 50 years.[2]

The growth in the 2000 harvest was due to both expanding area and rising yield per hectare.[3] The area harvested went from just over 72 million hectares to 75 million, a gain of 4 percent.[4] (See Figure 3.) Yield rose from 2.18 tons per hectare to 2.23 tons, an increase of 2 percent.[5]

Over the last half-century, world soybean production climbed from 17 million tons in 1950 to 167 million tons in 2000.[6] This growth of nearly 10-fold dwarfed that of all other major crops.[7]

Another distinguishing feature in the growth in world soybean production—in contrast with grains, for example—is that most of it came from expanding cultivated area.[8] Between 1950 and 2000, the area in soybeans increased more than fivefold, while yield increased by just over half.[9] The bottom line is that to get more soybeans, we plant more soybeans.

Links:
pp. 62, 122

Although the soybean was domesticated in China some 5,000 years ago and was exported from there to other countries, China today accounts for less than one tenth of the world harvest.[10] Some 45 percent of the world soybean crop is produced in the United States.[11] Brazil accounts for another quarter of the world harvest, with Argentina, China, and other countries accounting for the remaining one fourth.[12]

Within the United States, the harvested area in soybeans eclipsed that of wheat several years ago.[13] More recently, it overtook that of corn as well, putting soybeans in the number one position among all U.S. crops.[14]

In some countries, the additional area needed to expand soybean production comes from clearing new land. This is the case in Brazil, where agriculture is expanding into the *cerrado*, a savanna-type area in western Brazil.[15] In other leading producers, such as the United States, Argentina, and China, expanding soybean production usually comes at the expense of grain.[16]

In the United States, corn and soybeans are often grown in a two-year rotation. Like most rotations, this helps control insect pests and disease.[17] In addition, the soybean, a legume, fixes nitrogen for corn, a nitrogen-hungry crop.

The growth in the demand for soybeans reflects growth in the demand for livestock products. The efficiency with which livestock and poultry convert grain into animal protein is greatly enhanced if the grain is enriched with high-quality protein, such as that found in soybean meal.[18] The widespread use of soybean meal as a protein supplement in animal feed thus means that the growth in soybean production indirectly tracks the worldwide movement of people up the food chain, as they add more meat to their diets.

After the world grain economy, the oilseed economy ranks second among crops in land use and value of output.[19] The ratio of land devoted to grain and oilseeds is roughly four to one, with grain occupying 668 million hectares and oilseeds 173 million hectares.[20]

The world oilseeds economy is a source of both vegetable oil and oil meal, with the demand for both rising with income. At the lowest levels, such as in India, rises in income translate into demand for vegetable oil.[21] At the level of development in China, growth in oil meal use is much faster than that of vegetable oil.[22]

The leading world exporters of soybeans are the United States (26 million tons), Brazil (11 million), and Argentina (5 million), with all others together exporting a total of 5 million tons.[23] U.S. soybean exports exceed those of all other countries combined.[24] Ironically, the largest market for U.S. soybean exports is China, the soybean's original source.[25]

No one knows how long this rapid growth in soybean production will continue, but we do know that the demand for soybean meal will likely keep climbing as long as incomes rise in developing countries. The early indications for 2001 are for another increase in the area planted to soybeans, and yet another record crop.[26]

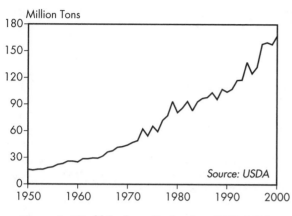

Figure 1: World Soybean Production, 1950–2000

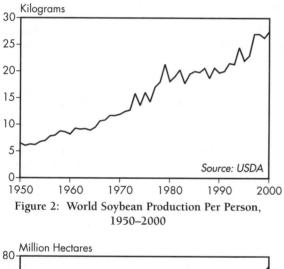

Figure 2: World Soybean Production Per Person, 1950–2000

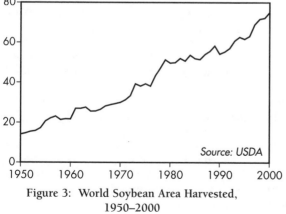

Figure 3: World Soybean Area Harvested, 1950–2000

World Soybean Production, 1950–2000

Year	Total (mill. tons)	Per Person (kilograms)
1950	17	6.5
1955	19	7.0
1960	25	8.2
1965	32	9.5
1970	44	11.9
1971	47	12.5
1972	49	12.7
1973	62	15.9
1974	55	13.6
1975	66	16.1
1976	59	14.3
1977	72	17.1
1978	78	18.0
1979	94	21.4
1980	81	18.1
1981	86	19.0
1982	94	20.3
1983	83	17.7
1984	93	19.5
1985	97	20.0
1986	98	19.8
1987	103	20.6
1988	96	18.7
1989	107	20.6
1990	104	19.7
1991	107	20.0
1992	117	21.5
1993	118	21.3
1994	138	24.5
1995	125	22.0
1996	132	22.9
1997	158	27.0
1998	160	27.0
1999	158	26.3
2000 (prel)	167	27.5

Source: USDA, *Production, Supply, and Distribution*, electronic database, December 2000.

World fertilizer use in 2000 totaled 141 million tons, up from 139 million tons in 1999.[1] (See Figure 1.) Most of this 1-percent growth occurred in China and the Indian subcontinent.[2] (See Figures 2 and 3.) Among the three principal plant nutrients—nitrogen, phosphorus, and potassium—the increase was almost entirely in nitrogen, pushing it to 86 million tons.[3] The use of 33 million tons of phosphate and 22 million tons of potash was little changed from the previous year.[4]

The rise in fertilizer use in 2000 reflected the acceleration of economic growth in developing countries to an estimated 5.6 percent in 2000, up from 3.8 percent in 1999.[5] International trade also grew much more rapidly, at more than 10 percent, compared with scarcely 5 percent in 1999.[6] In addition, low fertilizer prices stimulated growth in fertilizer use. Nitrogen prices were unusually low in 2000, but began climbing late in the year as natural gas prices rose.[7]

Fertilizer use in Western Europe was down nearly 2 percent in 2000.[8] As a result of already high rates of fertilizer application and pressures to protect water quality, fertilizer use has been declining slowly in Europe for several years.[9] In Northern Europe, where usage is heaviest, some governments require farmers to calculate plant nutrient balances each year.[10] In Denmark, for example, each farmer must calculate a nitrogen balance and submit a report to the government.[11] If nitrogen use exceeds the allowable level, the farmer is subject to a fine.

In the former Soviet Union, as rainfall improved, fertilizer use was up by more than 8 percent from the depressed levels of recent years.[12] The rise was especially strong in Russia, where the government adopted a subsidy that encouraged farmers to use more fertilizer.[13]

In East Asia, fertilizer use gains were particularly pronounced in China and Viet Nam. In China, the world's largest user of fertilizer, usage climbed by nearly 5 percent, the largest gain in seven years.[14]

In the Indian subcontinent, where fertilizer use has been climbing steadily for many years, applications increased by 9 percent in 2000.[15]

This unusually large gain reflected substantial increases in each of the major countries in the region: India, Pakistan, and Bangladesh.

In Africa, fertilizer use increased by 2 percent in 2000, but from a very low level.[16] Although the region contains 13 percent of the world's people, it uses only 2 percent of the fertilizer, a level that lags far behind nutrient removal by crops.[17]

This nutrient mining is slowly undermining the productivity of Africa's soils. Last year an estimated 4.4 million tons of nitrogen were removed by crops, in addition to 600,000 tons of phosphorus and 3 million tons of potassium.[18] In contrast, nutrient replacement in the form of fertilizer use stood at 800,000 tons of nitrogen, 260,000 tons for phosphate, and 200,000 tons of potash.[19] This nutrient depletion, combined with rapid population growth, helps explain the region's declining food production per person.

There are several reasons for Africa's low fertilizer use. One is the lack of a transport infrastructure, which leads to a prohibitive price when fertilizer finally reaches the farmer. There is also a lack of credit mechanisms and a shortage of agronomic advisors. In response to this deteriorating situation, the World Bank, the U.N. Food and Agriculture Organization, local farm groups, fertilizer industry groups, and nongovernmental organizations have combined forces to create the Soil Fertility Initiative, an effort to devise a strategy to reverse the fall in soil fertility in Africa.[20]

In Latin America, fertilizer use in 2000 was down, particularly in Brazil, because of depressed economic conditions and a lack of credit.[21] But improving economic conditions suggest a strong upsurge in fertilizer use for the 2001 crop.[22] Usage in North America was up by nearly 1 percent last year, reflecting a gain of more than 1 percent in the United States and a slight decline in Canada.[23]

Looking ahead at 2001, it now appears that the reduction in world grain stocks to the lowest level in several years could boost grain prices.[24] If so, this would encourage farmers to use more fertilizer.

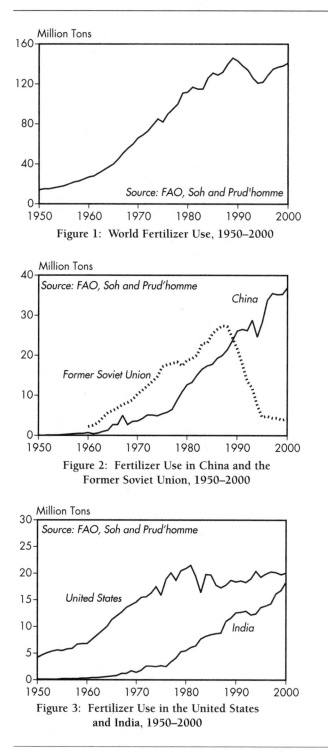

Figure 1: World Fertilizer Use, 1950–2000

Figure 2: Fertilizer Use in China and the
Former Soviet Union, 1950–2000

Figure 3: Fertilizer Use in the United States
and India, 1950–2000

World Fertilizer Use, 1950–2000

Year	Total (mill. tons)	Per Person (kilograms)
1950	14	5.5
1955	18	6.5
1960	27	8.9
1965	40	12.0
1970	66	17.8
1971	69	18.2
1972	73	18.9
1973	79	20.1
1974	85	21.2
1975	82	20.1
1976	90	21.6
1977	95	22.4
1978	100	23.2
1979	111	25.3
1980	112	25.1
1981	117	25.8
1982	115	24.9
1983	115	24.5
1984	126	26.4
1985	131	27.0
1986	129	26.1
1987	132	26.3
1988	140	27.4
1989	146	28.1
1990	143	27.1
1991	138	25.7
1992	134	24.6
1993	126	22.8
1994	121	21.6
1995	122	21.4
1996	129	22.4
1997	135	23.1
1998	137	23.1
1999	139	23.0
2000 (prel)	141	23.2

Sources: FAO, Fertilizer Yearbook (Rome: various years); Soh and Prud'homme, Fertilizer Consumption Report: World and Regional Overview and Country Reports (Paris: IFA, December 2000).

Milk Production Maintains Momentum
Janet Larsen

Milk production worldwide rose to 575 million tons in 2000—the ninth consecutive year of steady growth.[1] (See Figure 1.) Despite increases in output, an expanding population has caused milk production per person to decline rather consistently over the past decade.[2] (See Figure 2.)

The United States, long the world leader in this sector, was eclipsed by India in 1997.[3] (See Figure 3.) In 2000, India produced 79 million tons of milk, followed by the United States with 75 million tons.[4] Russia, with 31 millions tons, was a distant third.[5]

Consistent growth in milk production is maintained in part by dairy herds that do not vary greatly in size from year to year. Additionally, a drastic production drop in Eastern Europe and the former Soviet Union in the past decade served to offset increased output in Asia, Latin America, and Oceania.[6]

Link: p. 100

Cows account for 85 percent of worldwide milk production.[7] Buffalo milk makes up 11 percent of the global supply; the remaining 4 percent comes from goats, sheep, and camels.[8]

Buffalo milk, most of which is produced in India, has grown nearly 11 percent a year since 1970.[9] About half the milk produced for India's large domestic market comes from buffalo, which make up a far smaller proportion of total livestock population but yield a more reliable supply than cattle.[10] The Indian milk-pricing system is based on the fat content of milk, and thus favors production of fattier buffalo milk.[11] India's system is also remarkable because most milk is produced by individual farmers or farming cooperatives that manage small numbers of ruminants fed on farm by-products and crop residues that would otherwise be wasted.[12]

Throughout much of Asia, rice straw is a primary forage for dairy rations.[13] In China, rural reforms of the 1980s that stimulated markets and contracted land to small farmers made it profitable for individual farming households to raise a few milk cows and goats on crop residues.[14] Starting from a small base, ambitious government milk production goals resulted in a fourfold increase in China's milk production between 1980 and 2000.[15]

Small-scale mixed crop and livestock systems enable livestock wastes to be returned to local fields—maintaining soil fertility and organic matter content and reducing the need for expensive chemical fertilizers. Over 90 percent of the world's milk production comes from mixed crop-livestock farms; near-sighted economics, however, favors concentration of livestock in intensive dairy operations. Such systems, which evolved in Europe and North America in the past 50 years, are now gaining popularity in other parts of the world.[16]

Intensive confinement systems concentrate wastes and thus elevate the probability of ground and surface waters becoming polluted by excess nutrients. In the Central Valley in California, the nation's top milk-producing state, the 891,000 dairy cows in highly concentrated feedlots produce up to 30 million tons of manure a year—as much waste as 21 million people.[17] In addition, animals in feeding operations typically consume much more grain than those on rangelands or small farms.[18]

In many parts of the world, arid conditions or rough terrain make farming nearly impossible, so livestock are the sole means of local food production. At moderate populations, grazing animals stimulate regrowth of grasses and remove older and less-productive plant matter, but as herds grow, grasslands can be devastated by loss of biodiversity and species richness, compaction of soil, erosion, and hindered water retention.[19] About 90 percent of India's cattle subsist on natural grasslands that are at risk from both overgrazing and drought.[20]

Worldwide, consumer demand for milk products is up due to urbanization and rising disposable incomes. The associated elevated consumption of high-value foods and a more varied diet are facilitated by new supermarkets and improved refrigeration capabilities.[21] Where milk consumption is low, as in most developing countries, increased intake is nutritionally beneficial, especially for children. But if further growth continues to push dairy farmers to concentrate production in industrial feedlots or at levels that overwhelm pastures, the health of the environment may be of greater concern.[22]

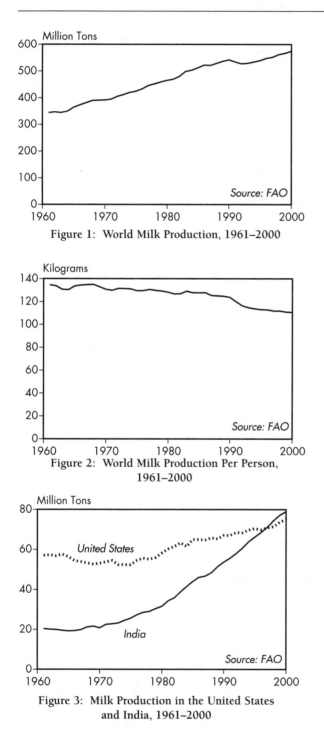

Figure 1: World Milk Production, 1961–2000

Figure 2: World Milk Production Per Person,
1961–2000

Figure 3: Milk Production in the United States
and India, 1961–2000

World Milk Production, 1961–2000

Year	Total (mill. tons)	Per Person (kilograms)
1961	344	134.7
1965	365	133.6
1970	392	130.7
1971	395	129.9
1972	405	131.5
1973	412	131.4
1974	420	131.1
1975	425	129.6
1976	433	129.5
1977	446	130.6
1978	453	129.8
1979	460	129.2
1980	466	128.2
1981	470	126.7
1982	480	126.9
1983	498	129.1
1984	504	127.8
1985	513	127.7
1986	523	127.8
1987	522	125.4
1988	529	125.0
1989	537	124.7
1990	542	123.8
1991	535	120.0
1992	528	116.4
1993	530	114.8
1994	534	113.8
1995	540	113.1
1996	548	112.9
1997	552	111.9
1998	562	111.9
1999	567	111.0
2000 (prel)	575	110.7

Sources: FAO, Food Outlook, no. 5,
November 2000; FAO, FAOSTAT Statistics
Database, <apps.fao.org>, updated 27
October 2000.

Coffee Production Hits New High

Brian Halweil

World coffee production hit an all-time high in 2000, jumping nearly 10 percent to 7.1 million tons.[1] (See Figure 1.) Production has increased 57 percent since 1961, due to increases in both global acreage and yield per hectare.[2]

Global production and prices are driven primarily by the weather in Brazil, which produces one quarter of the world's coffee.[3] Following severe frosts in Brazil, for instance, global production dropped in 1976 and 1993, while prices soared.[4] (See Figure 2.)

Such price spikes have generally encouraged farmers to expand planted area, but rebounds can take time because coffee is grown only on a narrow band of Earth's surface and because it takes several years for new plantings to produce harvestable beans.[5] Recent oversupply means that prices are wallowing near all-time lows.[6]

Links: pp. 62, 122

Though the coffee tree originated in East Africa, nearly 60 percent of the world's coffee is produced in Latin America and the Caribbean; Asia accounts for just over 20 percent of production, and Africa produces the rest.[7] At 1.8 million tons per year, Brazil is the top producer, followed by 672,600 tons from Viet Nam, where production has tripled in five years.[8] Colombia produces 630,000 tons, Indonesia produces 432,000 tons, and Mexico and Côte d'Ivoire harvest just over 350,000 tons.[9] The top 10 producers account for 75 percent of global production.[10]

There are two main species of coffee. *Coffea arabica* is a high-altitude species that produces a sweeter, milder, and more distinctive flavor.[11] It accounts for 80–85 percent of global acreage and is mainly produced in Latin America and the Caribbean.[12] *C. robusta* is grown in the lowlands, and has a more bitter and earthier flavor; it commands a lower price.[13] Robusta is primarily cultivated in Africa and Asia.[14]

At $11.2 billion in exports, coffee is second only to oil in the developing world's export commodities.[15] It represents 21 percent of all agricultural exports for Central America—but 40 percent in Guatemala and 60 percent in El Salvador.[16] Major exporters in Africa are even more dependent: coffee represents more than 60 percent of agricultural exports for Ethiopia, and over 70 percent for Uganda.[17]

Nearly three out of four cups of coffee are consumed in the industrial world.[18] The average person there drinks 300 cups each year, compared with 35 cups in the developing world. Americans drink 20 percent of the world's coffee, though current per person consumption—370 cups a year—is roughly 40 percent below the peak of 625 cups in 1960.[19] The average European consumes 475 cups, while the world's top coffee drinkers live in Scandinavia, where the average person drinks 884 cups a year—nearly 2.5 cups a day.[20]

Coffee is currently planted on 11.5 million hectares worldwide, and has traditionally been produced in the shade of intact forests.[21] But a growing share of coffee is produced in full sun, as traditional varieties have been replaced in recent decades by high-yielding dwarf varieties that require more chemicals and sunlight.[22] Just over 40 percent of the coffee area in Colombia, Mexico, Central America, and the Caribbean has been converted to sun coffee, with an additional one quarter of the area in conversion.[23] Much of the one-third increase in global coffee yield per hectare since 1960 is due to this transformation.[24]

Because sun coffee represents a form of deforestation, efforts to reform coffee production have assumed a central role in maintaining global forest health. Thirteen of the world's 25 biodiversity hot spots are major coffee producers.[25] Luckily, stands of shade-grown and organic (without agrochemicals) coffee have been found to be biodiversity havens.[26]

While still a small share of global sales, consumer support for such "ethical" coffee is the most rapidly growing segment of the market.[27] Certified organic coffee area is estimated at 110,000–205,000 hectares worldwide, just 2 percent of global area.[28] And the area growing "fair trade" coffee—a social classification that guarantees a fair price and working conditions to growers and coffee workers—stands at nearly 400,000 hectares, with an estimated half-million farmers participating.[29]

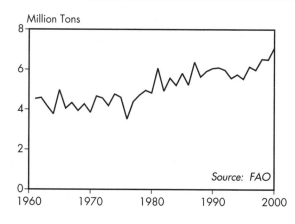

Figure 1: World Coffee Production, 1961–2000

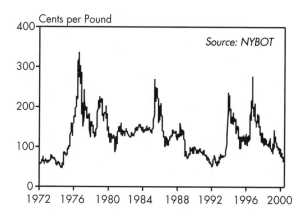

Figure 2: Weekly Coffee "C" Prices, September
1972–September 2000

World Coffee Production, 1961–2000

Year	Total
	(million tons)
1961	4.5
1962	4.6
1963	4.2
1964	3.8
1965	5.0
1966	4.0
1967	4.3
1968	4.0
1969	4.3
1970	3.8
1971	4.7
1972	4.6
1973	4.2
1974	4.8
1975	4.6
1976	3.5
1977	4.4
1978	4.7
1979	5.0
1980	4.8
1981	6.1
1982	4.9
1983	5.6
1984	5.2
1985	5.8
1986	5.2
1987	6.4
1988	5.6
1989	5.9
1990	6.1
1991	6.1
1992	6.0
1993	5.6
1994	5.8
1995	5.5
1996	6.1
1997	6.0
1998	6.5
1999	6.5
2000 (prel)	7.1

Source: FAO, FAOSTAT Statistics Database,
<apps.fao.org>, updated 27 October 2000.

Energy Trends

Fossil Fuel Use Falls Again

Nuclear Power Inches Up

Wind Energy Growth Continues

Solar Power Market Surges

Fossil Fuel Use Falls Again

Seth Dunn

Worldwide consumption of coal, oil, and natural gas declined in 2000 for the second consecutive year, inching down by 0.2 percent to 7,643 million tons of oil equivalent.[1] (See Figure 1.) Nonetheless, global fossil fuel use has expanded by more than three and a half times since 1950.[2] And fossil fuels currently account for 90 percent of commercial energy use.[3]

Consumption of coal, which provides 25 percent of world commercial energy, fell for the fourth year in a row, by 4.5 percent.[4] (See Figure 2.) U.S. coal use, which is just over one quarter of the world total, increased by 1.6 percent as growing electricity demand spurred coal-fired power generation.[5] But China, also with about a quarter of world coal use, witnessed a drop of 3.5 percent.[6] Indeed, Chinese coal use has fallen by 27 percent since 1996, with reductions in heating and industrial use more than offsetting increases in coal use for electricity.[7] Coal consumption rose by 5.4 percent in India, the third leading user, with 7 percent of the global total.[8]

Links: pp. 52, 120, 128

Use of oil, which provides 41 percent of world commercial energy, expanded by 1.1 percent.[9] The United States, the leading petroleum user, with a 26-percent share, increased consumption by 0.1 percent.[10] In the Asia Pacific region, which uses 27 percent of world oil, consumption rose by 2.6 percent.[11] In Europe, the destination of 22 percent of world oil, use edged up 0.2 percent.[12]

Natural gas consumption, which totals 24 percent of world commercial energy, rose by 2.1 percent.[13] The United States, which accounts for 27 percent of world natural gas use, experienced a 2.4-percent expansion.[14] Growth was strongest in former Eastern bloc nations like Lithuania, Estonia, and Latvia, which increased consumption by 29, 30, and 45 percent, respectively.[15] South Korea and Spain led gas growth in Asia and Europe, each expanding use by 16 percent.[16]

Oil and natural gas consumption were both influenced by higher market prices. The world price of oil hit its highest point since 1985, just below $35 per barrel, despite a 5.8-percent annual increase in oil production by the Organization of Petroleum Exporting Countries.[17] (See Figure 3.) As oil prices eased in December, U.S. natural gas prices were four times as high as in mid-1999, creating concerns about rising home heating and electricity costs for consumers.[18]

High prices also renewed interest in additional oil and gas exploration in the untapped Arctic fields of Russia and Alaska. But drilling in the Russian Arctic would require billions of dollars more than has already been spent there.[19] Drilling in Alaska's Arctic National Wildlife Refuge, meanwhile, is unlikely to begin before 2010 and would yield, according to a mean estimate, only 10.3 billion barrels of recoverable oil—the equivalent of one and a half years of U.S. oil consumption.[20]

In its *World Energy Outlook 2000*, the International Energy Agency (IEA) projects fossil fuel consumption trends between 1997 and 2020.[21] Overall use of these fuels is expected to grow by 57 percent (2 percent annually), maintaining their 90-percent share of world energy use.[22] Coal use is due to increase by 1.7 percent annually, with two thirds of the growth occurring in China and India.[23] Petroleum will remain the dominant source, says the IEA, its use expanding by 1.9 percent annually and its share of primary energy reaching 40 percent.[24] Natural gas consumption grows fastest among fossil fuels in the projections, by 2.7 percent a year, primarily due to increased use for power generation.[25]

The IEA analysis also contains assumptions, however, that suggest how reality may differ from these projections.[26] It assumes that prices will remain flat over the next decade—in contrast to recent events. In addition, it assumes that no additional steps are taken to reduce carbon emissions beyond those already adopted in response to the Kyoto Protocol on climate change. An anticipated peak in worldwide oil production and growing public pressure to address global warming could undermine both of these assumptions—accelerating the transition from coal to oil to natural gas and the displacement of fossil fuels by hydrogen and renewable sources of energy.

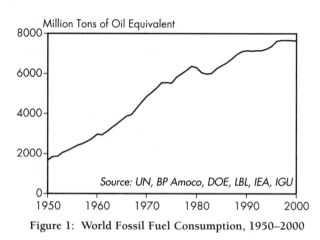

Million Tons of Oil Equivalent

Source: UN, BP Amoco, DOE, LBL, IEA, IGU

Figure 1: World Fossil Fuel Consumption, 1950–2000

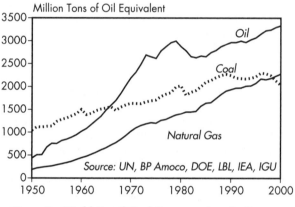

Million Tons of Oil Equivalent

Oil

Coal

Natural Gas

Source: UN, BP Amoco, DOE, LBL, IEA, IGU

Figure 2: World Fossil Fuel Consumption, by Source, 1950–2000

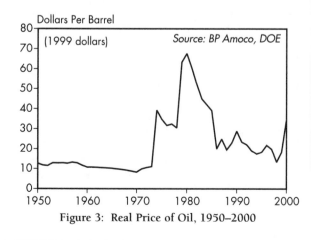

Dollars Per Barrel

(1999 dollars)

Source: BP Amoco, DOE

Figure 3: Real Price of Oil, 1950–2000

World Fossil Fuel Consumption, 1950–2000

Year	Coal	Oil	Natural Gas
	(mill. tons of oil equivalent)		
1950	1,043	436	187
1955	1,234	753	290
1960	1,500	1,020	444
1965	1,533	1,485	661
1970	1,635	2,189	1,022
1971	1,632	2,313	1,097
1972	1,629	2,487	1,150
1973	1,668	2,690	1,184
1974	1,691	2,650	1,212
1975	1,709	2,616	1,199
1976	1,787	2,781	1,261
1977	1,835	2,870	1,283
1978	1,870	2,962	1,334
1979	1,991	2,998	1,381
1980	2,021	2,873	1,406
1981	1,816	2,781	1,448
1982	1,878	2,656	1,448
1983	1,918	2,632	1,463
1984	2,001	2,670	1,577
1985	2,100	2,654	1,640
1986	2,135	2,743	1,653
1987	2,197	2,789	1,739
1988	2,242	2,872	1,828
1989	2,272	2,921	1,904
1990	2,244	2,968	1,938
1991	2,189	2,967	1,970
1992	2,179	2,998	1,972
1993	2,171	2,969	2,012
1994	2,186	3,027	2,019
1995	2,218	3,069	2,075
1996	2,298	3,150	2,170
1997	2,285	3,224	2,155
1998	2,243	3,241	2,181
1999	2,130	3,296	2,230
2000 (prel)	2,034	3,332	2,277

Source: Worldwatch estimates based on UN, BP Amoco, DOE, LBL, IEA, and IGU.

Nuclear Power Inches Up

Nicholas Lenssen

Between 1999 and 2000, total installed nuclear power generating capacity increased by less than 0.5 percent, bringing the total to a new high of 347,734 megawatts.[1] (See Figure 1.) Overall, the growth was just 1,598 megawatts, or about one-and-a-half large reactors.

Altogether, 435 reactors were listed as grid-connected at the end of 2000.[2] Six reactors were completed—three in India and one each in Brazil, the Czech Republic, and Pakistan.[3] But these were partly offset by the closure of four reactors, bringing to 99 the number of reactors (representing more than 30,000 megawatts) that have been retired after an average service life of less than 18 years.[4] (See Figure 2.)

In 2000, construction started on just one reactor, in China.[5] (See Figure 3.) Worldwide, some 25 reactors (with a combined capacity of 22,000 megawatts) are now under active construction—the equivalent of just 6.3 percent of current installed capacity.[6]

In North America and Western Europe, no new reactors are being built, nor are there any firm plans to add more. The future of nuclear power there depends on whether shutdowns of existing reactors will be accelerated or delayed. In the United States, consolidation of nuclear operators and higher-than-anticipated electricity prices have held up some early closures previously anticipated by financial analysts.[7]

In Western Europe, however, Germany's government and nuclear industry agreed to phase out nuclear power. The 19 reactors in the country will be shut down after 32 years of operation, so the last plant will be closed in roughly 20 years.[8] Two reactors closed in England, and another 14 there are likely to stop operations by 2010.[9] Sweden, though, delayed shutting down its second reactor until 2003 at the earliest due to the immediate unavailability of zero-carbon replacement power.[10] France's de facto moratorium on starting new projects is likely to hold until at least 2002.[11]

Plants have closed in the former Soviet bloc too. In Ukraine, the final reactor at the Chernobyl site shut down.[12] And Kazakhstan permanently shut down a small, Soviet-designed reactor in 2000.[13] Russia is likely to close one

aging reactor in 2001 and another in 2002, but also to open a new one in 2001.[14]

The Czech Republic connected a new reactor, Temelin 1, to the grid in late 2000, only to disconnect it a day later.[15] The future of this plant is quite uncertain, given strong political opposition to it from Austria and Germany and ongoing technical problems.[16]

China has become the world's stronghold for new reactor construction, hosting nearly a third of the projects being worked on. Next are Japan and South Korea, each with four new reactors being built, though Japan cut its long-term target for new reactors in half in 2000, to just 10, due to public opposition.[17]

Meanwhile, India opened three new, small reactors in 2000, and efforts are under way to fund the expansion of nuclear capacity from today's 2,503 megawatts to 20,000 megawatts by 2020.[18] But India had only two reactors, accounting for less than 1,000 megawatts, under construction at the end of 2000.[19]

After 24 years, Brazil finally completed its second reactor.[20] But other developing countries took the opposite approach in 2000, canceling existing projects or plans to begin new ones. Cuba stopped work on two Soviet-designed reactors it had been working on since 1983 and 1985.[21] And Turkey halted efforts to order its first reactor, a project that the country has been pursuing for some 30 years.[22]

In Taiwan, the country's newly elected government kept a campaign promise to halt work on two reactors.[23] In early 2001, however, it appeared as if supporters of the project forced the executive branch to back down and construction would restart.[24]

The shrinking market for new plants has led to an industry shakeout. For example, the French firm Framatome and Germany's Siemens merged their nuclear businesses in 2000.[25] Other companies have chosen to get out of the business completely, as ABB did in 2000.[26] And the venerable U.S. engineering firm, Stone & Webster, which had a hand in building most U.S. plants, filed for bankruptcy in 2000.[27]

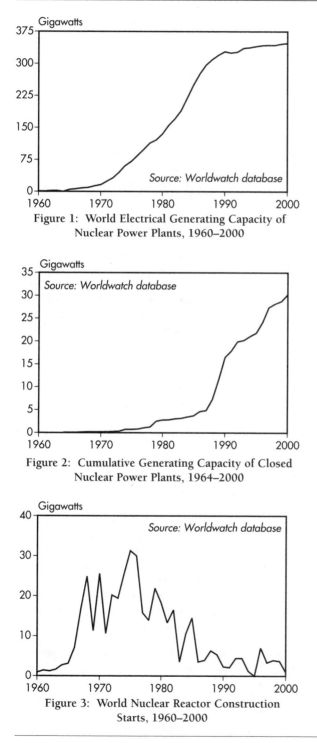

Figure 1: World Electrical Generating Capacity of Nuclear Power Plants, 1960–2000

Figure 2: Cumulative Generating Capacity of Closed Nuclear Power Plants, 1964–2000

Figure 3: World Nuclear Reactor Construction Starts, 1960–2000

World Net Installed Electrical Generating Capacity of Nuclear Power Plants, 1960–2000	
Year	Capacity (gigawatts)
1960	1
1965	5
1970	16
1971	24
1972	32
1973	45
1974	61
1975	71
1976	85
1977	99
1978	114
1979	121
1980	135
1981	155
1982	170
1983	189
1984	219
1985	250
1986	276
1987	297
1988	310
1989	320
1990	328
1991	325
1992	327
1993	336
1994	338
1995	340
1996	343
1997	343
1998	343
1999	346
2000 (prel)	348

Source: Worldwatch Institute database, compiled from the IAEA and press reports.

Wind Energy Growth Continues
Christopher Flavin

Wind energy generating capacity reached approximately 18,100 megawatts at the end of 2000, up 30 percent over 1999.[1] (See Figure 1.) Wind power now provides the world with nearly 10 times as much electricity as it did in 1990, although it still accounts for less than 1 percent of the world total.[2] Yet Germany, whose wind industry was launched in the early 1990s, now gets 2.5 percent of its electricity from the wind, while in Denmark the figure is 13 percent.[3] The northernmost German state of Schleswig-Holstein reports a figure of 16.5 percent.[4]

The estimated 4,200 megawatts of wind turbines installed worldwide in 2000 is 7 percent higher than 1999's record-breaking total.[5] (See Figure 2.) The slower growth in 2000 reflects a severe slump in the U.S. market, which continues to swing widely in response to short-term extensions of a federal wind energy tax credit.[6] (See Figure 3.) But a record 2,000 megawatts is planned for installation there in 2001, and the industry was buoyed when President George W. Bush proposed extending the wind energy tax credit beyond December 31, 2001.[7]

In 2000, Germany set the current record for annual installations: 1,670 megawatts.[8] With more than 6,100 megawatts of wind power in place, Germany has over twice as much wind power as any other country, an impressive figure given the fact that the industry there is not yet a decade old.[9] The year began on a promising note with a strengthened renewable energy law that ensures roughly 8¢ per kilowatt-hour for electricity produced by new wind power installations.[10] Development of the country's offshore potential could help Germany reach its goal of 22,000 megawatts of wind power by 2010.[11]

Denmark also had its strongest year ever in 2000, with 600 megawatts added, giving this tiny country more than 2,300 megawatts total.[12] The Danish wind industry faces political turbulence, however: the strong market reflected a rush to take advantage of expiring price supports.[13] The new Danish wind policy is untested, and the risk and uncertainty associated with it have virtually halted new wind energy contracts. Little if any development is expected in 2001, but long-term prospects for the Danish industry are bright, with much of the focus on large offshore wind projects.[14]

Spain's wind industry continued its frenetic growth in 2000, with between 900 and 1,100 megawatts added during the year, pushing total installed capacity to over 2,500 megawatts—trailing only Germany and the United States.[15] From Galicia in the northwest to Andalucia in the south, wind power is now being developed in five Spanish provinces.[16]

Italy's wind industry came to life, with 144 megawatts added in 2000, while Greece added 123 megawatts, making them the fifth and sixth largest markets worldwide.[17] France, widely known as Europe's nuclear leader, appears poised to join the wind energy big leagues, with a new renewable energy law and the announcement by Prime Minister Lionel Jospin of plans to add 3,000 megawatts by 2010.[18]

Outside of Europe, two countries seemed closer to a self-sustaining wind market in 2000. Following encouraging signs of change in Argentina's policy, Spanish companies announced plans to form a joint venture to develop 3,000 megawatts of wind power in Patagonia.[19] And in China, sizable wind power loans from the Asian Development Bank and the World Bank encouraged NEG Micon, a leading Danish company, to open a new factory near Beijing.[20] Still, China's antiquated electricity laws and infighting among government agencies must be overcome before the country's vast wind resources can be tapped.[21]

The end of the year brought further signs that wind power is crossing the threshold to competitiveness with conventional thermal power plants in most parts of the world. A new project at a windy site along the Washington/Oregon border will generate power at less than 3.5¢ per kilowatt-hour.[22] Meanwhile, the cost of natural gas–fired power—the dominant source of new electricity in most of Europe and North America—is going up, along with rising fuel costs. Early in 2001, California had to pay 7¢ per kilowatt-hour in order to obtain firm 10-year contracts for power—most of it from existing gas-fired plants.[23]

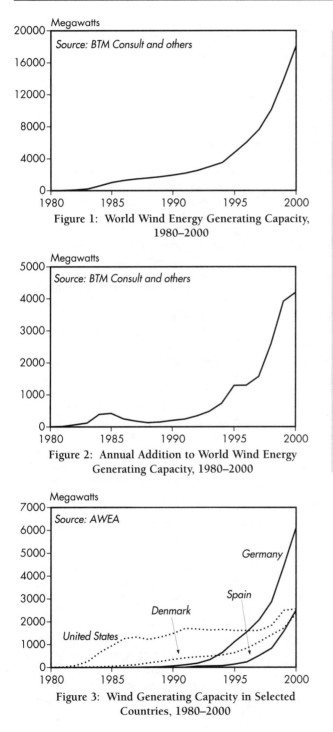

Figure 1: World Wind Energy Generating Capacity, 1980–2000

Figure 2: Annual Addition to World Wind Energy Generating Capacity, 1980–2000

Figure 3: Wind Generating Capacity in Selected Countries, 1980–2000

World Wind Energy Generating Capacity, Total and Annual Addition, 1980–2000

Year	Total	Annual Addition
	(megawatts)	
1980	10	5
1981	25	15
1982	90	65
1983	210	120
1984	600	390
1985	1,020	420
1986	1,270	250
1987	1,450	180
1988	1,580	130
1989	1,730	150
1990	1,930	200
1991	2,170	240
1992	2,510	340
1993	2,990	480
1994	3,490	730
1995	4,780	1,290
1996	6,070	1,290
1997	7,640	1,570
1998	10,150	2,600
1999	13,930	3,920
2000 (prel)	18,100	4,200

Sources: BTM Consult, EWEA, AWEA, Windpower Monthly, and New Energy.

Solar Power Market Surges

Christopher Flavin

Production of solar photovoltaic (PV) cells jumped 43 percent in 2000, to an estimated 288 megawatts.[1] (See Figure 1.) Production in 2000 was more than three times higher than in 1996, a year that marked the transition to a period of accelerated growth for the industry—an era that shows every sign of continuing.[2] In the face of surging demand, factory prices stayed steady at $3.50 per watt.[3] (See Figure 2.)

Government policies are the primary cause for this surge, led by Japan, which increased its lead in the solar power market with production of an estimated 128 megawatts in 2000.[4] The government expanded subsidies for rooftop solar applications: $130 million was made available to support one third of the cost of 25,000 new rooftop solar systems, a figure that will increase to $210 million in 2001.[5] This level of support, combined with falling PV costs, is projected to double the number of rooftop systems installed in Japan this year.[6]

The Japanese companies Sharp and Kyocera surpassed U.S.-based Solarex to take the top two positions among global manufacturers in 2000.[7] Sharp, now the leading producer, plans to increase production 70 percent in 2001 to meet the increase in projected demand.[8] With its home market growing so rapidly, Japanese companies are in good position to extend their command of the technology, expand production quantities, and stretch their market lead over competitors.

U.S. solar production increased more slowly in 2000, reaching 75 megawatts.[9] Even that growth appears to have been propelled largely by exports to Europe and Japan; the U.S. domestic market remains weak, despite the country's size, wealth, and abundance of sunny regions that are ideally suited for solar power.[10] The Million Solar Roofs Initiative announced in 1997 has not been backed by any significant financial support, and its loose collection of low-interest loans, state pricing laws, and public-private partnerships has failed to ignite a surge in PV installations.[11]

In California, hit hard by soaring electricity prices and rolling blackouts, the Los Angeles Department of Water and Power has estab-lished a $75-million budget to support as many as 100,000 solar rooftop installations over the next five years.[12]

The European outlook is brighter. PV production reached 61 megawatts in 2000, an increase of 52 percent over 1999.[13] The European solar industry is being led by Germany, which launched its own 100,000 rooftop program in late 1998.[14] That program—which includes a 10-year, interest-free loan from the German Federal Bank plus a guaranteed purchase price of 50¢ per kilowatt-hour—resulted in 45 megawatts of new installations in 2000.[15] In fact, strong interest in the program forced the government to reduce the level of incentives midway through 2000.[16] Continued strong growth is under way in 2001.

The most important application for solar PVs is in rural areas of developing countries, where billions of people are still not connected to electric lines. Despite the valiant efforts of governments and international agencies such as the Global Environment Facility, however, solar energy remains a "rich man's" power source.[17] In 1999, only about 45 megawatts—less than one quarter of the world's production—was installed in off-grid areas of Africa, Asia, and Latin America, a number that appears to have increased only modestly in 2000.[18]

The greatest barrier to developing-country use of PVs is cost: solar cells are capital-intensive, and rural areas are generally cash-poor. In addition, developing countries face the challenge of building the infrastructure to install and maintain PV systems.

Government subsidies and low-interest loans or lease plans are among the strategies that have proved effective in spreading PVs in some developing countries.

In South Africa, the planned installation of 350,000 solar home systems is a central part of the country's post-apartheid effort to provide electricity in rural areas.[19] In 1999, for example, President Nelson Mandela helped launch a program in the Eastern Cape for the local utility to install 50,000 50-watt systems, charging villagers $30 for installation and an $8 monthly service fee.[20]

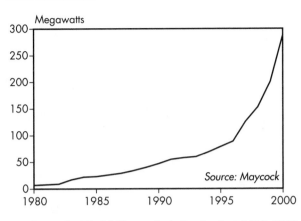

Megawatts

Figure 1: World Photovoltaic Production, 1980–2000

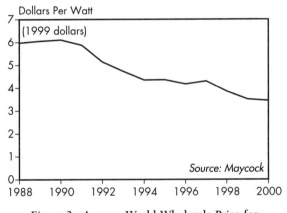

Dollars Per Watt

(1999 dollars)

Source: Maycock

Figure 2: Average World Wholesale Price for
Photovoltaic Modules, 1988–2000

World Photovoltaic Production, 1980–2000

Year	Production (megawatts)
1980	7
1981	8
1982	9
1983	17
1984	22
1985	23
1986	26
1987	29
1988	34
1989	40
1990	46
1991	55
1992	58
1993	60
1994	69
1995	79
1996	89
1997	126
1998	153
1999	201
2000 (prel)	288

Source: Paul Maycock, *PV News*, various issues.

Atmospheric Trends

Global Temperature Steady

Carbon Emissions Continue Decline

Seth Dunn

The average temperature of the atmosphere at Earth's surface held at 14.36 degrees Celsius, according to data from the Goddard Institute for Space Studies at the National Aeronautics and Space Administration (NASA). (See Figure 1.)[1] This makes the past two years the sixth and seventh warmest in this NASA dataset, which is based on land- and ocean-based measurements and dates back to 1950.[2]

An older NASA dataset, based only on meteorological stations and extending back to 1867, showed a slight drop to 14.35 degrees, making 2000 the ninth warmest year on record. (See Figure 2.)[3] In both datasets, the 10 warmest years have occurred since 1980.[4]

Global temperatures were influenced by the year-long presence of La Niña—a cooling phenomenon that originates in the Pacific Ocean but has a worldwide influence—that began strongly but weakened in July and August.[5] This contributed to lower-than-normal temperatures in the equatorial Pacific and in the tropics overall.[6] In the nontropical northern hemisphere, however, temperatures north of 20 degrees latitude were the third warmest among records dating back to 1880, which are kept by the National Oceanic and Atmospheric Administration (NOAA).[7] Canada, Scandinavia, and Eastern Europe experienced annual average temperatures that were more than 1 degree above their historical average.[8]

NOAA estimates that global temperatures in 2000 were 0.39 degrees above the long-term mean.[9] While global surface temperatures increased by about 0.6 degrees in the last century, during the last 25 years the rate neared 0.2 degrees per decade.[10]

NOAA satellites are used by NASA and the University of Alabama-Huntsville to measure temperatures in the lower troposphere, the bottom eight kilometers of Earth's atmosphere.[11] These measurements, dating back to 1979, indicate an increase of only 0.04 degrees Celsius per decade in the troposphere—one fifth the rate shown at the surface.[12] But data from NOAA, using measurements from instrumented balloons, show similar increases in lower tropos-

Links:
pp. 52, 92

pheric and surface temperatures: 0.09 and 0.1 degrees, respectively, per decade since 1958.[13]

In January 2001, the Intergovernmental Panel on Climate Change (IPCC), a U.N.-led international network of hundreds of scientists, released a draft summary of its Third Assessment Report.[14] The panel concludes that "there is new and stronger evidence that most of the warming observed over the last 50 years is attributable to human activities."[15]

It projects a rate of warming that is much higher than that observed during the twentieth century, and that is probably "without precedent" during at least the last 10,000 years.[16]

The IPCC has revised upward its 1995 scenarios for surface temperature change, due to an anticipated drop in sulfur emissions, which cause a temporary atmospheric cooling.[17] Temperatures are projected to increase by 1.4–5.8 degrees between 1990 and 2100, compared with the previous estimate of 1–3.5 degrees.[18] Improved models also indicate a smaller melting of glaciers and ice sheets, lowering sea level rise projections to 9–88 centimeters by 2100, versus 13–94 centimeters in the 1995 assessment.[19]

Higher surface temperatures are projected to increase global average precipitation, but with varying regional increases and decreases.[20] Higher maximum and minimum temperatures, with more hot days and fewer cold days, are "very likely" to occur over nearly all land areas.[21] Also very likely are reduced temperature ranges and an increase in the heat index over "most" land areas, and more intense precipitation events over "many" land areas.[22]

Nearly all land areas are likely to warm more rapidly than the global average: the projected warming in northern North America and northern and Central Asia exceeds the global mean by more than 40 percent.[23] A U.S. assessment projects that average U.S. temperatures will increase by 3–5 degrees Celsius by 2100.[24] Precipitation in the United States, which has already risen by 5–10 percent, is expected to become more extreme, combining with increased evaporation to make both drier and wetter events more frequent.[25]

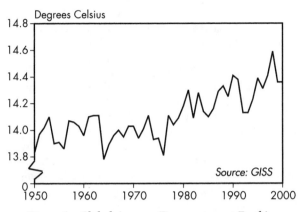

Figure 1: Global Average Temperature at Earth's
Surface, 1950–2000

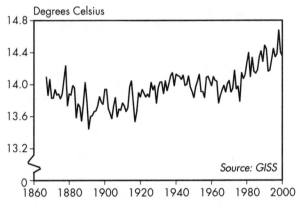

Figure 2: Global Average Temperature at Earth's Surface
(Land-Based Series), 1867–2000

Global Average Temperature, 1950–2000

Year	Temperature (degrees Celsius)
1950	13.83
1955	13.91
1960	13.96
1965	13.89
1970	14.03
1971	13.94
1972	14.01
1973	14.11
1974	13.93
1975	13.94
1976	13.81
1977	14.11
1978	14.04
1979	14.09
1980	14.18
1981	14.30
1982	14.09
1983	14.28
1984	14.14
1985	14.10
1986	14.16
1987	14.29
1988	14.33
1989	14.25
1990	14.41
1991	14.38
1992	14.13
1993	14.13
1994	14.23
1995	14.39
1996	14.31
1997	14.41
1998	14.59
1999	14.36
2000 (prel)	14.36

Source: Surface Air Temperature Analysis, Goddard Institute for Space Studies, 19 January 2001.

Carbon Emissions Continue Decline   *Seth Dunn*

Global carbon emissions from fossil fuel combustion fell for the third consecutive year, by 0.6 percent, to just below 6.3 billion tons.[1] (See Figure 1.) Since 1950, some 217 billion tons of carbon have been released to the atmosphere, with annual emissions nearly quadrupling over this period.[2]

The amount of carbon emitted per unit of global economic output continued to drop, by 3.6 percent, to 148 tons per million dollars of gross world product (GWP).[3] (See Figure 2.) The carbon/GWP ratio has declined by approximately 41 percent over the past half-century, reflecting improvements in efficiency and an ongoing transition to lower-carbon fuels.[4]

Link: p. 50 Under the Kyoto Protocol to the U.N. Framework Convention on Climate Change, industrial and former Eastern bloc nations (called Annex I countries) are committed to collectively reducing their emissions of carbon and other greenhouse gases by 5.2 percent below 1990 levels by 2008–12.[5] By the end of 2000, these nations were 2.6 percent below the 1990 mark for carbon, largely because of a 33.2-percent reduction in former Eastern bloc nations, which are permitted under the Protocol to return emissions to 1990 levels.[6]

Western industrial nations, on the other hand, have increased carbon emissions by 9.2 percent since 1990.[7] The United States, which accounts for 24 percent of global emissions and agreed in Kyoto to a 7-percent cut, now stands at about 13 percent above 1990 levels.[8] The European Union, which agreed to an 8-percent cut, is 0.5 percent below 1990 levels.[9] Japan, due for a 6-percent reduction, is 2.7 percent above the 1990 mark.[10]

In developing nations, carbon emissions have grown by 22.8 percent since 1990.[11] But progress is being made in reducing carbon/gross domestic product (GDP) trends—arguably a better way to measure these nations' efforts to "decarbonize" economic development. China, India, and Brazil all have carbon/GDP indicators below that of the United States.[12]

Atmospheric carbon dioxide (CO_2) levels climbed to 369.4 parts per million volume (ppmv).[13] (See Figure 3.) Current concentrations have not been exceeded for at least 420,000 years, and probably during the last 20 million years, and have risen by 31 percent since 1750.[14] The rate of increase of atmospheric CO_2 levels, unprecedented for at least 20,000 years, has averaged close to 0.4 percent for the past two decades, with a 0.8-percent average rise during the 1990s.[15]

CO_2 is one of several greenhouse gases driving temperature and climate change at Earth's surface. Scientists have pointed out that non-CO_2 gases, such as chlorofluorocarbons, methane, and nitrous oxide, have as a group been the main drivers of the warming of recent decades.[16] But they also note that CO_2 remains the single most important gas: its estimated warming effect is twice that of the second most significant greenhouse gas, methane.[17] The importance of reducing carbon emissions will grow, moreover, as emissions of offsetting atmosphere-cooling aerosols are cut.[18]

Under the latest scenarios from the Intergovernmental Panel on Climate Change, annual carbon emissions from fossil fuel burning are projected to reach 9–12.1 billion tons by 2020.[19] By 2050, emissions will range from 11.2 billion to 23.1 billion tons.[20]

For the Kyoto Protocol to enter into force, it must be ratified by 55 nations, including those representing 55 percent of Annex I emissions.[21] As of late 2000, 30 nations had ratified the treaty.[22] But most countries, including the United States, are waiting for the specific details of the pact to be worked out.[23]

Representatives from 182 governments, meeting in the Hague in November 2000, failed to reach agreement on finalizing the Kyoto rules.[24] Major points of difference, primarily between the United States and the European Union, involved the extent to which countries can meet their commitments through international emissions trading and the counting of "sinks" through agricultural and forest practices.[25] The next full round of climate negotiations will take place October 29–November 9, 2001, in Marrakesh, Morocco.[26]

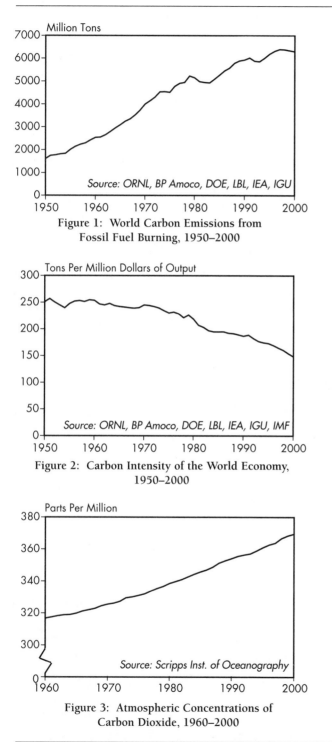

Million Tons

Source: ORNL, BP Amoco, DOE, LBL, IEA, IGU

Figure 1: World Carbon Emissions from
Fossil Fuel Burning, 1950–2000

Tons Per Million Dollars of Output

Source: ORNL, BP Amoco, DOE, LBL, IEA, IGU, IMF

Figure 2: Carbon Intensity of the World Economy,
1950–2000

Parts Per Million

Source: Scripps Inst. of Oceanography

Figure 3: Atmospheric Concentrations of
Carbon Dioxide, 1960–2000

World Carbon Emissions from Fossil Fuel Burning, 1950–2000, and Atmospheric Concentrations of Carbon Dioxide, 1960–2000

Year	Emissions (mill. tons of carbon)	Carbon Dioxide (parts per mill.)
1950	1,612	n.a.
1955	2,013	n.a.
1960	2,535	316.7
1965	3,087	319.9
1970	3,997	325.5
1971	4,143	326.2
1972	4,305	327.3
1973	4,538	329.5
1974	4,545	330.1
1975	4,518	331.0
1976	4,776	332.0
1977	4,910	333.7
1978	4,950	335.3
1979	5,229	336.7
1980	5,155	338.5
1981	4,984	339.8
1982	4,947	341.0
1983	4,933	342.6
1984	5,098	344.2
1985	5,271	345.7
1986	5,453	347.0
1987	5,574	348.7
1988	5,789	351.3
1989	5,892	352.7
1990	5,931	354.0
1991	6,020	355.5
1992	5,879	356.4
1993	5,861	357.0
1994	6,013	358.9
1995	6,190	360.9
1996	6,315	362.6
1997	6,395	363.8
1998	6,381	366.6
1999	6,340	368.3
2000 (prel)	6,299	369.4

Source: Worldwatch estimates based on ORNL, BP Amoco, DOE, LBL, IEA, IGU, and Scripps.

Economic Trends

PHOTOGRAPH BY KLAUS ANDREWS/PETER ARNOLD, INC.

World Economy Expands

Lester R. Brown

The global economy in 2000 expanded by 4.7 percent, the most in many years and well above the 1999 growth of 3.4 percent.[1] (See Figure 1.) The output in goods and services of $43 trillion lifted average output per person for the world's 6 billion people to $7,102.[2] (See Figure 2.)

This economic expansion was fed by a strong U.S. economy, an upswing in economic activity in Europe, continuing recovery in Asia from the 1997 financial crisis, a strong recovery in Latin America from the crisis of 1998, and a marked improvement in the transition economies.[3]

The North American economy was particularly strong, leading all other industrial regions.

Links:
pp. 58, 112

The United States, with a 5.2-percent expansion in 2000—up from 4.2 percent in 1999—continued the longest economic expansion in its history.[4] Canada, with an unusually strong performance as well, grew by 4.7 percent.[5]

Western Europe also registered a hefty performance in 2000. Growth of the European Union economies was an unusually robust 3.4 percent, up from 2.4 percent in 1999.[6] Growth in the four largest industrial economies ranged around 3 percent or higher, with Germany recording a growth of 2.9 percent, Italy and the United Kingdom 3.1 percent, and France 3.5 percent.[7] Ireland continued as the region's "tiger" economy, expanding by 8.7 percent.[8]

Asia expanded at 6.7 percent in 2000, up from 5.9 in 1999 and 4.1 percent the preceding year.[9] China's economy again led the region, growing 7.5 percent.[10]

The Indian subcontinent expanded by over 6 percent in 2000.[11] India's economy grew by 6.7 percent, followed by Pakistan at 5.6 percent, and Bangladesh at an even 5 percent.[12] This continuing strong economic performance of the region, which sadly has a large share of the 1.2 billion people in the world who live on $1 a day or less, is a welcome development.[13] Record wheat and rice crops helped reinforce the economic expansion.[14]

The southeast Asian economies, all recovering from 1997's financial crisis, were mostly expanding at 4–5 percent.[15] Included in this group were Indonesia, the Philippines, Thailand, and Viet Nam.[16]

Perhaps the biggest surprise of 2000 was the strong expansion of the transition economies, notably the 7-percent growth of the Russian economy.[17] Fueled by higher energy prices and renewed confidence, the Russian expansion was up from 3.2 percent in 1999, and from a shrinkage of 4.9 percent in 1998.[18] Higher export prices for oil and natural gas underpinned the strongest expansion in the Russian economy in at least a decade.[19] Eastern Europe's growth of roughly 4 percent was led by Hungary at 5.5 percent and Poland at 5 percent.[20]

Latin America bounced back from a shrinkage of 0.3 percent in 1999 to a strong 4.3-percent expansion in 2000.[21] Among the leaders were Mexico at 6.5 percent, which benefited from higher oil prices; Chile at 6 percent; and Brazil at 4 percent.[22]

In the Middle East, the 4.8-percent expansion in 2000 was nearly double the 2.8 percent of the preceding year.[23] Higher oil prices stimulated several economies in the region. The Saudi economy, for example, which had declined by 1 percent in 1999, grew by 3.5 percent in 2000.[24] Egypt continued at a strong pace with a 5-percent expansion.[25] Iran increased its overall economic output by 3.4 percent, despite having its agriculture decimated by one of the most severe droughts in decades.[26]

Africa's economy expanded at 3.4 percent in 2000, compared with 2.2 percent the year before.[27] Among its economies growing at 5 percent or more were Tanzania, Tunisia, and Uganda.[28] Nigeria, the most populous country in the region, grew 3.5 percent in 2000, up from 1.1 percent in 1999.[29] It benefited from both mounting confidence inspired by new leadership and higher oil prices. South Africa, the largest economy in the region, also picked up, expanding 3 percent in 2000, compared with 1.2 percent the year before.[30]

As of late 2000, the International Monetary Fund projects that global economic growth will continue in 2001 but at a somewhat slower rate.[31] The expansion in all regions is projected to slow except for Latin America, which is expected to grow even faster in 2001.[32]

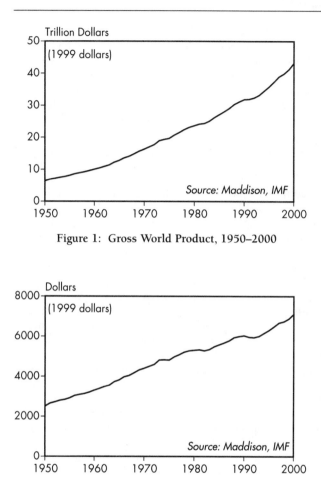

Figure 1: Gross World Product, 1950–2000

Figure 2: Gross World Product Per Person,
1950–2000

Gross World Product, 1950–2000

Year	Total (trill. 1999 dollars)	Per Person (1999 dollars)
1950	6.4	2,502
1955	8.1	2,921
1960	10.0	3,306
1965	12.8	3,822
1970	16.3	4,407
1971	17.1	4,505
1972	17.8	4,599
1973	19.0	4,819
1974	19.4	4,829
1975	19.7	4,816
1976	20.7	4,977
1977	21.5	5,083
1978	22.4	5,210
1979	23.1	5,282
1980	23.6	5,306
1981	24.2	5,329
1982	24.4	5,280
1983	25.1	5,341
1984	26.2	5,485
1985	27.1	5,582
1986	28.0	5,673
1987	29.0	5,778
1988	30.3	5,938
1989	31.2	5,996
1990	31.9	6,031
1991	32.0	5,957
1992	32.4	5,941
1993	33.2	6,000
1994	34.5	6,150
1995	35.8	6,295
1996	37.3	6,475
1997	39.0	6,666
1998	39.9	6,732
1999	41.2	6,871
2000 (prel)	43.2	7,102

Sources: Worldwatch update of Angus
Maddison, *Monitoring the World Economy
1820–1992* (Paris: OECD, 1995); updates
from IMF, *World Economic Outlook* tables.

Foreign Debt Unchanged

David Malin Roodman

The accumulated foreign debt of developing and former Eastern bloc nations, having posted its largest increase in history during 1998, was essentially unchanged in 1999. It fell slightly after adjusting for inflation, at $2.57 trillion (in 1999 dollars).[1] (See Figure 1.) Governments in borrowing nations owed or guaranteed 81 percent of this debt.[2] (In the latter case, they promise to repay the lender if a domestic borrower, such as an electric utility, does not.)

Financial crises in 1997 and 1998 in such nations as Brazil, Indonesia, Russia, and South Korea largely explain overall debt trends since 1996. Back then, 21 percent of the debt owed by developing and former Eastern bloc nations was short-term, lent for at most one year.[3] But then creditors became less willing to grant new short-term loans, so as old ones expired, their share of outstanding debt plunged to 16 percent in 1998 and 1999.[4] Cumulative short-term debt shrank from $480 billion at the end of 1997 to $410 billion at the end of 1999.[5]

But total long-term debt owed to private investors jumped a record $190 billion in 1998, to $1.22 trillion—as creditors granted more in new long-term loans than they received in repayment on old ones—and then held steady in 1999.[6] High interest rates promised by countries desperate for foreign exchange enticed some banks and investors to lend more. Other creditors turned their short-term loans into long-term ones, recognizing that prompt repayment was impossible.

Loans from government agencies, mostly in rich industrial nations, also rose after 1997.[7] Cumulative debt owed to aid and export financing agencies inched up from $520 billion in 1997 to $530 billion in 1999.[8] And debts owed to international agencies swelled from $370 billion to $430 billion as the World Bank and the International Monetary Fund financed huge "bailout packages" in crisis countries.[9]

Ideally, long-term lending supports projects, from public railroad construction to small business expansion, that generate enough income to more than repay the loans. In South Korea, for example, foreign lending has been an important source of capital for rapid economic development and poverty reduction, despite occasional debt crises.[10] Worldwide, however, foreign funds have too often been used poorly—supporting arms buying, corruption, capital flight, and prestige projects (such as unneeded airports), as well as projects that worked better on paper than in practice.[11]

These uses do double damage. First, they often exacerbate inequities in wealth and power and waste opportunities for economic development. Second, as borrowing escalates, creditors eventually lose faith in a country's ability to repay, and they cease lending, often triggering financial crisis and recession. During the global debt crisis that began in 1982, wages fell by half in Mexico.[12] In the Philippines, poverty sent a million hungry peasants into the mountains, where they cleared protective trees from erodible slopes in order to farm.[13]

One indicator of ability to handle debt is a country's debt-to-gross-national-product ratio. At the height of the 1980s debt crisis, this exceeded 60 percent in Latin America.[14] (See Figure 2.) In the 1990s, the ratio has climbed above 70 percent in sub-Saharan Africa—and above 100 percent if South Africa is excluded.[15]

In response to pressure from nongovernmental groups in creditor and debtor nations, industrial governments and international lenders have slowly written off some of Africa's debts.[16] The latest debt cancellation program, the enhanced Heavily Indebted Poor Countries initiative announced in 1999, aims to cut by about 45 percent the cumulative debt of 41 of the poorest, most indebted nations, 33 of which are in Africa.[17] The initiative takes an important step toward resolving the debt troubles of the poorest nations. But it will probably not prevent future crises, for it does little to change the systems that create the crisis in the first place. Export credit agencies, for example, lend to poor countries for reasons that have little to do with development. And even agencies intent on helping borrowers are insulated from the consequences of their actions, which gives freer play to bureaucratic tendencies toward the pursuit of growth in lending for its own sake and corruption.[18]

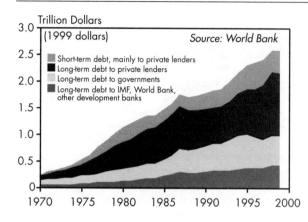

Figure 1: Foreign Debt of Developing and Former Eastern Bloc Nations, 1970–99

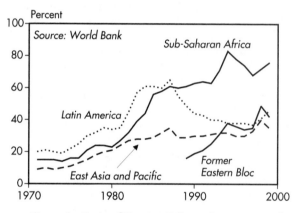

Figure 2: Ratio of Foreign Debt to Gross National Product, Selected Regions, 1971–99

Foreign Debt of Developing and Former Eastern Bloc Nations, 1970–99

	Total
	(trill. 1999 dollars)
1970	0.26
1971	0.29
1972	0.32
1973	0.37
1974	0.42
1975	0.51
1976	0.59
1977	0.74
1978	0.86
1979	0.98
1980	1.07
1981	1.18
1982	1.23
1983	1.33
1984	1.35
1985	1.47
1986	1.57
1987	1.73
1988	1.68
1989	1.70
1990	1.77
1991	1.80
1992	1.85
1993	1.97
1994	2.15
1995	2.30
1996	2.35
1997	2.40
1998	2.61
1999	2.57

Source: World Bank, *Global Development Finance 2000*, electronic database, 2000.

Funding for the United Nations has been on a roller coaster. The total amount of money available rose slightly in 1999 to $10.6 billion (the most recent year for which complete budget information is available), but is down more than 5 percent from the 1992 peak of $11.2 billion.[1] (See Figure 1.)

About $1.2 billion of this money is available for the U.N. regular budget, which supports headquarters in New York; offices in Geneva, Vienna, and Nairobi; and five regional commissions. This component, which is paid for by assessments levied on each member state, has seen little growth for the past decade—largely at the urging of the United States.[2]

A far larger chunk of money—some $9.3 billion in 1999—goes to an array of specialized U.N. agencies and organs.[3] Among these, 12 agencies are funded both through annual budget assessments and through voluntary contributions from member states, to the tune of about $3 billion a year.[4] Prominent among them are the Food and Agriculture Organization (FAO), the International Labour Organization (ILO), and the World Health Organization (WHO).[5] Another 12 U.N. bodies, known as special organs, are supported through voluntary funds only. This group includes the U.N. Development Programme, U.N. Environment Programme, U.N. High Commissioner for Refugees, UNICEF, and the World Food Programme. In 1999, a total of $6.4 billion was available to the special organs.[6]

Voluntary contributions accounted for 81 percent of the funds of all U.N. agencies and organs in 1999, and about 72 percent of total U.N. system funds.[7] (See Figure 2). But voluntary funding has also been extremely volatile, causing unexpected budget shortfalls in some years and making long-term planning exceedingly difficult.

In theory, assessed budgets offer more predictability, but, particularly since the mid-1980s, many member states have failed to pay their share of the budget in full and on time. Only in the last few years have payment habits improved again. U.N. members are expected to pay their regular budget dues within the first 30 days of each calendar year. In 1991, only 9 countries (accounting for 8 percent of the regular budget) lived up to this obligation.[8] By 2001, 40 countries (covering 18 percent of the budget) made this U.N. "honor roll."[9] Seven nations—Canada, Denmark, Finland, Ireland, Liechtenstein, New Zealand, and Sweden—have paid promptly every year since 1991.[10]

Many nations pay late; others build up arrears. The portion of regular budget dues paid by 30 September each year rose from 58 percent in 1994 to 67 percent in 1999.[11] Likewise, by the end of September, U.N. agencies receive on average about two thirds of the money that member governments owe in a calendar year.[12] But the record varies sharply from year to year and from agency to agency. The more technically oriented agencies—the International Telecommunication Union, the Universal Postal Union, the World Intellectual Property Organization, and the International Maritime Organization—have fared far better, with 83–93 percent of dues collected.[13]

U.N. member states' arrears on their regular budget dues have fallen sharply—from $602 million in 1995 to $219 million in 2000.[14] (See Figure 3.) Meanwhile, arrears on membership dues for U.N. agencies also dropped, from $1.4 billion in 1996 to $1.2 billion in 1999.[15]

The United States is both the largest financial contributor to the U.N. system and its largest debtor, accounting for roughly three quarters of regular budget arrears. The reduction of the U.S. share of the regular budget from 25 to 22 percent (approved by the U.N. General Assembly in December 2000 after some high-stakes arm-twisting by the U.S. Congress) raises hopes for a more responsible U.S. policy.[16] Even so, Congress has attached a series of conditions before it will authorize payment of past debts. Among them is a demand that the FAO, ILO, and WHO adopt no-growth budgets.[17] Thus in exchange for settling past debts, these agencies risk being shackled in their future operations.

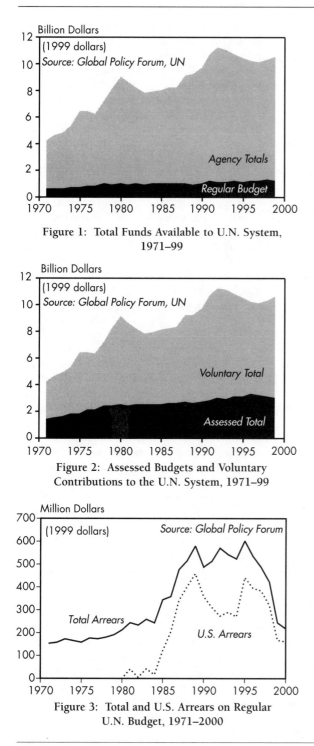

Figure 1: Total Funds Available to U.N. System, 1971–99

Figure 2: Assessed Budgets and Voluntary Contributions to the U.N. System, 1971–99

Figure 3: Total and U.S. Arrears on Regular U.N. Budget, 1971–2000

Total Funds Available to U.N. System, 1971–99

Year	Regular Budget	Agency Totals
	(bill. 1999 dollars)	
1971	0.6	3.6
1972	0.6	4.0
1973	0.6	4.0
1974	0.8	4.5
1975	0.7	5.6
1976	0.8	5.5
1977	0.8	5.5
1978	1.0	6.1
1979	0.9	7.2
1980	1.0	8.0
1981	0.9	7.7
1982	1.0	7.1
1983	1.0	6.8
1984	1.0	6.9
1985	1.0	7.0
1986	1.0	7.2
1987	1.0	7.3
1988	1.0	8.2
1989	1.0	8.2
1990	1.0	8.7
1991	1.1	9.5
1992	1.1	10.0
1993	1.1	9.9
1994	1.2	9.5
1995	1.2	9.3
1996	1.2	9.0
1997	1.2	9.0
1998	1.3	9.0
1999	1.2	9.3

Sources: Global Policy Forum, U.N. General Assembly, and UNDP/U.N. Population Fund.

Food Trade Slumps

Brian Halweil

Global trade in food and agricultural products stood at $417 billion in 1999, 15 percent below the high of $488 billion in 1996 (in 1999 dollars).[1] (See Figure 1.) Still, as all nations depend increasingly on food brought from farther away, food trade has grown nearly threefold since 1961, doubling just since 1970.[2]

Food trade soared following World War II, as the introduction of industrial farm practices quickly generated exportable surpluses and as diplomatic relations came to include economic ties. Many nations launched export-oriented agricultural strategies in the 1970s.[3]

A global farm crisis of high farmer debt and extremely low commodity prices in the 1980s sent food trade into severe decline until the early 1990s.[4] Agriculture was partly opened to World Trade Organization rules in 1994; since then, 20- and 30-year lows for major agricultural commodity prices have cut the value of food trade.[5]

Links: pp. 28, 120, 122

Agricultural products once dominated world trade, accounting for 47 percent of all exports in 1950.[6] But as manufactured and mined goods have grown in importance, agriculture's share dropped to 10 percent by 1999.[7] For certain regions, the figure is higher: 14 percent of sub-Saharan Africa's exports are agricultural, as are 22 percent of those from Latin America and the Caribbean.[8]

The developing world is a net importer of basic food stuffs, such as grain and meat, although it is a net exporter of many cash crops, including bananas, sugarcane, coffee, and cocoa.[9] Still, most food consumed in the world is produced domestically. Cereal exports, for instance, represent just 13 percent of global cereal production.[10] Yet wealthy and densely populated nations, such as South Korea and Japan, import 70–75 percent of their grain; as a region, North Africa and the Middle East imports half of its grain.[11]

As the value of agricultural trade has increased, so has the volume. Today, some 650 million tons of food are shipped around the planet each year—up fourfold from 165 million tons in 1961.[12] Most of this travels by boat,

although high-value items such as cut flowers or frozen produce are increasingly shipped by refrigerated plane.[13]

At 280 million tons, cereal products account for at least 40 percent of total shipments, while fruits and vegetables are the second biggest category, at 114 million tons.[14] (See Figure 2.) The vast majority of internationally traded cereals and oilseeds end up in livestock feedlots of the industrial world.[15]

In contrast, luxury items with substantially less nutritional value than staples command a disproportionately large share of value. (See Figure 3.) For example, at $57 billion, trade in coffee, cocoa, wine, and tobacco is worth more than all cereals trade.[16]

A relatively small number of nations and companies control exports for most major commodities. The five biggest exporters—Argentina, Australia, Canada, France, and the United States—ship 70 percent of the world's grain, while the United States alone exports two thirds of the world's corn.[17] The top five cocoa exporters account for 83 percent of cocoa trade, with Côte d'Ivoire responsible for nearly half.[18]

According to a recent study, a handful of transnational firms control about 90 percent of the global trade in wheat, maize, coffee, cocoa, and pineapple; 70 percent of the global tea, banana, and rice markets; and more than 60 percent of the world trade in sugar—giving these firms great control over prices.[19] Cargill alone controls an estimated 50 percent of all grain shipped around the globe.[20]

While food trade can generate much-needed foreign exchange, profits generated by traders often do not trickle down to farmers, and cheap imports can squash local markets, exacerbating poverty and hunger.[21]

As agriculture is integrated into the global economy, the distance from farmer to consumer grows, even when food can be grown locally. For instance, food consumed in the United Kingdom travels 50 percent more on average than two decades ago.[22] While this may offer greater variety to the global consumer, it also uses large amounts of energy, generates excess packaging and pollution, and can reduce food quality.[23]

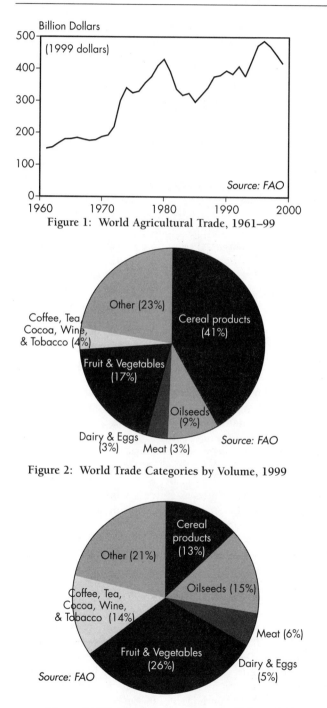

Billion Dollars

(1999 dollars)

Source: FAO

Figure 1: World Agricultural Trade, 1961–99

Other (23%)

Coffee, Tea, Cocoa, Wine, & Tobacco (4%)

Cereal products (41%)

Fruit & Vegetables (17%)

Oilseeds (9%)

Dairy & Eggs (3%)   Meat (3%)   Source: FAO

Figure 2: World Trade Categories by Volume, 1999

Cereal products (13%)

Other (21%)

Oilseeds (15%)

Coffee, Tea, Cocoa, Wine, & Tobacco (14%)

Meat (6%)

Fruit & Vegetables (26%)

Dairy & Eggs (5%)

Source: FAO

Figure 3: World Trade Categories by Value, 1999

World Agricultural Trade, 1961–99

Year	Total (billion 1999 dollars)
1961	150.4
1962	154.4
1963	167.9
1964	180.1
1965	180.8
1966	184.6
1967	179.7
1968	175.5
1969	177.7
1970	187.7
1971	192.4
1972	219.1
1973	300.6
1974	341.0
1975	325.0
1976	330.4
1977	356.6
1978	375.9
1979	410.3
1980	430.1
1981	392.1
1982	337.4
1983	318.0
1984	324.3
1985	297.0
1986	319.0
1987	341.7
1988	376.1
1989	380.5
1990	395.0
1991	384.5
1992	408.3
1993	377.6
1994	424.4
1995	473.3
1996	487.7
1997	470.6
1998	444.6
1999	417.3

Source: FAO, FAOSTAT Statistics Database, <apps.fao.org>, updated 27 October 2000.

Aluminum Production Keeps Growing

John E. Young

In 2000, estimated world production of primary aluminum (metal made from bauxite ore, rather than recycled) was at a record 23.9 million tons, 3 percent more than in 1999.[1] (See Figure 1.) Sixteen times as much of this light metal is now produced as in 1950.[2] World average production per person has risen from 0.6 to 3.9 kilograms over the same period.[3] And in 2000, some 127 million tons of bauxite were mined worldwide, at least three fourths of which was refined into alumina (aluminum oxide) for aluminum production.[4]

The United States, Russia, China, Canada, and Australia account for more than half of world primary aluminum production.[5] The United States is the leader, with 15 percent of world output in 2000, but it no longer dominates the industry as it did a few decades ago.[6]

Link: p. 122

Production of secondary, or recycled, aluminum has grown sharply since the 1960s. In 1999, the latest year with data, secondary production was 7.9 million tons—18 times more than in 1950.[7] (See Figure 2.) Probably two thirds or more of that amount, however, was made from aluminum-industry production scrap rather than from used, or "post-consumer," products.[8] In 1999, the United States recycled about 3.5 million tons of metal, nearly half the world total, but only 40 percent of that was post-consumer material.[9]

Aluminum is light, strong, easily worked, corrosion-resistant, and a good conductor of heat and electricity. This combination of qualities has made it ubiquitous and essential in industrial economies. It is particularly important in transportation, where weight reductions add up to large energy savings. Almost a third of the primary aluminum produced each year goes into automobiles, airplanes, and other transport vehicles.[10] Packaging, such as aluminum cans and foil, accounts for about one fifth of primary metal use, and construction products, such as window frames and roofing, take about an eighth.[11] The rest goes into electrical applications (mainly high-tension transmission cables), consumer goods, and machines and equipment.[12]

Most bauxite is mined in the developing world, but industrial countries use far more of the final product—aluminum—than developing countries. In 1999, the United States, Western Europe, and Japan used nearly two thirds of all primary aluminum.[13] The United States leads the world here too, in both total and per capita consumption. Taking into account the use of recycled metal, Americans use about 34 kilograms of aluminum per person a year, while the Japanese use 28 kilograms and West Europeans, 21.[14] In contrast, people in developing countries use 1–2 kilograms apiece each year.[15]

Aluminum production is one of the world's most energy-intensive industries, and a significant contributor to global climate change. Alumina is smelted to produce pure metal through the application of electric current, a process that requires, on average, more than 15,000 kilowatt-hours per ton of aluminum—enough for an average U.S. household for a year and a half.[16] Primary smelters used an estimated 370 billion kilowatt-hours in 2000, more than 2 percent of world electricity consumption.[17] In 1998, about 54 percent of power for aluminum smelters came from hydropower, 31 percent from coal, 8 percent from natural gas, 6 percent from nuclear power, and 1 percent from oil.[18] Aluminum smelting also releases substantial amounts of perfluorocarbons, gases with very high greenhouse potential.[19]

Aluminum smelters now use, on average, about three fourths as much electricity per ton of aluminum as 20 years ago.[20] The industry's total electricity use has continued to rise, however, as production has grown.[21] (See Figure 3.) Only a major expansion of aluminum recycling—and substitution of recycled aluminum for primary metal—is likely to check this rising consumption. Aluminum recycling takes only 5 percent as much energy as primary production.[22] Much more metal could be recycled than is currently the case. Americans alone threw away 2.2 million tons of aluminum in 1998.[23] The energy savings from recycling that much metal rather than producing new aluminum from ore could power 2.9 million American households—about as many as in New York City—for a year.[24]

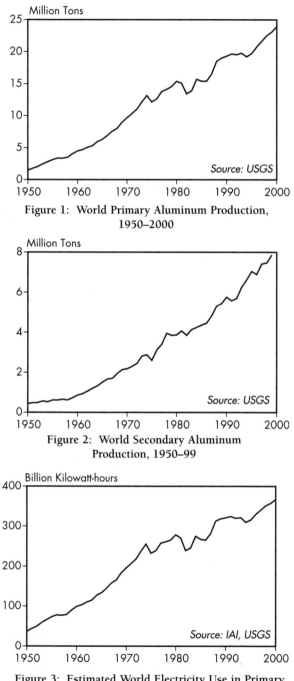

Figure 1: World Primary Aluminum Production, 1950–2000

Figure 2: World Secondary Aluminum Production, 1950–99

Figure 3: Estimated World Electricity Use in Primary Aluminum Production, 1950–2000

World Aluminum Production, 1950–2000

Year	Primary	Secondary
	(million tons)	
1950	1.5	0.4
1955	3.1	0.6
1960	4.5	0.9
1965	6.3	1.5
1970	9.7	2.2
1971	10.3	2.3
1972	11.0	2.4
1973	12.1	2.8
1974	13.2	2.9
1975	12.1	2.6
1976	12.6	3.1
1977	13.8	3.4
1978	14.1	4.0
1979	14.6	3.8
1980	15.4	3.9
1981	15.1	4.1
1982	13.4	3.8
1983	13.9	4.1
1984	15.7	4.2
1985	15.4	4.4
1986	15.4	4.5
1987	16.5	4.8
1988	18.5	5.3
1989	19.0	5.4
1990	19.3	5.8
1991	19.7	5.6
1992	19.5	5.7
1993	19.8	6.3
1994	19.2	6.6
1995	19.7	7.0
1996	20.7	6.9
1997	21.6	7.4
1998	22.5	7.5
1999	23.1	7.9
2000 (prel)	23.9	n.a.

Sources: USGS, *Mineral Commodity Summaries 2001* (Washington, DC: 2001); Plunkert, USGS, e-mail, 15 November 2000.

Transportation Trends

Vehicle Production Sets New Record

Bicycle Production Recovers

Vehicle Production Sets New Record   *Michael Renner*

Rising 4 percent in 2000, global passenger car production set a new record of 40.9 million vehicles.[1] (See Figure 1.) Light truck production also reached a new peak, 16.4 million.[2] The global passenger car fleet grew to 532 million in 2000.[3]

Japan, the United States, and Germany dominate car output, together producing 47 percent of the global total.[4] For a long time Canada, France, Italy, and the United Kingdom formed a second tier of manufacturers, but, except for France, they have been overtaken by newer producers in recent years.[5] Spain and South Korea are now the world's fifth and sixth largest producers.[6] (See Figure 2.) And Brazil, China, and India are poised for rapid additional growth in the next few years.[7]

Links:
pp. 52, 128

Global passenger car sales ran to 38.8 million in 2000, and 17.4 million light trucks were sold.[8] Western Europe, Japan, the United States, and Canada account for 75 percent of the world market.[9] But sales in a number of developing nations—Brazil, South Korea, India, China, and Mexico—have grown rapidly, even as economic crisis has caused considerable volatility for some of them in recent years.[10]

Production of cars and light trucks outpaced sales by about 1.1 million units worldwide in 2000.[11] Still, auto factories could easily churn out far more. Only 70 percent of the manufacturing capacity was being used last year.[12] At 87 percent, the rate in North America was by far the highest, compared with 76 percent in Western Europe and only 50–60 percent in the rest of the world.[13]

The auto industry is undergoing a wave of consolidation. Since 1985, some $250 billion worth of acquisitions have been announced, and the merger pace began to pick up real speed in the mid-1990s.[14] Companies partially or wholly acquired since just 1998 form quite a line of famous brands: Chrysler, Daihatsu, Isuzu, Lamborghini, Mazda, Mitsubishi, Nissan, Rover, Saab, Subaru, Suzuki, and Volvo, with South Korea's Daewoo and Samsung also up for sale.[15]

The top four car companies now control roughly half the world passenger car market, and the top 10, almost 80 percent.[16] (See Figure 3.) In the top 10 are two U.S. companies (General Motors and Ford), three Japanese (Toyota, Honda, and Nissan), two German (Volkswagen and DaimlerChrysler), two French (Renault and Peugeot), and one Italian (Fiat).[17]

Even as the remaining car companies are jousting for more competitive position, environmental concerns about the industry's impact are mounting. Cars and other motor vehicles are an important source of urban air pollution and a major contributor of greenhouse gases. Carbon emissions from U.S. cars and light trucks, at 291 million tons in 1997, exceeded the total emissions of all but a few countries worldwide.[18] Among the members of the European Union, motor vehicle carbon emissions could rise as much as 20–30 percent by 2005.[19]

As the number of vehicles on the roads and the distances driven in them continues to grow, so does their impact. The U.S. Department of Energy (DOE) estimates that the global motor vehicle fleet—passenger cars, trucks, and buses—will grow from about 700 million currently to 1.1 billion in 2020.[20] In the United States—the most auto-mobile society—annual distances driven in passenger cars more than quadrupled between 1950 and 1999, to more than 2.5 trillion kilometers, and could grow to 3.6 trillion kilometers by 2020.[21] In the United Kingdom, car travel expanded an astounding 15-fold since 1950.[22]

Improvements in fuel efficiency will therefore be critical, but there has been hardly any progress in the last two decades. U.S. fuel economy for new cars has been flat since the mid-1980s.[23] DOE forecasts that average horsepower for new cars in 2020 will be 55 percent higher than in 1999, offsetting much of the expected improvements in fuel economy gained through new efficiency technologies.[24] U.S. energy consumption by passenger cars and light trucks is projected to grow by 40 percent between 2000 and 2020.[25] These trends are likely to be mirrored in other industrial countries.

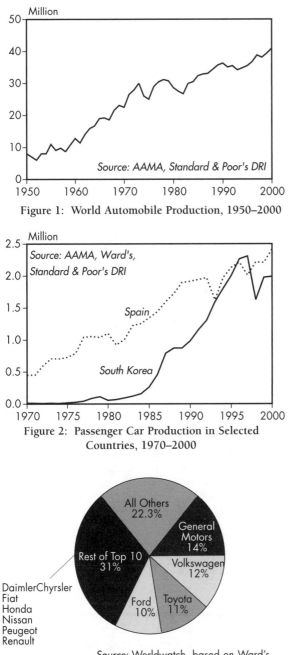

Figure 1: World Automobile Production, 1950–2000

Figure 2: Passenger Car Production in Selected Countries, 1970–2000

DaimlerChyrsler
Fiat
Honda
Nissan
Peugeot
Renault

Source: Worldwatch, based on Ward's

Figure 3: Share of World Passenger Car Production, 1999–2000

World Automobile Production, 1950–2000	
Year	Production
	(million)
1950	8.0
1955	11.0
1960	12.8
1965	19.0
1970	22.5
1971	26.5
1972	27.9
1973	30.0
1974	26.0
1975	25.0
1976	28.9
1977	30.5
1978	31.2
1979	30.8
1980	28.6
1981	27.5
1982	26.7
1983	30.0
1984	30.5
1985	32.4
1986	32.9
1987	33.1
1988	34.4
1989	35.7
1990	36.3
1991	35.1
1992	35.5
1993	34.2
1994	34.8
1995	35.5
1996	36.7
1997	38.8
1998	38.1
1999	39.4
2000 (prel)	40.9

Sources: American Automobile Manufacturers Association; Standard & Poor's DRI.

Gary Gardner

Bicycle production recovered to 95 million units in 1999, the latest year for which global production data are available.[1] (See Figure 1.) This represents a 22-percent increase over 1998, and reverses three years of global decline in output, when excess inventories cut demand at the factory.[2] The recovery was driven by increased purchasing in China, the European Union, and the United States—three of the leading markets.[3]

Asia continues to be the dominant bicycle-producing region. China bounced back from a poor year in 1998 to manufacture 43 million bicycles in 1999. [4] Output from Taiwan slipped somewhat, from fewer than 11 million units to just over 8 million.[5] But India held steady, with 11 million units.[6] The three Asian giants accounted for nearly two thirds of global production.[7] They were also the world's leading exporters, sending more than half of their combined output overseas, and claiming some 86 percent of global bicycle exports in 1999.[8]

Outside of Asia, the European Union remained the second largest producer, at 12 million units, roughly on a par with previous years.[9] But the United States continued a steep slide in production, with only 1.7 million new bicycles in 1999, compared with 6 million just two years earlier.[10]

Production declines in Taiwan, the United States, and Japan partly reflect manufacturers' flight in search of low-wage labor.[11] U.S. producers shifted operations first to Mexico, and then more recently to China.[12] Many Japanese manufacturers have also moved operations to China, while Taiwanese companies have set up shop in Viet Nam.[13]

Electric bikes continue to be a rapidly growing niche product. Total global sales reached 1.1 million units in 2000, triple the level of 1999.[14] (See Figure 2.) Some 750,000 of these were sold in China, where electric bicycles are now a clean and comfortable commuting option.[15] In the industrial world, electric bicycles are often marketed through automobile companies, such as Ford, which has created Think Mobility to produce electric vehicles, including bicycles.[16]

Changes in production centers and products

are matched by changes in the demographics of cycling. In industrial countries, an aging population has boosted demand for "comfort" bikes with padded seats and large tires, folding bicycles that can be stowed in a car trunk, and electric bicycles.[17] In contrast, American children may be losing interest: between 1990 and 1999, the number of people aged 7–17 who rode more than once a year declined by more than 13 percent, even as the population under 15 years of age expanded by some 7 percent.[18]

Government continues to be an important influence on bikes' popularity. Municipal authorities in Paris, Rome, Milan, and Bogota all sponsored "car-free days" in 2000 to highlight the availability and benefits of non-automotive transportation, including bicycles.[19] In the car-centric United States, concerns about traffic congestion and sprawl along with increased federal funding for cycling have led to a few initiatives to promote cycling. A 4,200-kilometer cycling trail is near completion on the East Coast, and California's Marin County has proposed a bicycle master plan with 200 different projects inspired by the highly successful plan in the Dutch city of Delft.[20]

On the other hand, where authorities pay insufficient attention to the potential and needs of bicycles, cycling can become dangerous or marginalized. In China, traffic fatalities have doubled in the past 15 years—with 35 percent of the deaths being cyclists—because official deference to automobiles has left bikes at a disadvantage on increasingly crowded roads.[21] And in the United States, state governments have been slow to claim funds authorized by the federal government to improve cycling and walking, jeopardizing a renewal of such funding when the next transportation bill comes before Congress.[22]

The market for bicycles is also being expanded by nonprofits like Pedals for Progress, which rehabilitates old U.S. bicycles and exports them to developing countries, where they are sold cheaply as a spur to economic development.[23] The group aims to put 20 percent of the developing world's walking labor force on bicycles.[24]

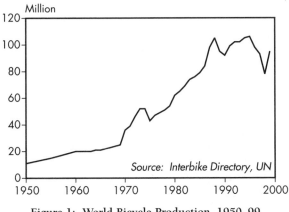

Figure 1: World Bicycle Production, 1950–99

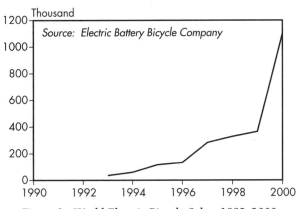

Figure 2: World Electric Bicycle Sales, 1993–2000

World Bicycle Production, 1950–99	
Year	Production (million)
1950	11
1955	15
1960	20
1965	21
1970	36
1971	39
1972	46
1973	52
1974	52
1975	43
1976	47
1977	49
1978	51
1979	54
1980	62
1981	65
1982	69
1983	74
1984	76
1985	79
1986	84
1987	98
1988	105
1989	95
1990	92
1991	99
1992	102
1993	102
1994	105
1995	106
1996	98
1997	93
1998	78
1999 (prel)	95

Sources: United Nations, *The Growth of World Industry 1969 Edition, Yearbook of Industrial Statistics 1979* and *1989 Editions,* and *Industrial Commodity Statistics Yearbook 1998; Interbike Directory,* various years.

Health and Social Trends

Population Increases Steadily

Cigarette Production Remains High

AIDS Erodes Decades of Progress

Gary Gardner

Global population reached 6.1 billion people in 2000, an increase of 77 million over 1999.[1] (See Figures 1 and 2.) The increase is equivalent in size to the population of three Tokyos, the world's most populous city.[2]

The global increase masks great variations in population trends. In general, industrial-country populations are growing very little—the exception is the United States, where a third of the nearly 1 percent growth rate is fueled by immigration.[3] And some countries—primarily the former Eastern bloc nations in Europe and Asia—actually have shrinking populations.[4]

The bulk of the global increase in 2000—a full 95 percent—occurred in developing countries.[5] Asia accounted for 57 percent of the global increase, some 45 million people.[6] Africa contributed 23 percent, Latin America 9 percent, and the Near East 5 percent.[7] Six countries account for half of the annual growth: India, China, Pakistan, Nigeria, Bangladesh, and Indonesia.[8]

Links:
pp. 78, 142

Like a locomotive, global population growth requires a prolonged braking period before it can come to a halt. In much of the world, the brakes began to be applied decades ago. Rates of growth and fertility rates (the average number of children per woman) have fallen globally for nearly 40 years (see Figure 3), and they fell for each major region in 2000.[9] Yet the world remains decades away from population stabilization.[10] Today's continuing population increases result largely from the momentum of past growth, as record numbers of young people reach adulthood and parenthood; one in six people alive today is between the ages of 15 and 24.[11] Even if fertility were to fall immediately to the replacement level of 2.1 children, more than three quarters of the population growth currently projected would still take place.[12]

A number of positive trends account for most of the reduction in fertility rates and growth rates. Economic prosperity and better health care persuaded many couples that large families were no longer necessary to ensure security in old age.[13] Improvements in girls' access to education and in women's status have increased women's control over their lives, including when and how many children to have.[14] And broad access to contraceptives has boosted the share of couples using these family planning methods from 10 percent in 1960 to nearly 60 percent in 2000.[15]

Indeed, strong efforts to make contraceptives available can rapidly bring down birth rates, even in conservative countries. Iran, which had a strongly pro-natalist orientation in the years following its 1979 revolution, changed its policy in the late 1980s and cut its growth rate rapidly and dramatically, from 3.2 percent in 1986 to 0.8 percent in 2000.[16] Under the new policy, all forms of contraception are available free of charge, and religious leaders are active in legitimizing the use of various methods.[17]

The deceleration of population growth is not entirely good news, however, because part of the decline is due to the spread of AIDS. Some 3 million people died of AIDS in 2000, bringing the disease's cumulative total to nearly 22 million people.[18] At least 45 AIDS-afflicted countries—35 of them in Africa—are projected by 2015 to have populations at least 5 percent lower than they would have had without this deadly disease.[19] The 35 African countries will have populations 10 percent lower.[20]

Continued deceleration of population growth is needed to bring human economies closer to sustainability. But the road ahead continues to be challenging. The United Nations estimates that the number of contraceptive users among married women will need to increase by 60 percent—and among African women, it will need to double—if the medium population projection for 2025 of 7.8 billion is to be achieved.[21] And additional gains in health, education, and economic security for girls and women will be needed to ensure that women are strong, independent decisionmakers. The 1994 International Conference on Population and Development saw nothing less than universal education, a reduction in child mortality, and total access to family planning and reproductive health services as necessary prerequisites for achieving global population stabilization.[22]

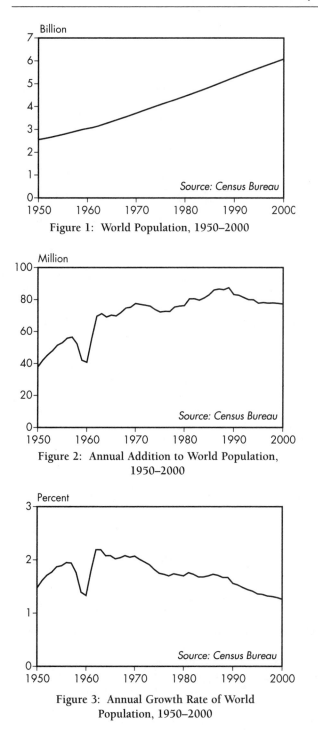

Figure 1: World Population, 1950–2000

Figure 2: Annual Addition to World Population, 1950–2000

Figure 3: Annual Growth Rate of World Population, 1950–2000

World Population, Total and Annual Addition, 1950–2000

Year	Total[1] (billion)	Annual Addition (million)
1950	2.555	38
1955	2.780	53
1960	3.039	41
1965	3.346	70
1970	3.708	78
1971	3.785	77
1972	3.862	77
1973	3.939	76
1974	4.015	74
1975	4.088	72
1976	4.160	73
1977	4.233	72
1978	4.305	75
1979	4.381	76
1980	4.457	76
1981	4.533	80
1982	4.613	81
1983	4.694	80
1984	4.774	81
1985	4.855	83
1986	4.938	86
1987	5.024	87
1988	5.110	86
1989	5.196	87
1990	5.284	83
1991	5.367	83
1992	5.450	81
1993	5.531	80
1994	5.611	80
1995	5.691	78
1996	5.769	78
1997	5.847	78
1998	5.925	78
1999	6.003	78
2000 (prel)	6.080	77

[1]Total at mid-year.
Source: U.S. Bureau of the Census, *International Data Base*, electronic database, Suitland, MD, updated 10 May 2000.

Cigarette Production Remains High
Anne Platt McGinn

Global cigarette output increased to 5,564 billion pieces in 2000, only a 0.1-percent boost from 1999.[1] (See Figure 1.) Production per person rose to 915 cigarettes between 1999 and 2000.[2] (See Figure 2.) Compared with the all-time high in 1996, total production was down 2 percent, while per capita supplies have dropped 11 percent since their peak in 1990.[3]

China, Germany, Japan, Russia, and the United States now produce more than half the world's cigarettes.[4] The leading cigarette producer and consumer is China; between 1999 and 2000, output there increased 4 percent, to 1,713 billion cigarettes, just short of the peak in 1995.[5] With some 350 million smokers—equal to the combined population of Russia and Mexico—people in China smoke an estimated 38 percent of the world's cigarettes.[6]

Link: p. 138

In contrast, output in the United States—the world's number two producer—dropped 18 percent between 1995 and 2000, and consumption per person fell 16 percent.[7] (See Figure 3.) In 2000, U.S. cigarette exports reached their lowest level in 25 years. Nevertheless, the United States remains the world's leading source of cigarettes, responsible for 21 percent of exports.[8]

In 2000, for the first time in history, Russia produced more cigarettes than Japan.[9] Prompted by foreign investments and higher raw tobacco imports, Russian output jumped 52 percent between 1998 and 2000, from 180 billion to 273 billion pieces.[10] Foreign companies and joint ventures now account for more than half of Russia's cigarette production.[11]

Mirroring trends in the United States, production in most industrial countries is now either stagnant or falling, as more people in these nations reject smoking. Since the mid-1990s, Japanese output has stabilized.[12] Germany's production has fallen 8 percent since 1995.[13]

Price is a key factor influencing smoking rates. The World Health Organization (WHO) and World Bank have shown that a global cigarette tax of 10 percent would prompt 40 million smokers to quit and would prevent the premature deaths of 10 million people alive today.[14] (Each year, 4 million people die prematurely from more than 25 tobacco-related illnesses.)[15]

Although higher prices have captured public attention, in much of the developing world cigarettes are cheaper in real prices today than in 1990.[16] And they are more available. Consequently, cigarette sales have jumped 80 percent in developing countries since 1990.[17]

An estimated 800 million smokers—70 percent of the world's total—now live in developing countries, along with countless passive smokers who share the risks of smoking-related diseases.[18] Each day some 80,000–100,000 young people become regular long-term smokers, primarily in developing countries.[19]

The increase is particularly high in Africa, where smoking rates are climbing about 5.5 percent each year; in other developing regions, the figure is as much as 3 percent annually.[20] If these trends continue over the next 20 years, more Africans could die from tobacco-related illnesses than AIDS, malaria, and maternal mortality combined.[21]

Illegal trafficking is a significant and growing source of cigarettes. In 1999, Chinese officials seized about 100 billion illegal cigarettes, 26 percent more than in 1998.[22] In November 2000, the European Commission filed a civil action suit against two U.S. cigarette companies, seeking compensation for alleged avoidance of customs duties and value-added taxes.[23] High taxes in Canada, Ukraine, and the United Kingdom have also had the unintended consequence of fueling the black market.[24]

After suffering defeat in a major U.S. lawsuit in 1998, tobacco companies also came under fire for questionable and possibly illegal corporate practices in a damning WHO report indicating the firms sought for years to discredit several U.N. bodies with paid scientists and lobbyists.[25] To counter these and other influences, 150 countries and the European Union are negotiating a global treaty on tobacco control.[26] The current draft supports widespread adoption of anti-smoking programs, higher taxes, and restrictions on the sale and use of cigarettes. Negotiators expect the treaty to be finalized in 2003.[27]

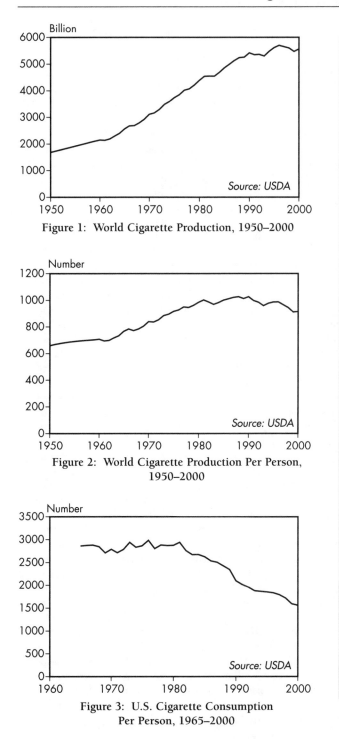

Figure 1: World Cigarette Production, 1950–2000

Figure 2: World Cigarette Production Per Person, 1950–2000

Figure 3: U.S. Cigarette Consumption Per Person, 1965–2000

World Cigarette Production, 1950–2000

Year	Total (billion)	Per Person (number)
1950	1,686	660
1955	1,921	691
1960	2,150	707
1965	2,564	766
1970	3,112	840
1971	3,165	836
1972	3,295	853
1973	3,481	884
1974	3,590	895
1975	3,742	916
1976	3,852	926
1977	4,019	950
1978	4,072	946
1979	4,214	962
1980	4,388	985
1981	4,541	1002
1982	4,550	987
1983	4,547	969
1984	4,689	983
1985	4,855	1,001
1986	4,987	1,011
1987	5,128	1,022
1988	5,250	1,026
1989	5,258	1,013
1990	5,419	1,027
1991	5,351	998
1992	5,363	985
1993	5,300	960
1994	5,478	978
1995	5,615	987
1996	5,699	988
1997	5,649	966
1998	5,598	945
1999	5,471	911
2000 (prel)	5,564	915

Sources: Trent, USDA, letters to author, February 2001; USDA, *Special Report: World Cigarette Situation*, August 1999; data for 1950–58 are estimates based on U.S. data.

Ann Hwang

Every six seconds in the year 2000, someone was infected with HIV, the virus that causes AIDS—5.3 million people in total.[1] (See Figure 1.) By the end of the year, one of every 100 adults worldwide between the ages of 15 and 49 was infected.[2] Since the epidemic started 20 years ago, AIDS has killed almost 22 million people, more than the population of greater New York City.[3] (See Figure 2.)

Two thirds of the world's HIV-infected people live in sub-Saharan Africa. In 2000, for the first time, the number of new infections in the region decreased, from 4 million to 3.8 million.[4] But in a region that already has some of the highest infection rates (in Botswana, one in three adults is infected), this slowing may reflect the sad fact that the virus is encountering fewer and fewer uninfected targets.[5]

Links:
pp. 106, 138

In just two decades, AIDS has single-handedly erased 50 years of life expectancy gains in many African countries. People in eight countries have lost more than 10 years of expected life, and in Botswana and Zimbabwe, life expectancy has dropped by more than three decades.[6]

Because it can take several years for the virus to sicken and ultimately kill its hosts, the full impact of AIDS may still lie ahead. AIDS strikes at young, sexually active people, the cornerstone of the work force. By 2020, it could reduce the labor forces in Botswana, Mozambique, Namibia, South Africa, and Zimbabwe to less than three quarters of what they would otherwise have been.[7] And as countries lose teachers to AIDS, fewer children will have the chance to obtain an education. Already, students are leaving school to support their families after the loss of other breadwinners.[8]

The Caribbean region harbors the second-highest rates of infection, with two adults in every 100 infected.[9] In Asia, AIDS has spread from the heroin-producing Golden Triangle to remote corners of China and India, infecting 6.4 million people.[10] And the number of people in Eastern Europe living with HIV or AIDS jumped nearly 70 percent in the past year, from 420,000 to 700,000.[11]

While new drugs have helped HIV-positive people in wealthy nations live longer and better, reliance on them can foster a false sense of security that undermines prevention efforts. Today's youth—spared the experience of watching friends die from AIDS—may see the disease as a manageable chronic illness.[12] In the United Kingdom, the number of cases of sexually transmitted diseases reached its highest level in a decade, suggesting that risky sexual practices are again on the rise.[13] Indeed, a U.S. study found that 40 percent of young gay men interviewed had had unprotected sex within the previous six months.[14] And many users of intravenous drugs—92 percent in one British study—are sharing needles.[15] Even after years of warnings about HIV, there has been no decrease in the number of new infections, which totaled 75,000 in 2000 in Western Europe and North America.[16]

Bringing down the cost of pharmaceuticals could make treatment affordable for more of the 36 million people living with HIV/AIDS.[17] In May 2000, five makers of anti-HIV drugs unveiled plans to discount their products for developing countries.[18] But so far the tangible results have been few. Senegal, one of the few countries to have signed an agreement, said it expected to increase eightfold the number of people treated—but that means adding only 420–889 patients by 2006.[19] Other developing countries are risking the wrath and lawsuits of drugmakers by producing or importing cheaper generic versions of anti-HIV drugs.[20] By manufacturing its own generic drugs, Brazil is able to treat an estimated 90,000 people.[21]

Around the globe, the socially disenfranchised are hit the hardest by AIDS. Women in developing countries, people living in poverty, and members of racial and ethnic minorities form the "silent majority" of AIDS victims. The Joint United Nations Programme on HIV/AIDS estimates that $4.5 billion could both boost AIDS prevention and fund basic medical care for AIDS victims throughout Africa.[22] Harvard economist Jeffrey Sachs has proposed raising $5 billion to start providing anti-retroviral drugs to millions.[23] The amounts involved are surprisingly modest: $4.5 billion can barely purchase two B-2 Stealth bombers.[24]

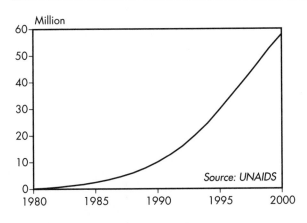

Million

Figure 1: Estimates of Cumulative HIV Infections Worldwide, 1980–2000

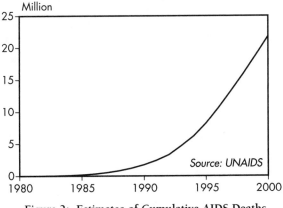

Million

Figure 2: Estimates of Cumulative AIDS Deaths Worldwide, 1980–2000

Cumulative HIV Infections and AIDS Deaths Worldwide, 1980–2000

Year	HIV Infections	AIDS Deaths
	(million)	
1980	0.1	0.0
1981	0.3	0.0
1982	0.7	0.0
1983	1.2	0.0
1984	1.7	0.1
1985	2.4	0.2
1986	3.4	0.3
1987	4.5	0.5
1988	5.9	0.8
1989	7.8	1.2
1990	10.0	1.7
1991	12.8	2.4
1992	16.1	3.3
1993	20.1	4.7
1994	24.5	6.2
1995	29.8	8.2
1996	35.3	10.6
1997	40.9	13.2
1998	46.6	15.9
1999	52.6	18.8
2000 (prel)	57.9	21.8

Sources: Worldwatch update based on Neff Walker, UNAIDS, e-mail, 20 March 2000; UNAIDS, *AIDS Epidemic Update: December 2000* (Geneva: 2000).

Military Trends

War Trends Mixed

Peacekeeping Expenditures Rebound

Limited Progress on Nuclear Arsenals

Michael Renner

According to AKUF, a conflict research group at the University of Hamburg, the number of wars worldwide declined from 34 in 1999 to 31 in 2000.[1] (See Figure 1.) Three wars came to an end (in Kosovo, Congo-Brazzaville, and Guinea-Bissau), and two (Nigeria and Kashmir) were re-classified as "armed conflicts" that did not entirely meet AKUF's criteria for war.[2] At the same time, however, the Israeli-Palestinian conflict escalated once again, and the war in Sierra Leone spilled over into neighboring Guinea.[3]

Combining the wars and armed conflicts categories, the number of violent clashes actually rose slightly—from 48 in 1999 to 49 in 2000.[4] More than 7 million people, mostly civilians, are believed to have died in these conflicts since they began.[5]

Links: pp. 84, 142

Due to divergent definitions and methodologies, other research groups report somewhat different figures, but broadly confirm the AKUF trend. The Uppsala Conflict Data Project puts the number of armed conflicts in 1999 at 37, of which 14 were wars, 13 intermediate conflicts, and 10 minor conflicts.[6] Project Ploughshares in Canada cites 40 conflicts in 1999.[7] And PIOOM, a Dutch organization, casts a far wider net, reporting 26 wars, 78 low-intensity conflicts, and 178 violent political conflicts as of mid-2000.[8] On the other hand, however, conflict researchers in Heidelberg, Germany, reckon that 108 disputes in 2000 were dealt with largely nonviolently, up from 69 in 1992.[9] (See Figure 2.)

More than 90 percent of all wars since 1945 have taken place in developing countries.[10] The major exception has been the series of conflicts in the former Yugoslavia. Africa and Asia continue to be plagued by the most wars (12 and 10 respectively), followed by the Middle East (7), and Latin America (2).[11]

One third of sovereign states—63 countries—have not been involved in any warfare since 1945.[12] But at the other end of the spectrum, at least 10 countries are currently home to multiple armed conflicts, ranging from wars to low-level violent political conflicts. PIOOM researchers counted 32 separate conflicts in India, 17 in Nigeria, 12 each in Indonesia and Pakistan, and 10 in Colombia.[13] Other countries with multiple conflicts are China, Ethiopia, Russia, Sudan, and Uganda.[14]

Of 110 conflicts listed by the Uppsala researchers as active in 1989–99, 103 were internal (including 9 cases in which there was foreign intervention).[15] Only 7 conflicts were interstate wars.[16] (See Figure 3.)

Still, in several cases, regions surrounding countries at war are in danger of being drawn into the violence. The most obvious example is the ongoing civil war in the Democratic Republic of Congo, where the intervention of Angola, Burundi, Chad, Namibia, Rwanda, Uganda, and Zimbabwe has created a regional war. Several of these states became involved in part to fight rebel groups in their own countries that use Congolese territory as a base of operations.[17] Tensions are now also escalating in the Central African Republic, in part because of the influx of Congolese refugees.[18]

In West Africa, conflicts in Guinea-Bissau and Senegal's Casamance region became intertwined, as did those in Liberia, Sierra Leone, and Guinea.[19] In Latin America, Colombia's neighbors increasingly fear that its worsening civil conflict will spill across their borders. Ecuador, itself reeling economically and politically, has seen fighting among Colombian paramilitaries and rebels in its border area.[20]

Among the most devastating current or recent wars, as many as 100,000 people were killed in fighting between Eritrea and Ethiopia between May 1998 and June 2000; up to 1 million people have been uprooted.[21] In the Democratic Republic of Congo, at least 1.7 million "excess deaths" occurred over the 22 months prior to May 2000—that's 77,000 deaths a month.[22] That war has displaced up to 2 million people within the country and pushed a quarter of a million more into neighboring nations.[23] And in Angola, following failed peacemaking efforts in the mid-1990s, the United Nations estimated in 1999 that some 200 citizens fall victim to the war each day.[24]

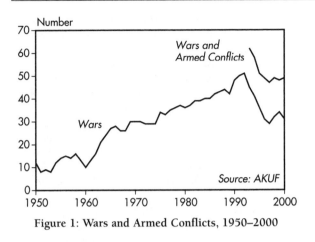

Figure 1: Wars and Armed Conflicts, 1950–2000

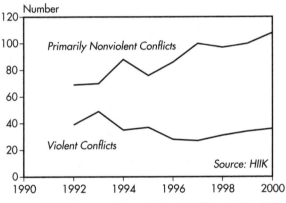

Figure 2: Violent and Nonviolent Conflicts, 1992–2000

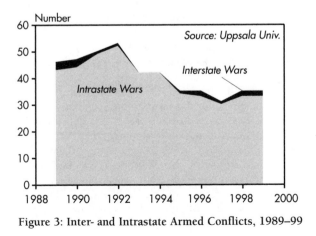

Figure 3: Inter- and Intrastate Armed Conflicts, 1989–99

Wars and Armed Conflicts, 1950–2000

Year	Wars	Wars and Armed Conflicts
		(number)
1950	12	
1955	14	
1960	10	
1965	27	
1970	30	
1971	30	
1972	29	
1973	29	
1974	29	
1975	34	
1976	33	
1977	35	
1978	36	
1979	37	
1980	36	
1981	37	
1982	39	
1983	39	
1984	40	
1985	40	
1986	42	
1987	43	
1988	44	
1989	42	
1990	48	
1991	50	
1992	51	
1993	45	62
1994	41	58
1995	36	51
1996	31	49
1997	29	47
1998	32	49
1999	34	48
2000 (prel)	31	49

Source: Arbeitsgemeinschaft Kriegsur-sachenforschung, Institute for Political Science, University of Hamburg.

Peacekeeping Expenditures Rebound

Michael Renner

Continuing the erratic pattern of the last several years, expenditures for U.N. peacekeeping operations are on a rebound. Rising from $1.6 billion for the July 1999–June 2000 period, budgets for July 2000–June 2001 will run to about $2.9 billion as several missions become fully established.[1] (See Figure 1.) But this is equivalent to less than 0.5 percent of world military expenditures.[2] Since the beginning of U.N. peacekeeping in 1948, a total of 54 missions have been initiated, at a cumulative cost of about $31 billion.[3]

Some 38,000 soldiers, military observers, and civilian police from 89 countries served in 15 peacekeeping missions active at the end of 2000, more than twice as many individuals as in 1999.[4] (See Figure 2.) Further, a total of 12,577 local and international civilian personnel served in these missions.[5]

Link: p. 82

Just five countries—Bangladesh, Ghana, India, Jordan, and Poland—accounted for one quarter of all peacekeepers dispatched in 1996–2000.[6] In fact, 12 contributors provided half the total number.[7] The five permanent members of the Security Council provide a rather modest 10 percent of all personnel and have largely avoided the riskiest missions.[8] Whereas in 1991 only 2 developing countries— Ghana and Nepal—were among the top 10 contributors of personnel, in 2000 there were 8.[9]

Three of the four missions initiated in 1999—the transitional administration in East Timor, the interim administration for Kosovo, and a peacekeeping force in Sierra Leone— quickly grew into the largest current undertakings.[10] The ranks of U.N. peacekeepers are likely to grow to about 45,000 once these missions reach their authorized strength and a new 4,200-strong force to observe a peace agreement between Ethiopia and Eritrea is in place.[11] Also, the number of observers in the Democratic Republic of Congo is set to double to about 500, but the prospects for peace there—and for full deployment of a 5,537-strong mission authorized by the U.N. Security Council—remain highly uncertain.[12]

In May 2000, a high-level Panel on U.N. Peace Operations chaired by former Algerian Foreign Minister Lakdhar Brahimi was convened by Secretary-General Kofi Annan to conduct a critical review of the peacekeeping experience. Its report made a broad range of recommendations to boost the organization's peacekeeping capacity.[13] It urged member states to establish clear and achievable mandates, strengthen the headquarters staff, create an information-gathering and analysis office, and improve logistics and integrated mission planning.[14] To enable the United Nations to field missions quicker, the Brahimi report called for improving the existing standby system and suggested generating "on-call" lists of military officers, civilian police, judicial experts, and human rights specialists.[15]

Most fundamentally, the Brahimi report made it clear that if the United Nations is to succeed, it needs enough staff, equipment, and resources.[16] Yet U.N. members, and particularly the permanent members of the Security Council, have not heeded this lesson, even as they continue to heap expectations onto the organization. Struggling under an ongoing cloud of financial crisis, in late 2000 the United Nations had only enough cash in hand to pay for about three months' worth of peacekeeping expenditures.[17] At the end of 2000, U.N. members owed the organization close to $2 billion for peacekeeping operations.[18] (See Figure 3.) The United States accounted for 58 percent of the total, or $1.1 billion in unpaid dues.[19] Most of this debt piled up in 1995 and 1996, when the United States paid only 40¢ and 70¢, respectively, of each dollar owed.[20]

The United States has long pressed to have its share of the peacekeeping budget reduced, conditioning payment of its arrears on such a move. Following acrimonious negotiations, the U.N. General Assembly agreed to that demand in December 2000.[21] In return, the U.S. Congress is likely to release a portion of the money needed to clear its debt.[22] But the United States insists it owes less money than the United Nations claims, and may well withhold future dues.[23] It is still too early to celebrate an end to the U.N. financial crunch.

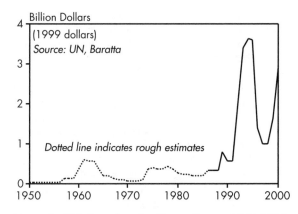

Figure 1: U.N. Peacekeeping Expenditures, 1950–2000

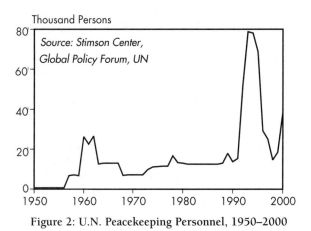

Figure 2: U.N. Peacekeeping Personnel, 1950–2000

U.N. Peacekeeping Expenditures, 1986–2000

Year	Expenditure (mill. 1999 dollars)
1986	336.5
1987	324.4
1988	347.4
1989	798.2
1990	561.4
1991	572.3
1992	2,015.0
1993	3,406.0
1994	3,645.2
1995	3,591.0
1996*	1,393.1
1997*	1,017.3
1998*	1,014.9
1999*	1,647.0
2000*	2,900.5

*July to June of following year.
Sources: U.N. Department of Peacekeeping Operations; Office of the Spokesman for the U.N. Secretary-General.

Figure 3: Arrears of U.N. Members for Peacekeeping Expenses, 1975–2000

Limited Progress on Nuclear Arsenals *Michael Renner*

The number of nuclear warheads held by the world's five full-fledged nuclear powers declined slightly last year, from 31,960 in 1999 to 31,535 in 2000.[1] Since a 1986 peak of almost 70,000 warheads, the size of the global nuclear arsenal (strategic and "tactical" warheads) has dropped by 55 percent.[2] (See Figure 1.)

The United States retains 10,500 strategic and tactical warheads, while Russia has 20,000.[3] (See Figure 2.) The three other original nuclear powers—France, China, and the United Kingdom—have roughly 1,000 warheads combined.[4] Israel, India, and Pakistan possess an unknown, but clearly smaller, number of warheads.[5]

Since 1945, an estimated total of 128,000 warheads have been built; the United States produced some 70,000 and the Soviet Union/Russia about 55,000.[6] Today, there is enough weapons-grade plutonium worldwide—some 260 tons—to supply about 85,000 warheads.[7]

The size of the global nuclear stockpile has declined as a result of U.S.-Russian arms control efforts. But the remaining arsenals still add up to a mind-numbing 5,000 megatons of explosive power.[8] Some 4,600 U.S. and Russian warheads are still on the "hair-trigger" alert status that allows immediate launch on warning but that also carries a high risk of accidental war.[9] And a number of troubling developments cast doubt on how much additional progress on nuclear disarmament can be expected in coming years.

One issue is nuclear testing. Since 1945, seven countries have conducted more than 2,050 tests.[10] India and Pakistan conducted a series of test explosions in May 1998. Since then, there have been no nuclear tests anywhere.[11] (See Figure 3.) But efforts to outlaw any future tests—the objective of the 1996 Comprehensive Nuclear Test Ban Treaty (CTBT)—have met with only partial success. At the end of 2000, the treaty had been signed by 160 countries and ratified by 69.[12] But it will not go into effect unless the 44 countries with nuclear power reactors or research reactors ratify it. So far, 41 of these nations have

signed (the nonsignatories are India, North Korea, and Pakistan), and 30 have ratified it.[13] Prominent among the 11 nonratifiers is the United States: the U.S. Senate rejected ratification in October 1999.[14]

Although the nuclear powers have ceased their test explosions, they are pursuing computer test simulations and so-called subcritical tests to develop nuclear warhead technology further. The United States, for example, conducted 8 subcritical tests in 1997–2000 and is planning at least another 14. A number of countries oppose such experiments as violations of the spirit of the CTBT.[15]

U.S. moves to develop a ballistic missile defense system, considered to be in violation of the 1972 Anti-Ballistic Missile Treaty between the United States and the Soviet Union, have led Russia to threaten that it will withdraw from other nuclear arms control agreements if the United States carries out its plan.[16] China announced in May 2000 that it might significantly expand its nuclear arsenal in response to any U.S. missile shield.[17] Quantitative and qualitative improvements in China's nuclear forces would in turn increase pressure on India and Pakistan to step up their own programs.[18]

If U.S.-Russian discord over missile defense deepens, one casualty could be a planned third strategic arms reductions treaty (START III). Negotiations aim to reduce each country's arsenal of strategic warheads down to 2,000–2,500, from the 3,000–3,500 limit established by START II.[19]

Even though the five original nuclear powers signed an agreement in May 2000 committing themselves to the "unequivocal" elimination of nuclear arms, their day-to-day policies do not in any way suggest that they are prepared to abolish their arsenals.[20] This, however, is a legal obligation under Article VI of the Nuclear Non-Proliferation Treaty. The yawning gap between rhetoric and reality perpetuates international insecurity and all but ensures continued serious disputes between the nuclear haves and have-nots.

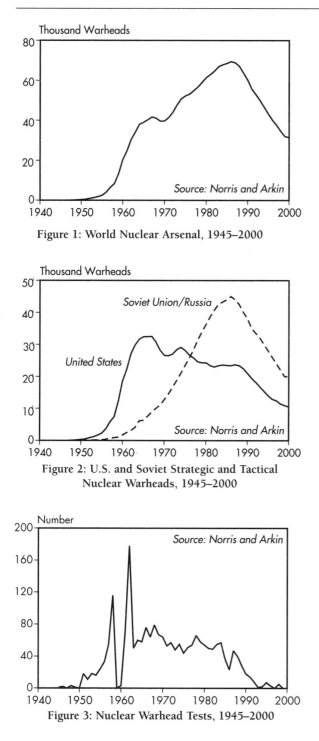

Thousand Warheads

Source: Norris and Arkin

Figure 1: World Nuclear Arsenal, 1945–2000

Thousand Warheads

Soviet Union/Russia

United States

Source: Norris and Arkin

Figure 2: U.S. and Soviet Strategic and Tactical
Nuclear Warheads, 1945–2000

Number

Source: Norris and Arkin

Figure 3: Nuclear Warhead Tests, 1945–2000

World Nuclear Arsenal, 1945–2000

Year	Nuclear Warheads (number)
1945	2
1950	303
1955	2,490
1960	20,368
1965	39,047
1970	39,691
1971	41,365
1972	44,020
1973	47,741
1974	50,840
1975	52,323
1976	53,252
1977	54,978
1978	56,805
1979	59,120
1980	61,480
1981	63,054
1982	64,769
1983	66,979
1984	67,585
1986	69,478
1987	68,835
1988	67,041
1989	63,645
1990	60,236
1991	55,772
1992	52,972
1993	50,008
1994	46,542
1995	43,200
1996	40,100
1997	37,535
1998	34,535
1999	31,960
2000 (prel)	31,535

Source: Norris and Arkin, Nuclear Notebook, *Bulletin of the Atomic Scientists*, March/April 2000.

PART TWO
Special Features

Environmental Features

World's Coral Reefs Dying Off

Hydrological Poverty Worsening

Wetlands Decline

Birds Species Threatened

Farm Animal Populations Soar

Growth in Transgenic Area Slows

World's Coral Reefs Dying Off

Lisa Mastny

As of late 2000, an estimated 27 percent of the world's coral reefs were severely damaged, according to the Global Coral Reef Monitoring Network.[1] In 1992, the figure was only 10 percent, so the health of reefs is deteriorating quickly.[2] The greatest losses have occurred in the Indian Ocean, in the Arabian Sea and Persian Gulf, and in Southeast Asia.[3] (See Table 1.)

More than 100 countries—many of them small islands—rely on coral reefs for essential goods and services valued at some $375 billion a year.[4] Reefs shelter coastlines from storm damage, erosion, and flooding, providing protection and other benefits for an estimated half-billion people.[5] They are important feeding and breeding grounds for commercial fisheries, producing roughly a tenth of the global fish catch and a quarter of the catch in the developing world.[6] Reefs also generate significant tourism revenue, with Caribbean reefs alone bringing in some $140 billion annually.[7]

Links: pp. 50, 96

Coral reefs cover less than 0.2 percent of ocean area, but are among Earth's most complex and productive ecosystems.[8] The unique assemblages of tiny coral animals and symbiotic plants provide habitat for as many as 1 million species—including more than a quarter of known marine fish species.[9] Reef-derived molecules have been used to develop medicines from antibiotics to HIV drugs.[10]

An estimated 11 percent of the world's coral reefs have been lost as a result of direct human pressures.[11] These include fishing and coral mining, coastal development, waste dumping, vessel collisions, and inland deforestation and farming, which can cause runoff of harmful nutrients and sediments.[12] Such activities now threaten nearly 60 percent of all reefs.[13]

The booming demand for reef species for food and for aquariums has depopulated many coral ecosystems.[14] In Southeast Asia, live reef fish exports jumped nearly 13-fold between 1989 and 1995, then dropped 22 percent in 1996—a crash attributed to overfishing.[15] Worldwide, a survey of reefs in some 40 countries in 1998 found that many high-value species, such as lobster, grouper, and giant clams, were missing from areas where they were once abundant.[16]

Fishers often use methods that are highly destructive to reefs. In Southeast Asia, "blast" fishers set off as many as 10 separate explosions to obtain 1 ton of fish, shattering up to 20 square meters of reef per blast.[17] This practice has degraded an estimated 75 percent of Indonesia's reefs.[18] And in the Philippines, more than a million kilograms of cyanide have been injected into reefs since the 1960s—a procedure that stuns or kills many nontarget species as well.[19] Powerful trawlers can also devastate reefs, removing up to a quarter of seabed life in a single pass.[20]

But the greatest threat to coral reefs today is global warming.[21] Reefs live at the upper edge of their temperature tolerance, making them good indicators of climate change.[22] Warming of a little as 1 degree Celsius above normal can stress the microscopic plants that inhabit the tissue of corals and provide them with food and color.[23] If the stress endures, the corals expel the plants and turn white, often eventually dying.[24]

Such "coral bleaching" events have increased in frequency and intensity since the early 1980s.[25] In 1997–98, a combination of El Niño/La Niña–related climatic changes and record-high tropical sea surface temperatures caused the worst episode on record, affecting some 16 percent of the world's reefs, in at least 60 countries.[26] Indian Ocean reefs alone suffered damages estimated as high as $8.2 billion.[27] In some areas, 1,000-year-old corals died and losses neared 90 percent, at depths nearing 40 meters.[28]

About a third of the bleached reefs show early signs of recovery, having retained or recruited enough live coral to survive.[29] Roughly half could rebound in the next 20–50 years—if ocean temperatures remain steady and human pressures are low.[30] But if the warming continues, scientists predict that as many as 60 percent of all reefs could be lost by 2030.[31] Mass bleaching events could begin to occur annually by then, offsetting any real reef recovery.[32] Moreover, some corals may already have exceeded their capacity to adapt to warmer waters, and rising ocean carbon dioxide levels could further impede coral growth.[33]

As reef loss worsens, partnerships like the International Coral Reef Initiative, the International Coral Reef Action Network, and the Coral Reef Alliance are working to raise awareness, promote conservation, and assess threats.[34] Another global project, Reef Check, enlists sport divers and locals to conduct annual reef surveys.[35]

Innovative strategies are also emerging in developing countries, which typically lack the resources for effective reef protection.[36] In Bonaire, a $10 dive tax brings in $170,000 annually, helping to pay for rangers and educational materials.[37] And in one Indonesian park, a new reef patrol has helped reduce blast fishing by 80 percent since 1996.[38]

Another key solution is creating marine reserves where activities like fishing and anchoring are banned. The United States plans to protect a fifth of its reefs in such reserves by 2010.[39] But such actions may prove futile without parallel efforts to reduce emissions of climate-altering greenhouse gases.

Table 1: Status of Coral Reefs Around the World

Location	Share Destroyed (percent)	Condition of Reefs
Southeast and East Asia (30 percent of total reef area)	34	Reefs in southern Japan, Taiwan, Viet Nam, and parts of the Philippines and Indonesia hit hard by the 1998 bleaching, with losses of 30–90 percent in areas. Remote reefs have a fair chance for slow recovery. Others face serious human pressures: Indonesia, home to 14 percent of the world's reefs, has lost roughly half its reefs, mainly to blast and cyanide fishing.
Pacific Ocean (25 percent)	4 in Australia and Papua New Guinea; 9 in rest of Pacific	Reefs generally in good condition. Palau and inshore areas of the Great Barrier Reef saw extensive bleaching in 1998, though recovery is reported in both areas. Central and Southeast Pacific reefs largely escaped this event. In early 2000, bleaching in the Solomon Islands and Fiji affected some 65 percent of Fiji's reefs, killing at least 15 percent. Other threats include development, sediment and nutrient runoff, overfishing, and predation by crown-of-thorns starfish.
Indian Ocean (24 percent)	59	The 1998 bleaching caused widespread damage, particularly in the Maldives, Sri Lanka, and parts of western India. Reefs off Kenya, the Seychelles, Tanzania, and Comoros saw live coral losses of 80–90 percent. Also serious damage from pollution, coral mining, and overfishing. Reefs not affected by human pressures have a fair chance for recovery—with some early evidence of this in East Africa, the Seychelles, the Maldives, and the Lakshadweep Islands.
Caribbean Sea and Atlantic Ocean (15 percent)	22	Caribbean reefs experienced extensive bleaching in 1998, but many have shown near full recovery. Greatest threats are from overfishing, sedimentation, pollution, and coral disease. In the Florida Keys, live coral now covers only 5 percent of the surface area of the largest reef, down from over 50 percent in 1975. Reefs off Central America suffered mass bleaching in 1995 and 1998, as well as damage from Hurricane Mitch in 1998.
Middle East (6 percent)	35	Nearshore reefs in the Arabian Sea and Persian Gulf virtually wiped out by bleaching in 1996 and 1998. Low chance of short-term recovery. Northern Gulf affected by bleaching in late 2000. Red Sea reefs remain healthy, but are threatened by tourism, oil development, and shipping.

Sources: See endnote 3.

Hydrological Poverty Worsening
Janet Larsen

In 2000, the World Health Organization estimated that 1.1 billion people were not able to meet their needs for safe water.[1] (See Table 1.) These people can be thought of as hydrologically impoverished. Although moderate gains have been made in various regions, one fifth of humanity has no access to a safe water supply, and two fifths has inadequate sanitation.[2]

Twenty-nine percent of people living in rural areas around the world lack the most basic water supply—they cannot get water from a household connection, public standpipe, borehole, protected dug well, protected spring, or rainwater collection.[3] Over 62 percent of the world's rural population lacks improved sanitation, meaning a household connection to a public sewer, septic system, pour-flush toilet, or simple pit latrine.[4] In cities, the equivalent figure is 14 percent.[5]

Link: p. 96

In Asia, some 693 million people lack access to clean water, and nearly all of them—86 percent—live in rural areas.[6] In Africa, 300 million people are in this situation; 85 percent of them live in rural areas.[7] Indeed, 53 percent of Africa's rural population lacks access, while in Africa's cities the figure is 15 percent.[8] In Latin America and the Caribbean, 63 percent of the 78 million who cannot easily get safe water inhabit rural areas.[9] In Oceania and Europe, the people without water service are almost entirely found in rural areas.[10]

Hydrological poverty strikes at a variety of levels beyond lack of access to water supplies. At the most fundamental level is water scarcity, where drought and water diversions for agriculture and industry limit the amount of water available to meet people's basic needs. Currently, 2.3 billion people live in water-stressed countries, with less than 1,700 cubic meters of water available per person during the year.[11] Of this group, 1.7 billion reside in areas of water scarcity, where yearly per capita availability falls below 1,000 cubic meters.[12] By 2025, the number of people living in water-stressed situations is predicted to reach 3.4 billion, with over 2.4 billion in the more dire plight of water scarcity.[13] And these estimates are based on national-level predictions; they understate the current severity of the problem in many local areas.[14]

In some areas, water may be plentiful but arrive in punctuated bursts, or it cannot be collected for later use since there are no adequate water storage facilities. In India, for instance, precipitation is concentrated in the four months of the monsoon season, during which only a few hours of rain provide over half the year's rainfall.[15] In drought-prone northwestern China, 60 percent of the limited annual precipitation occurs between July and September, which unfortunately is not when the water is most needed by crops.[16]

An alternative to depending on precipitation is to turn to water from the ground. More than a quarter of the world's population relies on groundwater for drinking supplies, yet aquifers are being depleted worldwide because natural recharge rates cannot keep pace with increased use.[17] In many areas, including parts of China, the Indian subcontinent, Mexico, and Yemen, water tables are falling by as much as a meter each year.[18]

Where water is not necessarily scarce, it may be of poor quality, contaminated by pollutants or salt. Globally, less than 10 percent of total waste, including farm runoff, industrial pollution, and human waste, is treated before it enters rivers that are used for drinking, sanitation, irrigation, or industry.[19] On each continent, groundwater is threatened by contamination from nitrates, pesticides, petrochemicals, arsenic, chlorinated solvents, radioactive wastes, fluoride, or saltwater intrusion, or by a combination of these.[20]

Even in places where fresh water may be plentiful, poverty often precludes access to it. It is hardly a coincidence that the 1.1 billion who are without access to water supplies correspond closely to the 1.2 billion in extreme poverty who live on less than $1 a day.[21] The poor who are cut off from municipal services are forced to collect water from unsafe sources, such as unprotected wells, springs, and drainage ditches, or to purchase water from independent vendors.[22] Such supplies are

Table 1: Population Lacking Access to Safe Water Supply, by Region, 2000

Region	People Without Access to a Supply of Safe Water		
	Rural	Urban	Total
		(million)	
Africa	256	44	300
Asia	595	98	693
Latin America and the Caribbean	49	29	78
Oceania	3	0	3
Europe	23	3	26
North America	0	0	0
World	926	173	1,099

Source: World Health Organization and UNICEF, *Global Water Supply and Sanitation Assessment 2000 Report* (New York: 2000), p. 8.

exempt from quality controls and of indeterminate origin, oftentimes coming from local polluted rivers, yet their price is high.[23] In developing nations, those who are not connected to water supplies on average pay 12 times more per liter of water than other people.[24] In Jakarta, Indonesia, people pay water vendors some 60 times the cost of water from a standard hook-up; in Karachi, Pakistan, it is 83 times as expensive; and in Port-au-Prince, Haiti, and Nouakchott, Mauritania, unconnected citizens pay 100 times more than their neighbors for each liter of water.[25]

Where connection to a water supply is provided, water service may be confined to specific times of the day, depending on supply. In many countries, the poor in outlying urban areas suffer from frequent service disruptions, as 30–50 percent of water supplies is lost to leaking pipes, overflowing service reservoirs, faulty equipment, or poorly maintained distribution systems.[26] A study of urban water use in sub-Saharan Africa found that the reliability of water service to households connected to municipal systems deteriorated over three decades.[27] Additionally, the time it took those

without piped supplies to collect water more than tripled between 1967 and 1997 because of growing distances between homes and the water source coupled with longer waits at kiosks or springs due to increased local demand.[28]

The absence of an affordable and accessible supply of clean water and sanitation services is closely linked to high instances of morbidity and mortality. An estimated 3.4 million people die each year worldwide from water-related diseases.[29] Diarrhea alone claims 2.2 million lives, a figure that targeted water, sanitation, and hygiene interventions could easily reduce by one quarter to one third.[30]

In order to increase water availability and provide improved service around the world, the World Water Council, an international water policy research group, estimates that total global investment in water services must more than double—from the current annual budget of $70–80 billion to over $180 billion.[31] Much new investment will need to come from the private sector, which now accounts for less than 5 percent of the total, especially in developing countries, where tight government budgets do not allow much room for water and sewage infrastructure improvements.[32]

Unfortunately, as water stress becomes increasingly common, fast-growing populations hungry for food and eager for development will elevate demands on water, both for basic needs and for agriculture and industry. Competition between urban and rural dwellers is likely to increase as cities grow in size and density, worsening hydrological poverty in the countryside.[33] These pressures will make it even more difficult for the marginalized poor to pay higher prices for access to this scarce and vital resource.

Wetlands Decline

Janet Larsen

From coastal swamps to inland floodplains, Earth has lost over half its wetlands in the last 100 years.[1] Much of the disappearance and degradation during the first half of the twentieth century occurred in the northern hemisphere, but pressure on wetlands in the South has increased since the 1950s, and these fragile ecosystems continue to lose ground throughout the world.[2] (See Table 1.)

Wetlands are areas where inundation or saturation with water is frequent but does not exceed 6 meters depth at low tide.[3] Natural freshwater wetlands, including marshes, bogs, swamps, and peatlands, occupy the most area, followed by rice paddies and saltwater wetland areas that include mangroves and coral reefs.[4] Left intact, wetlands regulate water flow, recharge groundwater supplies, and provide flood control.[5] In addition to hosting diverse biological communities, they retain essential sediments and nutrients while effectively buffering ecosystems against contamination by removing toxins from effluents and reducing the concentration of excess nitrogen and phosphorus from crop field drainage.[6]

Links: pp. 92, 94, 116

Estimates of total global wetlands vary considerably because of lack of data and the transient nature of these seasonal areas. Most analysts concur that from 5 million to 9 million square kilometers of wetlands are distributed fairly evenly over the continents, except Antarctica, with slightly higher concentrations in Europe and Asia.[7]

A principal cause of wetland loss is the draining or filling for human settlements and agriculture. In Europe, conversion to agriculture alone has reduced wetlands by some 60 percent.[8] In Asia, where some 85 percent of the wetlands of international importance are threatened, rice cultivation has claimed 40 million hectares in the central plains of India and significant portions of natural wetland areas in Thailand, Viet Nam, and China.[9]

In the United States, an estimated 23,700 hectares of wetlands, 98 percent of which were freshwater wetlands, were lost each year between 1986 and 1997 to urban and rural development, agriculture, and forest plantations.[10] In Oceania, where most people live in the coastal zone, the coastal lake areas and the biologically rich coral reefs and mangroves have been seriously degraded by altered hydrological regimes, land reclamation, and pollution.[11]

Competition is high for the use of Africa's wetlands. These areas, some of the world's most productive ecosystems, are oftentimes the exclusive source of natural resources on which growing economies depend.[12] In the Inner Delta of the Niger River, over a half-million people with 1 million sheep and 1 million goats depend on floodplains as dry-season grazing land.[13] Unfortunately, population growth, excessive exploitation, and misguided development projects threaten wetlands throughout the continent.[14]

In Central America, where wetlands have been highly modified, deforestation of coastal hills and mountains causes increased runoff during storms, depositing heavy sediment loads into low-lying wetlands.[15] A number of water diversion and dam projects endanger wetland ecosystems worldwide. In South America, the proposed Hidrovía waterway on the Paraná River threatens to destroy the world's largest continuous wetland, the Patanal, which covers western Brazil and parts of Bolivia and Paraguay.[16]

The impact of human change on wetland functioning is not confined to the site of impairment. Wetland draining and filling or the diversion and damming of rivers can alter the frequency of water flow, thereby harming downstream wetlands, deltas, and coastal ecosystems.[17] Additionally, draining can cause water tables to fall and increase the potential for the salinization of soils.[18] Such disruptions of hydrological regimes are predicted to increase the severity of water shortages in at least 60 countries and to elevate the incidence of flood-related disasters within 50 years.[19]

The draining of half the wetland areas in South Africa for agriculture, coupled with increased runoff from overgrazed grasslands in the upper watersheds of the Limpopo River, led to extreme flooding in Mozambique in 2000, killing several hundred people and displacing hundreds of thousands.[20] In the United States, each hectare of lost wetlands incurs $3,300–11,000 of increased annual flood damages.[21] Degradation and destruction of wetlands in the Mississippi River basin impaired natural flood control and allowed for massive floods in 1993 that resulted in $19 billion of property damage.[22]

Because of the essential services they provide, wetlands are estimated to have the highest dollar value per hectare of all of Earth's ecosystems, including oceans, tropical forests, and grasslands. They are thought to contribute $4.9 trillion of the $33.3 trillion estimated value of the biosphere each year—almost as much as the gross domestic product of China.[23] At great cost, wetlands have lost out where urbanization occurs. The minimum annual environmental cost of paving over wet-

lands is estimated to be $21,620 per hectare.[24]

Attempts have been made in various nations to restore or recreate degraded wetlands, yet the complexity of their functioning makes restoration difficult.[25] Efforts to reinstate wetlands' ecosystem services and to reestablish endangered species populations have had mixed success.[26]

Even accounting for wetlands saved by future protection and remediation, the Hadley Centre for Climate Prediction and Research estimates that at least 40–50 percent of the world's remaining coastal wetlands will be lost by 2080 to agriculture, urban sprawl, and the effects of a 1-meter sea level rise.[27] The consequences will be more severe in developing countries that cannot afford projects, such as water purification plants, designed to recreate the valuable services that wetlands naturally provide.[28]

Table 1: Selected Examples of Wetland Loss Around the World

Region	Share Lost (percent)	Location and Estimated Loss
Oceania	70	New Zealand: 90 percent of original wetlands Southeast Australia: 89 percent of original wetlands
Europe and North America	60	France: over 85 percent of 78 major wetlands significantly or extremely degraded between 1960 and 1990 Poland: over 90 percent of extensive peatlands Switzerland: up to 95 percent of original marshland drained and converted United States: over half of wetland area in the lower 48 states Canada: since settlement, 65 percent of Atlantic saltmarshes, 70 percent of lower Great Lakes–St. Lawrence River shoreline marshes and swamps, up to 71 percent of prairie potholes and sloughs, and 80 percent of Pacific coast estuarine wetlands Eastern Caribbean: damage of over 220 sites on 16 islands Mexico: 35 percent of original wetland area
Asia	27	Israel: 100 percent of peatlands Singapore: 97 percent of mangroves West Malaysia: 71 percent of peatlands; 85 percent are threatened Red River Delta, Viet Nam: 1.75 million hectares of natural floodplains converted to riceland or drained for other agriculture and settlement
South America	6	Cauca River Valley System, Colombia: 88 percent between the 1950s and 1980s from land reclamation, river regulation, and pollution
Africa	2	Tugela Basin, Southern Africa: over 90 percent of wetlands in parts of the basin

Sources: See endnote 2.

Bird Species Threatened

Ashley Mattoon

Birds are the best-known group of organisms on the planet. We know more about the distribution and population trends of birds than we do about mammals, amphibians, reptiles, and fish or about any major invertebrate group.[1] A recent assessment of the world's bird species by the conservation organization BirdLife International is therefore one of the most accurate and comprehensive pictures we have of a major taxonomic group. Unfortunately, the news is not good.

Of the approximately 9,900 bird species in the world, 12 percent are threatened with extinction.[2] (See Table 1.) In terms of the percentage of species threatened, the proportion is less than in other major vertebrate taxa, but the absolute number of threatened birds exceeds the number of threatened species in any group.[3] It is possible that one out of eight of the world's bird species will be lost within the next 100 years.[4] Over the last 200 years, 103 bird extinctions have already been documented—a rate more than 50 times what would be expected as a normal or "background" rate of extinction.[5]

Link: p. 96

A similar assessment completed in 1994 listed 1,111 bird species as threatened, compared with 1,186 today.[6] Within some groups, there were substantial increases in the degree of risk. For example, 16 species of albatross are now listed as threatened, versus 3 in 1994 (although this is partly the result of taxonomic revision, with a few subspecies elevated to species status).[7] These seabirds tend to become trapped and killed in the hooks of long-line fishing operations.[8] Another group that saw a substantial increase in risk level is penguins: the number of threatened species rose from 5 to 10—out of a total of just 17 penguin species.[9] Climate change, fishery depletion, and oil spills are among the many culprits in this case.[10]

While birds are threatened all over the planet, there is a clear pattern of endangerment; less than 5 percent of Earth's land surface is home to almost 75 percent of the threatened species.[11] The highest densities are in the Neotropics and Southeast Asia. Indonesia, Brazil, Colombia, and China top the list of countries with the highest number of threatened species.[12]

Numerous causes lie behind the decline of the world's birds, and in most cases no single threat is to blame, but rather a combination of factors. For nearly all threatened birds, the impact of humans is evident—scientists estimate that 99 percent of threatened birds are at risk because of human activities such as agriculture, logging, hunting, and trapping.[13]

Habitat loss and degradation is the leading danger, affecting 85 percent of all threatened species.[14] About three quarters of threatened species depend on one type of habitat, and of these 75 percent are forest-dependent.[15] Yet forests are being lost around the world at a rapid rate—especially in tropical regions that are particularly rich in bird diversity. Recent estimates indicate that more than 13 million hectares of natural forest are being lost each year—primarily in tropical areas.[16] Singapore, for example, has lost 95 percent of its native lowland rainforest in the past two centuries, resulting in the local extinction of 61 forest-dependent bird species.[17] Grasslands, shrublands, savannas, and wetlands also provide important bird habitat. Unfortunately, these systems are being lost or degraded in many parts of the world.

Direct exploitation in the form of hunting for food or collection for the pet trade is the second leading threat to birds—affecting about one third of threatened species.[18] The Northern Cassowary of Indonesia and Papua New Guinea is vulnerable and in decline primarily due to severe hunting pressure, as the bird is an important food source for subsistence communities and its feathers and bones are used for decoration.[19]

Birds are also trapped for the pet trade. Today it is estimated that world trade in live birds ranges from 450,000 to 600,000 individuals per year. Roughly 40–50 percent of the traded birds are imported to the United States.[20] The colorful and talkative parrots, cockatoos, and macaws are particularly threatened by this activity. Intensive trapping, exacerbated by the impact of habitat loss, has reduced the wild population of Brazil's brilliant blue Lear's Macaw to approximately 150 individuals and has probably resulted in making Brazil's Spix's Macaw extinct in the wild.[21] Unfortunately, the more rare and endangered a species becomes, the more valuable it is. In the 1990s, about 15–20 Lear's Macaws were being stolen from the wild a year.[22]

Introduced species that prey on or compete with native birds are the third most significant threat to birds. In fact, the impact of exotic invaders fully or partially explains the majority of the bird extinctions that have been documented in the last two centuries. Island birds have been particularly vulnerable to introduced predators, as they lack natural defenses to these unfamiliar adversaries. On the western Pacific island of Guam, for example, all but 2 of the island's 14 land bird species were driven to extinction following the accidental introduction of the brown tree snake, a native of Australia, eastern Indonesia, New Guinea, and the Solomon Islands around 1950.[23] And the native birds of the Hawaiian Islands have been

decimated by a combination of threats brought on by a vast array of introduced species.[24] At one point, these islands were home to at least 111 native birds—today, 51 of these are extinct and 30 are threatened.[25] Even a creature as apparently benign as the domestic house cat can wreak havoc on native bird populations. In North America, household and farm cats probably kill more than 1 billion birds each year.[26]

It is important to keep in mind that it is not just the loss of birds that should concern us, but what their loss could mean for the ecosystems that depend on the many services birds provide. Birds are important insect predators, for example, and protect many plants and animals from a variety of pests.[27] They are also important pollinators. As a result of the bird declines in Hawaii, for example, 31 species of the plant family *Campanulaceae* have become extinct in the last century.[28] And a recent study of the Atlantic Forest of Brazil concluded that the forests' fruit-eating birds should be viewed as "umbrella" species—the birds are essential seed dispersers and their habitat requirements should serve as the minimum area required to maintain essential ecological processes responsible for the persistence of the native forest.[29]

Birds are more appealing to the general public than other groups of organisms and they have been the focus of many successful conservation efforts. So while the general trend is downward, there are many inspiring success stories. In the United States and Canada, for instance, there are now roughly 1,600 breeding pairs of the once endangered Peregrine Falcon, up from 324 pairs in 1975.[30] The bird's recovery is largely due to a 1972 ban on DDT, restrictions on the use of other pesticides, captive breeding, and Endangered Species Act protection. The status of other species has also improved in recent years, largely thanks to targeted conservation programs that include strategies such as the protection and restoration of habitat, the control of introduced predators and competitors, and captive breeding and reintroduction.[31]

Table 1: Status of Bird Species Worldwide

Risk Category	Species (number)
Extinct in the Wild	3
Critical	182
Endangered	321
Vulnerable	680
Total threatened	*1,186*
Conservation-dependent	3
Near-threatened	727
Least concern, data deficient, or not evaluated	~ 8,000

Source: BirdLife International, *Threatened Birds of the World* (Barcelona, Spain, and Cambridge, U.K.: Lynx Ediciones and BirdLife International, 2000), p. 2; World Conservation Union–IUCN, Species Survival Commission, <www.redlist.org/tables/table1a.html>, viewed 12 February 2001.

Farm Animal Populations Soar

Brian Halweil

Propelled by the rising human appetite for meat, milk, and eggs, the planet's population of cows, hogs, sheep, goats, chicken, and other farm animals has surged since mid-century.[1] (See Table 1.) The number of four-footed livestock on Earth at any given moment has increased 60 percent since 1961, from 3.1 billion to 4.9 billion, while fowl populations have nearly quadrupled, from 4.2 billion to 15.7 billion.[2]

Even this startling record of growth underestimates the impact of farm animals on resource use and the environment, since several generations of livestock can be raised and slaughtered in a single year, depending on the production system. For example, although at any given time the U.S. cattle herd is roughly half the size of Brazil's, the United States still produces nearly twice as much beef each year.[3] In contrast to the range-fed production that predominates in Brazil, U.S. production practices—including intensive feeding of grain, antibiotics, and hormones—dramatically cut the time required for cattle to reach market weight.

Links: pp. 28, 30, 132

Among the dominant livestock species, sheep populations increased modestly since 1961, cattle numbers increased 40 percent, while pig and goat populations more than doubled.[4] Of the world's 1.3 billion cattle, India contains the largest herd—220 million head.[5] China is home to nearly half of the world's 905 million pigs.[6] Forty percent of the world's 1.8 billion goats and sheep are in Africa and the Middle East, where small ruminants are the dominant farm animal.[7] New Zealand has the world's highest sheep to human ratio—12:1.[8]

Chickens—which require less space and resources than other livestock—have seen the greatest growth, almost quadrupling in number since 1961.[9] Nearly 40 percent of the world's chickens are found in the United States and China.[10] Poorer rural and urban households depend disproportionately on smaller farm animals: poultry, rabbits, and guinea pigs.

The world's livestock are raised in three main farming systems. Mixed farming systems—in which animals are in close proximity to crop production—produce 54 percent of the world's meat and 90 percent of the milk.[11] But these are giving way to industrial or feedlot production, characterized by large numbers of confined animals that are far removed from the soil used to produce their food and resulting in serious waste disposal problems as well as animal welfare concerns.[12] Feedlots are the most rapidly growing production system, responsible for 43 percent of the world's meat—up from one third in 1990—and more than half the world's pork and poultry.[13] Though concentrated in North America and Europe, feedlots are popping up near urban centers in Brazil, China, India, the Philippines, and elsewhere in the developing world.[14]

Though grazing occupies more land than the other systems, it produces just 9 percent of the world's beef and 30 percent of the mutton.[15] This seemingly low yield represents perhaps the only way to derive human nutrition from the world's arid grasslands. Since temperate rangelands have generally been pushed to—or beyond—capacity, grazing populations are increasing substantially only in the subhumid tropics, including the grasslands of southeastern Brazil, West Africa, and the eastern Indian subcontinent.[16]

The millennia-old coexistence with livestock has yielded both benefits and costs for humankind. For an estimated 200 million people in arid areas, including Central Asia and much of Africa, grazing livestock is the only possible source of livelihood.[17] In the absence of banking institutions, livestock are an important form of investment—yielding interest in the form of weight gain and births—and insurance against crop failure.[18] In total, animal products account for 30–40 percent of the global agricultural sector's economic output.[19]

Manure provides the equivalent of $750 million worth of chemical fertilizer in Asia.[20] Farm animals also provide the power to cultivate at least 320 million hectares, or one quarter of total global cropland, including 80 percent of plowed fields in Asia and Africa.[21] And where energy is scarce, in the Indian subcontinent for instance, dung cakes are a primary form of cooking and heating fuel.[22]

At the same time, livestock consume a substantial share of Earth's natural resources, sometimes converting resources that humans cannot eat into edible food—such as grass or food waste—but often competing directly with humans and other organisms.[23] Livestock graze one quarter of Earth's land area and consume the crop production of about one quarter of the world's croplands, in total making use of more than two thirds of the world's surface that is dedicated to food production.[24]

Livestock consume roughly 37 percent of the world's grain harvest, most of the soybeans, and millions of tons of other oilseeds, roots, and tubers each year.[25] Cattle eat 14 percent of the world's grain; pigs, 12 percent; and chickens, 9 percent.[26] Livestock's share of the global grain harvest has remained remarkably stable even as meat production has outpaced grain production—largely the result of a global shift toward pigs and chickens, which are more efficient calorie converters than cows.

Particularly as their populations have

Table 1: Global Livestock Populations, 1961 and 2000

Species	Population		Increase
	1961	2000	
	(million)		(percent)
Buffalo	88	167	90
Cattle	941	1,331	41
Ducks	194	886	357
Geese	36	235	553
Goats	348	714	105
Pigs	406	905	123
Sheep	994	1,060	7
Rabbits	101	475	370
Turkeys	131	240	83
Other	193	246	27
	(billion)		
Chickens	3.9	14.3	267
	(billion)		
Total	7.3	20.6	180

Source: FAO, FAOSTAT Statistics Database, <apps.fao.org>, updated 27 October 2000.

grown, livestock have often transformed ecosystems, disrupting or eliminating other forms of biodiversity.[27] Since mid-century, 20 percent—some 680 million hectares—of global rangeland has been degraded by overgrazing, which can reduce soil fertility and ultimately the size of the herd that can be sustained.[28] In Central and South America, ranching is implicated in nearly half of rainforest destruction.[29]

Feedlot production, in particular, has emerged as a dominant threat to soil, air, and water quality. In the United States, livestock produce 130 times as much manure as humans do.[30] Excess nutrients from the 600 million chickens in the Delmarva Peninsula in the United States have been implicated in toxic algae blooms in the Chesapeake Bay, while in the Netherlands—home to the world's highest concentration of livestock—nutrient overload has turned biologically diverse heathlands into monotonous grasslands.[31]

Livestock have also become the largest agriculture-related source of greenhouse gas emissions, contributing about 16 percent of total global production of methane—a gas about 25 times more potent than carbon dioxide.[32]

Even as livestock numbers increase, their diversity declines. Globally, of the 4,000 breeds with adequate population data, 18 percent are extinct and 32 percent are threatened.[33] Extinctions have accelerated in recent years, as homogenous production systems from the industrial world replace more complex animal farming all over.[34] For instance, Holstein cattle account for 90 percent of the North American dairy population.[35]

On a global basis, animal products provide about 15 percent of the energy and more than 30 percent of the protein.[36] A combination of urbanization, rising incomes, and the export of western diets has meant a fivefold jump in meat consumption since 1950—from 44 million to 232 million tons.[37] Per capita consumption has doubled over the same period—although at 77 kilograms, average meat consumption per person in the industrial world is still three times that in the developing world.[38]

Growth in Transgenic Area Slows

Brian Halweil

Farmers planted 44.2 million hectares of transgenic crops in 2000.[1] Also known as genetically engineered or genetically modified crops, this area has soared 25-fold since 1996, the first year of commercial plantings.[2] (See Figure 1.) But the increase of 4.3 million hectares—some 11 percent—between 1999 and 2000, while still substantial, represents a dramatic slowdown from 40-percent annual growth between 1996 and 1999, indicating that public concern over these crops may be affecting planting decisions.[3]

In contrast to traditional plant breeding, which can only mate closely related plant species, biotechnology can move genes between unrelated species, including viruses, bacteria, and animals. This distinction has spurred concerns that our understanding of potential risks—from the creation of new food allergies to unexpected ecological disruption due to the spread of transgenic plants—is too limited for the technology's widespread use.[4]

Links: pp. 28, 30

Global planting of transgenic crops remains highly concentrated in a number of ways: just a few nations, a few plants, and a few crop traits account for nearly all the global area. For instance, the United States, Argentina, and Canada together plant 98 percent of global area—a situation that has not changed during the past four years.[5]

Farmers in 13 nations planted transgenics commercially in 2000, just one nation more than in 1999 but up from six in 1996.[6] (Many more nations contain field tests of transgenic plants, but most governments in Europe, Asia, Latin America, and Africa do not allow widespread cultivation.)

With 30.3 million hectares—68 percent of global area—the United States remains the top producer of transgenic crops.[7] Plantings in this country increased modestly in 2000, the result of expanded area in soybeans, cotton, and canola (rapeseed) and a contraction in corn area.[8] Some 54 percent of the soybean plantings and 72 percent of the cotton plantings in the United States are now transgenic.[9] The corn area dropped by more than

2 million hectares—from one third to one fourth of the total crop—the result of farmer uncertainty about market acceptance and reduced profitability due to low populations of the pest targeted by the engineered corn.[10]

Argentina added 3.3 million hectares of transgenic area in 2000, accounting for more than three fourths of the global gain.[11] A full 95 percent of Argentina's soy crop is now transgenic, as is 20 percent of its corn crop.[12] Canada's farmers, on the other hand, planted 1 million fewer hectares of transgenic canola in 2000 than in 1999; still, half of Canada's canola fields have been planted with transgenics.[13]

China has just 1 percent of global transgenic area, though plantings jumped by 66 percent in 2000, to a half-million hectares of transgenic cotton—some 10 percent of national cotton area.[14] Of the remaining nine nations that have any such crops, only South Africa and Australia have more than 100,000 hectares.[15] Bulgaria, France, Germany, Mexico, Romania, Spain, and Uruguay have a few thousand hectares each.[16]

Soybeans and corn continue to dominate global transgenic area, accounting respectively for 58 and 23 percent of the total.[17] (See Figure 2.) The remaining 19 percent consists of cotton and canola.[18] For these four crops, transgenic varieties now make up a sizable share of global plantings. Thirty-six percent of global soybean area is transgenic, as is 16 percent of cotton area,

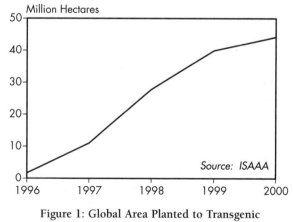

Figure 1: Global Area Planted to Transgenic Crops, 1996–2000

11 percent of canola, and 7 percent of corn.[19]

Worldwide, three out of four hectares with transgenics are devoted to crops engineered to withstand spraying of weed-killers.[20] These herbicide-resistant crops, used in conjunction with a herbicide produced by the same company, have dominated since 1996. Bt-crops—varieties of corn and cotton with a gene from the soil bacterium *Bacillus thuringiensis* to churn out an insecticide—cover 19 percent of the total area.[21] The remaining 7 percent of transgenic area is planted in "stacked" varieties, which contain both these traits.[22]

A number of market events in 2000 are likely to affect future planting decisions—which industry analysts see as flat to slow-growing in the years ahead.[23] In September, an engineered variety of corn—Starlink—only approved for livestock feeding because of potential human allergies was detected in brand name taco shells and hundreds of other food items in the United States and abroad.[24] The slip-up sent the seed manufacturer, Aventis, and top food manufacturers on a multimillion-dollar recall effort, while some American farmers scrambled to find alternative buyers when their harvest was rejected due to contamination.[25] Subsequent analysis found other unapproved corn varieties in European food items, pointing to the ubiquity of transgenics and questioning the feasibility of segregation.[26]

On the heels of the recall, Aventis announced in November that it would divest its agribusiness division (seeds and agrochemicals), so that it could focus on currently more profitable and acceptable medical and pharmaceutical applications of biotechnology.[27] Several other biotech leaders, including Pharmacia-Monsanto and Novartis, completed a similar transition last year.[28]

The transgenic seed market remains highly concentrated, with 80 percent of the global area planted in the varieties of a single company: Monsanto (now a subsidiary of Pharmacia).[29] The remaining acreage is shared by Aventis

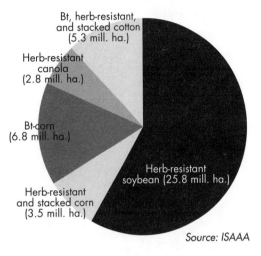

Source: ISAAA

Figure 2: Global Transgenic Area by Crop, 2000

(7 percent), Syngenta (formerly Novartis and AstraZeneca) and BASF (5 percent each), and Dupont (3 percent).[30]

Fierce debate continued on the potential impact of transgenic crops on wildlife and pesticide use.[31] Farmers who have rapidly adopted transgenic crops generally point to easier pest control and sometimes reduced operating costs.[32] Use of these crops in the United States has not significantly reduced pesticide applications on corn, cotton, or soybeans, however.[33] In a conclusion viewed as reasonable by both industry and critics, a study published in *Science* in December indicated that there is insufficient evidence to determine any positive or negative impacts of such crops on the environment.[34]

Also in December, shortly after the announcement of the sequencing of the human genome, scientists sequenced the entire genetic code of *Arabidopsis*, a common laboratory plant.[35] This milestone will boost scientific understanding of genetic control over plant traits—disease resistance, flowering date, and cold tolerance, for instance—which will reduce the cost and increase the speed and power of genetic engineering.[36]

Economy and Finance Features

Pharmaceutical Sales Thriving
PVC Plastic Pervades Economy
Microcredit Expanding Rapidly
Stock Markets Follow a Rocky Road
Socially Responsible Investing Surges
Toll of Natural Disasters Grows

Pharmaceutical Sales Thriving

Brian Halweil

Worldwide sales of pharmaceuticals have jumped more than 2.5-fold since 1983, from $132 billion to $337 billion.[1] (See Figure 1.) Sales were up 9 percent from 1998 to 1999, and annual growth has averaged 7 percent for the past two decades, in what is one of the most profitable and fastest-growing industries in the world.[2]

Pharmaceutical sales are largely concentrated in the industrial world, highlighting broader disparities in income levels, health care options, disease burdens, and life spans. North America, Western Europe, and Japan, with 14 percent of the world's population, account for 83 percent of pharmaceutical sales.[3] The United States alone, with just 5 percent of humanity, buys nearly 40 percent of the world's legal drugs.[4]

Links: pp. 78, 132, 134, 138

In stark contrast, Asia (excluding Japan) uses 8 percent, Latin America and the Caribbean 7 percent, and Africa just 2 percent.[5]

The great profitability of the legal drug industry has several explanations, including the monopolistic pricing that comes with drug patents and people's willingness to pay for medicines that reduce disability and suffering.[6] Drug companies claim that huge profit margins are justified by the industry's large research and development outlays and the high cost of bringing a new drug to market, although the companies spend roughly twice as much on marketing as on R&D.[7]

Not surprisingly, the top-selling drug classes are designed to treat First World illnesses, including heart disease, high blood pressure, and indigestion. At the head of the list, with $15.8 billion in annual sales, is antiulcerants (drugs for indigestion or antacid), which includes top-selling Prilosec.[8] Cholesterol reducers and calcium antagonists (anti-hypertensives)—including Zocor, Lipitor, and other drugs for cardiovascular disease—are the second and fourth top sellers.[9] Antidepressants, including Prozac and Zoloft, are the third leading drug class, while antirheumatic non-steroidals (pain medicine) round out the top five.[10]

Despite big disparities in drug use per person, as diets, lifestyles, and incomes change around the world the top drug categories are becoming similar. Antiulcerants are a top-5 category on all continents, while Norvasc, an anti-hypertension drug, is a top-10 seller everywhere.[11] Most legal drug use in the developing world is by wealthier segments of the population, who are likely to have the same diseases as First World patients.

Still, differences do exist: while antibiotics do not make the top 10 in the industrial world, they rank in the top 3 in the developing world.[12] And generic versions of top-selling drugs often predominate in these countries.[13] Another difference is the scale of use: at $1 billion or more, sales of blockbuster drugs like Viagra, for male impotence, exceed the entire health budgets—let alone the medicine budgets—of most developing nations.[14]

Across regions, rising drug costs are beginning to weigh on health care systems, transforming the profits of the drug industry into a sensitive political issue. For instance, the introduction of western medicines—and western health problems—has greatly contributed to the 35-percent annual growth in China's medical costs.[15] And in the United States, spending on prescription drugs has more than doubled in the last decade, becoming the fastest-growing item in the nation's health care budget.[16]

A rash of mergers in recent years has made the legal drug business among the world's most concentrated. The top 10 pharmaceutical firms control upwards of 35 percent of the global market.[17] The top 5 firms—Merck, Pfizer, and Bristol-Myers Squibb, based in the United States, and the British firms AstraZeneca and Glaxo Wellcome—all enjoy annual sales of more than $10 billion.[18]

The greater availability and array of pharmaceuticals has played a central role in increasing life expectancy and reducing disease and disability around the world. But the biggest health payoff has probably come from some of the least expensive innovations. For example, the $2.7-billion global vaccine market represents less than 1 percent of global drug sales, although the World Health Organization

(WHO) estimates that every $1 spent on childhood vaccines saves $7–20 on treatment of the targeted illnesses—not to mention great reductions in human suffering and child mortality.[19]

Still, the research focus of big pharmaceutical companies has tended to neglect the health needs of large chunks of the planet, including research on a malaria vaccine. Of 1,233 new drugs that reached market between 1975 and 1997, only 13 products were approved specifically for tropical diseases, including some of the world's biggest killers.[20] At the same time, legal issues have sometimes proved a barrier to drug access, as with the patent protection that prevents local production of antiretrovirals for HIV/AIDS in hard-hit developing nations.[21]

Even where drugs are available and off-patent, cost remains the biggest barrier to access. WHO estimates that one third of humanity lacks regular access to essential drugs that together provide treatment for the majority of infectious and chronic disease affecting the world's population.[22] The share without access to this drug package has remained unchanged since the mid-1980s, and grows to 50 percent in the poorest nations, despite an estimated cost of just $2 per person.[23] In 1998, one in four children did not receive routine immunization with the six basic vaccines against polio, diphtheria, whooping cough, tetanus, measles, and tuberculosis.[24]

Innovative public-private partnerships have great potential to help close this "global drug gap."[25] In recent decades, pharmaceutical companies have been encouraged to donate medicine or participate in public-private partnerships in the development and distribution of medicine. One of the more successful is the Mectizan Donation Program, a partnership between WHO and Merck, which developed and donated ivermectin for treatment of river blindness, providing enough product to treat 30 million people in 20 countries in 1999.[26] In some cases, suspending patent rules may hold even greater promise.[27]

Drug marketing is directed primarily at doctors—a practice that can encourage overreliance on medications or inappropriate use.[28] Of the $13.9 billion that U.S. drug companies spent promoting their products in 1999, about $12 billion was aimed at doctors, nurse practitioners, and other medical employees who can prescribe medications.[29] At the same time, a surge in direct advertising to consumers has raised the risk of inappropriate use, as well as

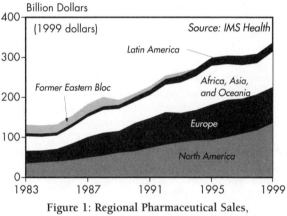

Figure 1: Regional Pharmaceutical Sales, 1983–99

stimulating a surge in consumer demand for newer, costlier drugs when less expensive products might work just as well.[30]

Overmedication has emerged as a serious problem in wealthier settings, particularly among elderly individuals, for whom multiple pharmaceutical regimens are more the rule than the exception.[31] A 1998 report estimates that adverse reactions to prescription drugs kill 106,000 Americans each year—more than automobile accidents—and injure more than 2.2 million.[32] With more people taking several drugs at any given time—three out of four doctor's visits in the United States end with a prescription—the risk of unwanted synergies between drugs increases.[33] And over the long term, pharmaceuticals may be distracting attention from other measures, such as changes in diet and exercise, that could prove more effective, safer, and more economical.

PVC Plastic Pervades Economy
Anne Platt McGinn

Polyvinyl chloride (PVC) plastic is now one of the most commonly used synthetic materials in the world. Some 250 million tons of PVC are in use today; another 100 million tons are piling up in landfills, feeding incinerators and backyard fires, or clogging the recycling stream.[1] In terms of production volume, PVC is the second most common plastic in the world after polyethylene, but it is put to more uses.[2] Some 60 percent of PVC is used in building materials, with the remainder found in packaging, electrical wiring, and countless other consumer goods.[3]

About 25 million tons are now produced annually, a sum that is expected to grow considerably in the next decade.[4] Global production increased 39 percent in just seven years—from 18 million tons in 1992 to 25 million tons in 1999, despite a significant downturn during the recent Asian economic crisis.[5] Fueling this trend is the surge in demand: in the early to mid-1990s, world consumption was growing 3.6 percent a year; in the first half of this decade, the annual rate will be nearly 5 percent.[6] By 2005, the market for PVC is projected to reach some 33 million tons.[7]

Between 1989 and 1999, U.S. PVC production grew 66 percent, from 3.8 million tons to 6.3 million tons.[8] The United States is currently the world's largest producer, but in terms of regional production, Asia dominates. (See Table 1.) In 1999, 34 percent of the world's PVC production capacity was in Asia, with 9 percent in Japan alone.[9] (Factories have run at about 80 percent capacity in recent years.)[10] About 150 companies in 50 different countries currently produce the material, but the largest manufacturers are in Asia.[11] Japan's Shin-Etsu Chemical Company is the world's largest producer, and Formosa Plastics of Taiwan is number two.[12]

Between 1998 and 1999, Japan's PVC production stabilized at 2.46 million tons, but its production of ethylene dichloride—a key ingredient in PVC—hit 3.5 million tons in 1999, the highest level ever.[13] PVC production in Taiwan jumped 21 percent between 1998 and 1999, while South Korean production rose 15 percent.[14]

The primary driver of Asian demand will likely be the construction industries serving major urban areas—megacities like Beijing, Bangkok, and Manila—and outlying parts in developing countries. China's demand for PVC is expected to jump from 2.5 million tons in 1998 to 6.5 million tons by 2010, a boost of 160 percent.[15]

As production climbs, the politics concerning this material continue to heat up as well, in large part because the manufacture and disposal of PVC creates dangerous toxic chemicals and because its use can release harmful chemical additives into the environment.

The production of PVC generates many toxic and persistent byproducts, including dioxins and furans, compounds known as persistent organic pollutants (POPs).[16] Under a recent U.N. treaty on POPs, countries will be obligated to reduce—and eliminate, where feasible—the creation of dioxins and furans in manufacturing practices, including PVC production.[17]

At the end of its life, PVC again poses a health risk. Today most PVC waste is either incinerated or landfilled; only a small fraction is recycled.[18] Burning chlorinated compounds generates dioxins. Because nearly 45 percent of PVC by weight is chlorine, incineration is a virtual guarantee of significant dioxin emissions.[19] Most PVC waste in the world is buried in dumps, where the dangers include accidental fires and the leaching of chemical additives into water, soil, fish, and plants.[20] These issues become more pressing as the mountain of discarded PVC continues to grow worldwide. In the European Union alone, PVC waste is expected to jump 76 percent over the next two decades.[21]

In terms of suspected direct human health effects, the greatest concerns are the additives in PVC, which give the material a range of characteristics from flexibility to flame retardation and color. In 1999, global sales of plastics additives hit $15.5 billion.[22] The most important additives are plasticizers, which confer flexibility. Some 90 percent of plasticizers belong to a group of 25 compounds called phthalates, and some of the most common phthalates are POPs or POP-like compounds.[23]

Because phthalates are not chemically bonded to the resin, they can migrate to the surface of the material and leak into the surrounding environment.[24] For example, hospital patients receiving infusions have been shown to be at risk of exposure to a commonly used phthalate known as DEHP, which can leach directly out of intravenous tubes and into a patient's bloodstream.[25]

In both wildlife and laboratory animals, phthalates have been linked to a range of reproductive health effects, including reduced fertility, miscarriage, birth defects, abnormal sperm counts, and testicular damage, as well as liver and kidney cancer.[26] Recently, scientists at the U.S. Centers for Disease Control and Prevention detected phthalates in the urine from women of childbearing age at levels that cause fetal abnormalities in laboratory animals.[27] A 1999 study in Oslo, Norway, concluded that young children may absorb phthalates from vinyl floor covering; children in homes with such coverings had an 89-percent greater chance than other children of developing bronchial obstruction and symptoms of asthma.[28]

Faced with such risks, a growing number of policymakers and consumers are questioning the use of PVC. In July 2000 the European Parliament voted to permanently ban all phthalate-softeners from PVC toys and other items that children are likely to chew on.[29] Eight European nations have unilaterally banned the additives in PVC toys for toddlers.[30] In a global first, Denmark recently imposed a tax on all PVC products and phthalates to discourage demand.[31] A number of companies—from automobile manufacturers to medical equipment providers—are now phasing out PVC in response to the public attention concerning health and environmental impacts.[32] The electronics giant Sony International recently announced that it would stop using PVC in all its products beginning in 2002.[33]

Alternatives currently exist for almost every application of PVC; the challenge is to adopt them widely. Substitute materials in the construction sector vary from traditional materials such as wooden window frames to high-tech modifications of familiar materials, such as a new generation of polyolefins (nonchlorinated plastics) that are being developed.[34] Another promising trend is the development of plastics from a wide variety of plant materials—oat hulls, corn, soybeans, oil seeds, or wood, for example.[35] At present, unfortunately, the possibilities for substituting such biopolymers for PVC are fairly limited.[36] But as with other environmental technologies, there is reason to hope that demand will help drive innovation. Until then, safer materials can be used in construction projects and consumer goods to reduce the health risks of PVC use.

Table 1: PVC Production Capacity by Region, 1999, with Projections for 2002

Region	1999		2002	
	Total	Share	Total	Share
	(thousand tons)	(percent)	(thousand tons)	(percent)
North America	7,908	28	9,350	27
Western Europe	6,100	21	6,320	18
Japan	2,581	9	2,772	8
Other Asia[1]	7,235	25	10,150	30
Other Regions[2]	4,912	17	5,595	16
World Total	28,736		34,187	

[1]China, Hong Kong, India, Indonesia, Malaysia, Philippines, Singapore, South Korea, Taiwan, and Thailand.   [2]Africa, Eastern Europe, Latin America, Middle East, and Oceania.
Sources: 1999 from CMAI, "Polyvinyl Chloride," *PVC Insight*, vol. 8, issue 15 (2000), p. 1; 2002 estimates from Joel A. Tickner, *Trends in World PVC Industry Expansion* (Washington, DC: Greenpeace, 19 June 1998), p. 2.

Microcredit Expanding Rapidly

Gary Gardner

Microcredit, the provision of small-scale financial services to the poor, is expanding rapidly throughout the developing world, as well as in some industrial countries. Global data are scarce, but one survey by the group Microcredit Summit found that the number of poor assisted worldwide through such programs rose by 12 percent between 1998 and 1999, to 23.6 million.[1] (See Table 1.) Of these, more than half were classified as the poorest of the poor—the bottom 50 percent of individuals living below their nation's poverty line—and a disproportionate share were women.[2]

Asia is far and away the leading region for microfinance activity, accounting for 78 percent of the world's clients and 9 of the 10 largest microfinance institutions in the global survey.[3] Africa, with 16 percent of clients, was a distant second, but activity is expanding there faster than in any other region.[4] Industrial countries account for less than 1 percent of all clients.[5]

Microfinance institutions (MFIs) could potentially provide financial services to many of the nearly 3 billion people who live on $2 or less per day, whose financial needs are too small to be handled by traditional financial institutions.[6] MFIs can manage loans of as little as $50, for example, and savings deposits as small as $5.[7] The interest rates they charge are often higher than those of commercial institutions, because of the expense associated with administering small, short-term loans. Yet low-income people accustomed to the exorbitant rates of private moneylenders often find MFI rates to be a bargain. As someone at a non-governmental organization (NGO) in Bolivia noted, "It's a paradox....To reach the poorest we have to charge the highest" of any institutional lender in the country.[8]

MFI loans help independent entrepreneurs, many of whom work out of the home, to generate greater income; they might allow a basketweaver, for instance, to purchase supplies in bulk to lower costs. And because MFIs target women, who account for up to 70 percent of the world's poor and who tend to use a higher share of earnings for family needs than men do, supporters hope that MFIs could become a major new weapon in combating poverty.[9]

Asia's predominance in microfinance is due in part to its long experience in this field. Asia is home to the first institutionalized MFI, the Grameen Bank, founded in Bangladesh by economist Muhamad Yunus in the 1970s. Yunus created a system of small-scale lending that requires no collateral for participation. Villagers are organized into units of five, two of whom are initially eligible for a loan.[10] New loans are made only when the first loans are paid off. Thus the "social capital" of neighborhood ties and the peer pressure produced by these relationships serve as the "moral collateral" that ensures a high rate of repayment—95 percent in Grameen's case.[11]

Grameen is now the largest rural finance institution in Bangladesh, with more than 1,100 branches serving nearly 40,000 villages—double the number in 1990.[12] It has more than 2.3 million borrowers, nearly triple the number in 1990, 94 percent of whom are women.[13] By the mid-1990s, Grameen lending had financed more than a half-million homes in Bangladesh, and was generating economic activity valued at more than 1 percent of Bangladesh's gross domestic product.[14] Because of its success, the Grameen model has been replicated in 58 countries during the last decade.[15]

As microcredit programs have matured, many have expanded their services. Some programs, such as the Village Banking model created by the NGO FINCA, combine savings and credit services. Borrowers are required to save 20 percent of the loan amount they are granted, and are then eligible for a second loan equal to the original loan plus the accumulated savings.[16] In this way, clients gain access to larger and larger loans as they expand their own capital base. The women of the FINCA Uganda program, for example, have accumulated savings equivalent to 97 percent of their loan portfolio in just five years.[17] Some MFIs now offer leasing as well, giving the poor access to equipment—from sewing machines to solar power systems—that can help generate greater income.[18] And some offer insurance,

Table 1: Growth and Composition of Microfinance Institution Clients, 1999

Region	Number of Clients	Increase over 1998	Poorest as Share of Clients[1]
	(thousand)	(percent)	
Africa	3,834	29	68
Asia	18,427	10	57
Latin America and the Caribbean	1,110	12	48
Middle East	47	6	61
North America	47	16	61
Europe and Countries in Transition	44	8	42
World	23,556	12	58

[1]The bottom 50 percent of a country's population living below the poverty line.
Source: Microcredit Summit, "Empowering Women with Microcredit: 2000 Microcredit Summit Campaign Report," <www.microcredit summit.org/campaigns/report00.html>, viewed 26 February 2001.

especially to cover the debts of clients in case of their death or disability.[19]

MFIs appear to better the lives of participants, especially by providing stability to people subject to economic volatility, such as seasonal unemployment or spikes in the price of production inputs.[20] Whether it also raises incomes is unclear. It is most likely to do so when access to credit is combined with assured access to complementary inputs such as seeds and irrigation water, and when other important conditions such as market access are in place.[21]

Microcredit is especially effective when combined with efforts to educate. The Credit with Education program in Ghana uses credit group meetings to teach participants about diarrhea prevention, breast-feeding, immunization, family planning, and HIV/AIDS prevention—with striking results.[22] Ninety percent of participating women reported increases in their income, the share of families reporting periods of food deprivation in the previous 12 months fell by half, and the measures of nutritional levels of one-year-olds improved significantly.[23]

Because providing financial services to the poor is expensive, many believe that MFIs cannot cover their costs without ongoing subsidies. But the record to date suggests that financial self-sustainability and service to the poor are not mutually exclusive. Since 1997, approximately 50 percent of microfinance institutions reporting to the *MicroBanking Bulletin*, a publication that monitors this emerging industry, were financially self-sufficient.[24] This average covered a wide range of performance, however: in the Middle East and North Africa, 17 percent were self-sustaining; in Africa, 32 percent; in Eastern Europe, 36 percent; in Asia, 55 percent; and in Latin America, 77 percent.[25] And the *Bulletin* reported in 2000 that 3 of the 10 most sustainable institutions served the poorest of the poor exclusively.

MFIs are not a panacea for the world's poor. They are unlikely, for example, to help the extremely poor—the homeless and destitute—because microcredit works best for those whose lives are stable and who have a steady, if meager, income.[26] Social safety nets will still be needed, even if microfinance spreads widely.[27] But if the Microcredit Summit Campaign reaches its goal of helping 100 million of the world's poorest families by 2005—a figure that represents probably 40 percent of the world's 1.2 billion people living in absolute poverty—it could provide an encouraging lift to many of the world's poor.[28]

Stock Markets Follow a Rocky Road   *Michael Renner*

Since 1697, when the world's first stock exchange was set up in London, stock markets have been one of the key ways to raise capital, in addition to banks and bond markets.[1] During the 1980s and even more so the 1990s, stock markets worldwide rose dramatically in prominence: the number of exchanges in operation expanded, the total volume of stocks traded surged, and stock prices skyrocketed.[2] In 2000, however, declining stock values interrupted this explosive growth.[3]

While the 1990s' "bull market" has been interpreted by many as testament to the genius of free-market capitalism, the ascendance of stock markets is not necessarily a good indicator of how sound a national economy is or how well people's needs are being met. Stock markets tend to overshoot in their upward and downward movements, potentially wreaking havoc in the economy and distorting social and economic development. Wall Street and other financial centers may punish otherwise healthy companies if their returns do not live up to short-term profit expectations.[4] Stock markets may allocate capital unwisely, such as overinvesting in poorly conceived Internet start-ups that subsequently go bankrupt, while making it harder for some traditional businesses to raise capital; this appears to have happened in 1998 and 1999.[5] Exaggerated stock values may also give the public a false sense of security that their private pension plans are adequately funded.[6]

Stock market values around the world, with the notable exception of Japan, were on a wild upswing until March 2000.[7] Morgan Stanley Capital International's MSCI World index, a composite of stocks from several industrial and developing countries, grew about 5-fold in value between 1980 and 1999; MSCI's Europe index rose 4.4-fold, a composite Latin America index developed by Global Financial Data rose 4-fold, and an Emerging Asia index increased 2.5-fold.[8] But the developing-country indices were marked by much greater volatility. The Standard & Poor's (S&P) 500 index, one of the most widely used benchmarks to assess stock market performance in the United States, grew

Link: p. 114

6-fold in value between 1980 and the end of 1999.[9] (See Figure 1).

Global stock market "capitalization"—the value of the stocks of all the roughly 50,000 companies listed on the world's stock exchanges—catapulted from $11.4 trillion in 1990 to $34.9 trillion in 1999, expanding 10 times faster than the world economy.[10] The United States alone accounts for half the global total, followed by Japan (13 percent) and the United Kingdom (8 percent).[11] The value of developing countries' stock markets has more than quadrupled, from $587 billion in 1990 to $2.7 trillion in 1999.[12]

Soaring stock values have made some people fantastically rich—on paper, at least—and have contributed to a considerable widening of wealth disparities. Worldwide, there are now 7 million people with a net worth of more than $1 million.[13] The ranks of individuals holding financial assets of at least $30 million have expanded from 36,500 in 1996 to 55,400 in 1999.[14] And the number of billionaires grew from 232 in 1990 to 514 in 1999.[15]

The number of people owning stock is rising—particularly in the United States and the United Kingdom, where shares are increasingly popular as a form of employee compensation and where employer-funded pension plans are being invested in stocks (either directly or indirectly, through mutual funds).[16] Still, stock ownership remains highly concentrated. The richest 1 percent of U.S. households captured 42 percent of the stock market gains between 1989 and 1997, and the top 10 percent secured 86 percent.[17]

The inequality effect of the stock market boom is more pronounced in the United States than in most other industrial countries, because while stock prices surged there, wages stagnated. In 1999 it took the average U.S. worker almost 92 hours to earn enough money to purchase a representative share of the S&P 500 stock index—up from about 20 hours in 1980.[18] As a result, the gap between haves and have-nots in the mid- to late 1990s was greater than at any time since 1929. The top 1 percent of American wealth holders controlled 38 percent of total household wealth, and the top 10 percent had 71 percent.[19]

Stock prices reflect investors' expectations of future corporate profits—though short- and long-term expectations may at times diverge substantially. Low inflation, lower taxes, the rise of information technologies, and deregulation helped bring about strongly rising profits in the 1990s. Still, stock prices outpaced even these record earnings.[20] As many have noted, the last few years have also been characterized by investors' "irrational exuberance"—the expectation that the good times will simply keep on rolling.[21] But the feedback loops that generate such expectations can also turn negative and amplify a downturn far beyond a reasonable range.

It is worth recalling the roller-coaster experience of the Japanese stock market. The Nikkei 225 index more than tripled in value between 1982 and 1989.[22] But an ailing economy and the burst of a massive real-estate bubble led to a collapse of the Nikkei. It has lost more than two thirds of its value since then. (See Figure 2.)

Judging by past experience, most stock markets were considerably overvalued by late 1999. The P-E ratio, the price of a share of stock relative to the earnings per share, has historically averaged about 15:1 for the S&P 500 in the United States.[23] By early 1997, P-E ratios were at double this average and rose past 40:1 by 1999, but then declined during 2000.[24] No one can forecast future stock prices. But in the past, whenever the P-E ratio climbed far beyond the normal range suggested by the historical average, it was followed by a pronounced market downturn—or even a disastrous crash, such as the one in 1929 that triggered the Great Depression.

Although a stock market crash would most directly hurt those own-

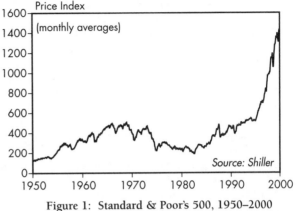

Figure 1: Standard & Poor's 500, 1950–2000

ing large quantities of stocks, others would suffer as well. Those who have invested their retirement funds in stocks would face unexpected shortfalls. And there are broader consequences. Particularly in the United States, the economy has been propelled by a stock market-driven consumption boom.[25] A crash would likely cause most people to cut back substantially on their spending; the resulting falloff in demand could then trigger a recession and a rise in unemployment.[26] Because trade, exchange rates, and capital flows increasingly bind together the world's economies, a downturn in the United States could also have ripple effects in other countries, even if their own stock markets managed a softer landing.[27]

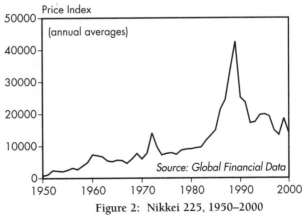

Figure 2: Nikkei 225, 1950–2000

Socially Responsible Investing Surges   *Hilary French*

Recent years have seen a rapid growth in "socially responsible investing" in many industrial countries. This can take several forms, from channeling money into investment funds that screen companies and industries according to social or environmental criteria, to engaging in "shareholder activism" to influence the policies of companies an investor owns shares in, to "community investment" in local development initiatives, such as affordable housing projects and small business lending.

Although no global tally exists of total assets invested according to social criteria, a range of country-based studies demonstrate steady growth. The largest and most thoroughly tracked market is the United States. According to data compiled by the Washington-based Social Investment Forum, money in funds based in the United States that is invested according to social criteria climbed from $59 billion in 1984 to $682 billion in 1995 and then to $2.16 trillion in 1999—$1 out of every $8 under professional management in the United States.[1] (See Figure 1.)

Link: p. 112

The 1999 U.S. total includes $1.2 trillion of investments in screened portfolios, $657 billion of investments controlled by investors active in shareholder advocacy, $265 billion in investments where both strategies were pursued, and $5 billion in community investment.[2] Between 1997 and 1999 alone, the total assets invested according to social criteria increased by 77 percent—nearly twice the overall growth rate of funds being professionally managed over that period.[3]

In the first national survey conducted in Canada, the Toronto-based Social Investment Organization recently reported that nearly $50 billion was now being invested according to social criteria, including some $10 billion in retail funds available to relatively small investors, $11 billion in funds that are privately managed by investment companies for institutional investors and other clients, $27 billion invested in-house by institutional investors, $1 billion in investments involving shareholder advocacy initiatives on social and environmental issues, and $85 million in locally based community investment organizations.[4] Between 1998 and 2000, the Canadian retail market grew by more than 75 percent—more than twice the mutual fund industry's overall rate of growth.[5]

In Europe, there are now more than 220 retail-based social investment funds, up from only 26 in the mid-1980s, according to estimates by Avanzi, an Italian-based research and consulting firm.[6] As of late 1999, more than 11 billion Euros ($10 billion) was invested in these funds.[7] The United Kingdom leads the way in socially responsible investing in Europe, with 44 green and ethical retail funds in place as of mid-2000, which between them had more than £3 billion ($4.3 billion) in assets under management by early 2000.[8] These numbers vastly understate the total amount of money being invested according to social and ethical criteria in Europe, as they do not include private and institutional investment portfolios.[9]

Socially responsible investment funds apply a variety of screens targeted to the diverse interests and concerns of their investors, including issues of labor relations, environmental protection, and human rights. The screens used by different funds vary widely in both their breath and stringency.[10] They can also have both positive and negative components, meaning they seek out companies with positive records on targeted issues while excluding those that produce harmful products or engage in socially unsound business practices. Tobacco is the most common screen applied by U.S.-based funds—96 percent of them ban this industry from their portfolios.[11] Most U.S. funds also avoid investing in the gambling, liquor, and weapons industries.[12] And nearly 80 percent address environmental issues in some manner, whether by screening out companies with poor records or screening in companies and industries deemed particularly "green."[13]

In one variation on socially responsible investing, some financiers are promoting "sustainability investing," which encourages a positive approach to investing by targeting companies that are deemed leaders rather than laggards on environmental and social issues.[14] In September 1999, for example, Dow Jones Indexes and the Switzerland-based SAM Sustainability Group launched the Dow Jones Sustainability Group Index, which tracks the financial performance of more than 200 "sustainability-driven" companies representing 64 industries in 33 countries.[15] The index is dominated by European companies in such sectors as automobiles, paper products, food, banks, insurance, and waste management.[16] As of February 2001, financial institutions in 11 countries, including Australia, Germany, Japan, the Netherlands, and Switzerland, have now created investment funds based on the Sustainability Group Index.[17]

Shareholder activism, the other major type of socially responsible investing, involves exerting leverage on environmental and social issues as a partial owner of a company, either through dialogue with management or by filing or supporting shareholder resolutions at annual meetings. In 1999, concerned investors in the United States introduced more than 200 shareholder resolutions on a broad range of issues, including environmental concerns, corporate governance, and international health and tobacco matters.[18] In one particularly successful case, Home Depot, a large lumber and hardware store, announced it would stop selling forest products from environmentally sensitive areas and would give preference to timber certified as sustainably produced just three months after 12 percent of its shareholders asked the company to stop selling wood from old-growth forests.[19] In 2000, climate change and genetically modified organisms were popular issues for shareholder activism.[20]

One important spur to the recent growth of socially responsible investment has been growing evidence that investment funds screened according to social and environmental criteria have financial returns that are competitive with if not superior to those of conventional portfolios. The Domini 400 Social Index (DSI 400), which monitors the financial performance of 400 U.S. corporations that pass a range of common social screens, posted average annual returns of more than 17 percent over the last decade, outperforming the Standard and Poor's 500.[21]

The growing evidence that socially responsible investing need not entail financial sacrifice has attracted powerful new entrants to the field. A number of large firms, including Ford Motor Company, Hewlett-Packard, and the Gap, are now offering their workers a socially responsible option in their retirement plans, and several well-established, mainstream investment companies, including TIAA-CREF and the Vanguard Group, have added socially screened funds to their standard menu of offerings.[22]

As the combined financial might of social investors grows, so will their clout within corporate executive suites and boardrooms. Just as investor pressure helped to bring about the end of apartheid in South Africa, so can it help us point the way toward an environmentally and socially sustainable global economy.

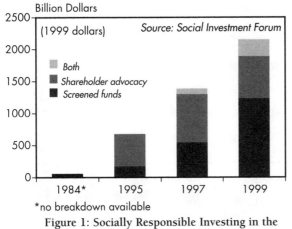

*no breakdown available

Figure 1: Socially Responsible Investing in the United States, Selected Years

Toll of Natural Disasters Grows   *Janet N. Abramovitz*

During the 1990s, the economic toll of natural disasters topped $608 billion, more than the previous four decades combined. Measured in 1999 dollars, losses during the 1990s were more than three times the figure for the 1980s, and more than 15 times the total for the 1950s.[1] (See Figure 1.) The biggest single year for losses in history was 1995, when damages reached $157 billion.[2] An earthquake in Kobe, Japan, accounted for more than two thirds of that total.[3] For weather-related disasters, 1998 was the biggest year on record, at nearly $93 billion in recorded losses, with China's Yangtze River flood responsible for more than a third of this total.[4]

Links: pp. 50, 96, 142

While some 500–850 natural disaster events are recorded every year, only a few are classified as "great"—natural catastrophes that result in deaths or losses so high as to require outside assistance, according to Munich Re, a reinsurance company that compiles global disaster data. Over the past 50 years there has been a dramatic increase in the occurrence of great disasters. In the 1950s there were 20 "great" catastrophes, in the 1970s there were 47, and by the 1990s there were 87.[5]

Between 1985 and 1999, Asia sustained 45 percent of the world's economic losses to disasters, North America 33 percent, and Europe 12 percent; the Caribbean, Central America, South America, and Oceania each incurred 2–3 percent of the global losses.[6] Rural areas and developing nations are in general underrepresented in global disaster data, as reporting systems tend to be weaker, and there is less infrastructure and capital exposure. Africa, with just 1 percent of the global total, is particularly underrepresented because it is rarely hit by major storms or earthquakes.[7] Most of the disasters in Africa are smaller, or are slow-onset disasters, like droughts, that are not counted in the global tallies.

Asia has been especially hard hit. The region is large and heavily populated, particularly in dangerous river basin and coastal areas. There is frequent seismic and tropical storm activity. Between 1985 and 1999, Asia suffered 77 percent of all deaths, 90 percent of all homelessness, and 45 percent of all recorded economic losses due to disasters.[8]

Disaster losses often take a big bite out of the economy in poor countries—and in poor households. While the wealthiest countries sustained 57 percent of the measured economic losses to disasters between 1985 and 1999, this represented only 2.5 percent of their gross domestic product (GDP).[9] In contrast, the poorest countries endured 24 percent of the economic toll of disasters, which added up to 13.4 percent of their GDP, further increasing their vulnerability to future disasters.[10] And in the poorest countries, little if any of the losses are insured. Worldwide, only one fifth of all disaster losses were insured, and 92 percent of these were in industrial nations.[11]

During the twentieth century, more than 10 million people died from natural catastrophes, according to Munich Re.[12] Between 1985 and 1999, nearly 561,000 lives were lost—77 percent of them in Asia.[13] Only 4 percent of the fatalities were in industrial countries.[14] Half of all deaths were due to floods.[15] (See Figure 2.) Earthquakes were the second biggest killer, claiming 169,000 lives.[16] In earlier decades and centuries, it was not uncommon for hundreds of thousands of lives to be lost in a single great catastrophe. In the last 20 years, however, there has been only one such event—the cyclone and

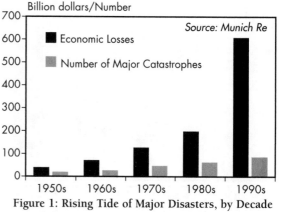

Figure 1: Rising Tide of Major Disasters, by Decade

storm surge that hit Bangladesh in 1991 and took 139,000 lives.[17] Early warnings and disaster preparedness have been a significant factor in keeping the death toll of recent decades from reaching even higher. So, too, have advances in basic services, such as clean water and sanitation. Still, in the 1990s alone more than 2 billion people worldwide were affected by disasters.[18]

Around the world, a growing share of the devastation triggered by "natural" disasters stems from ecologically destructive practices and from putting ourselves in harm's way. By destroying forests, damming rivers, filling in wetlands, and destabilizing the climate, we are unraveling the strands of a complex ecological safety net. Many ecosystems have been frayed to the point where they are no longer resilient and able to withstand natural disturbances, setting the stage for "unnatural disasters"—those made more frequent or more severe due to human actions. The usual approach to natural disturbances is to try to prevent them through methods that all too often exacerbate them. Dams and levees, for example, change the flow of rivers and can increase the frequency and severity of floods and droughts.[19]

Two major global social trends have also increased our vulnerability to natural hazards: the migration of people to coasts and cities and the enormous expansion of the built environment. Some 37 percent of the world—more than 2 billion people—lives within 100 kilometers of a coastline.[20] Since 1950, the global urban population has increased nearly fourfold; today, almost half the world lives in cities.[21] Many cities are located near rivers and coasts, further compounding the risks. Of 19 megacities—those with over 10 million inhabitants—13 are in coastal zones.[22] In much of the developing world, urbanization presents additional dangers. Up to half the people in the largest cities there live in unplanned squatter colonies, which are often sited in vulnerable areas such as floodplains and hillsides.[23]

In the future, our vulnerability to natural disasters will grow further as a result of climate change. The January 2001 report from the Intergovernmental Panel on Climate Change projects that over the next 100 years, sea levels will rise by 9–88 centimeters, and temperatures will increase by 1.4–5.8 degrees Celsius, bringing additional coastal flooding and more intense storms, among other effects.[24] A new report by insurers finds that economic losses related to climate change could top $304 billion a year in the future.[25]

While we cannot do away with natural hazards, we can eliminate those that we cause, minimize those we exacerbate, and reduce our vulnerability to most. Doing this requires healthy and resilient communities and ecosystems. Viewed in this light, disaster mitigation is clearly part of a broader strategy of sustainable development—making communities and nations socially, economically, and ecologically sustainable.

The adage "an ounce of prevention is worth a pound of cure" clearly applies to disasters. The World Bank and U.S. Geological Survey calculated that global economic losses from natural disasters could be reduced by $280 billion if just one seventh that amount were invested in preparedness and mitigation efforts.[26] The costs of disaster preparedness and mitigation can be far less than the costs of disaster relief and recovery.

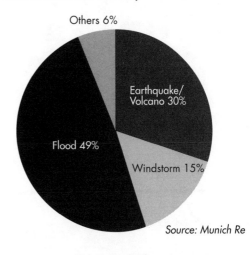

Source: Munich Re

Figure 2: Global Deaths by Disaster Type, 1985–99

Resource Economics Features

Wheat/Oil Exchange Rate Skyrockets

Commodity Prices Weak

Wheat/Oil Exchange Rate Skyrockets   *Janet Larsen*

In 2000, the average market oil price for the year hit a 16-year high as annual wheat prices continued on a downward trend.[1] The number of bushels of wheat needed to purchase a barrel of oil, which can be thought of as the wheat/oil exchange rate, jumped to a record 10 bushels per barrel—reminding the world of the dramatic shift in the terms of trade between oil and wheat exporters since a time when the prices of these commodities were equal.[2] (See Table 1.)

At any time between 1950 and 1973, a bushel of wheat could be traded in the world market for a barrel of oil.[3] The tripling of oil prices in 1973 by the Organization of Petroleum Exporting Countries (OPEC) signaled the first major shift in the exchange rate between grain and oil, serving as a harbinger of recurrent instability. The effect of the price hike on key wheat-exporting countries was tempered by a substantial rise in grain prices due to the impact of unfavorable weather on major crops.[4] But then steadily rising oil prices in the late 1970s and a spike in the early 1980s led to a wheat/oil ratio favoring oil exporters.[5]

Links: pp. 28, 40, 122

Oil is the leading source of energy in the modern economy, providing some 40 percent of commercial energy use.[6] Grain output of 1,840 million tons, nearly a third of which is wheat, satisfies global nutritional needs directly and is a source of feed for livestock and produce.[7] Because of the world's heavy reliance on these two commodities, price fluctuations in oil and grain can directly affect the economic prospects of many countries.

Oil and grain markets are linked. Rises in energy prices increase the cost of petroleum-based agricultural inputs like fertilizers and pesticides, as well as fuels needed for tillage and irrigation.[8] The 11 OPEC nations, which produce over 40 percent of the world's oil, are coincidentally all net importers of grain, and thus have reaped the benefits of the rising oil/wheat price ratio.[9] Crude exports from the Middle East and North Africa combined total 893 million tons, over half of global exports, while more than 35 million tons of wheat are brought into this dry region, accounting for nearly a third of the world's wheat imports.[10] Thus the shifting oil/wheat price ratio shows a transfer of wealth from the United States and Western Europe, both heavy oil importers and wheat exporters, to oil producers in the Middle East, Nigeria, Mexico, Venezuela, and Indonesia.

In 2000, wheat cost $2.89 a bushel (in 1999 dollars), nearly one fifth of the price in 1974.[11] The price decline over three decades can be attributed to gains in production efficiency.[12] Late last year wheat prices partially recovered from decade lows, but not enough to raise the estimated annual price.[13] Worldwide, wheat stocks have cushioned declining harvests, but with world carryover cereal stocks falling over the last few years, it might not be long before grain prices begin to climb.[14]

As oil consumption grew at an average annual rate of 2.6 percent over the past decade, prices climbed and oil's purchasing power surged.[15] In March 1999, OPEC nations agreed to cut oil production, bringing output at least 5 percent below 1998 levels and price increases of 38 percent.[16] Excluding Iraq, where production rose by nearly a fifth because of changes in U.N. sanctions, OPEC production during this period declined 7 percent.[17] Spot market prices continued to inflate until they peaked in September 2000 at $37 a barrel—the highest since the weeks immediately following Iraq's invasion of Kuwait in 1990.[18]

The high prices propelled governments of oil-importing nations to urge OPEC to increase output.[19] It also led motorists and others dependent on oil to protest.[20] Many nations, including France, Italy, Malaysia, Thailand, and the United Kingdom, were persuaded to cut taxes on fuel or to provide energy subsidies.[21] In an action unprecedented in times of peace, the United States—the world's largest oil importer—dipped into its strategic petroleum reserves amid election pressures and fear of unreasonable winter heating costs.[22] Environmentalists worried about the effects of oil-burning on the world's climate argued that these steps send the wrong signal to OPEC.[23]

Without taxes to buffer the price of oil, OPEC has a larger margin in which to raise oil prices, and thus profits from the difference between low production costs and high market prices.[24]

Table 1: The Wheat-Oil Exchange Rate, 1950–2000

Year	Bushel of Wheat	Barrel of Oil	Bushels Per Barrel
	(1999 dollars)		(ratio)
1950	11.34	10.11	1
1955	9.59	10.07	1
1960	7.46	6.98	1
1965	7.14	5.77	1
1970	5.37	4.62	1
1971	5.76	5.58	1
1972	6.25	6.16	1
1973	11.88	8.29	1
1974	13.98	27.50	2
1975	10.62	27.63	3
1976	8.96	28.07	3
1977	6.54	28.42	4
1978	7.56	27.17	4
1979	8.74	34.08	4
1980	8.63	51.86	6
1981	7.99	53.76	7
1982	6.89	52.12	8
1983	6.51	43.90	7
1984	6.08	40.80	7
1985	5.26	37.78	7
1986	4.35	18.93	4
1987	4.14	23.66	6
1988	5.16	18.20	4
1989	5.80	21.30	4
1990	4.47	26.30	6
1991	4.09	21.06	5
1992	4.69	20.47	4
1993	4.25	17.70	4
1994	4.45	16.63	4
1995	5.15	18.09	4
1996	5.91	21.02	4
1997	4.47	19.51	4
1998	3.48	13.07	4
1999	3.05	17.72	6
2000 (prel)	2.89	28.46	10

Source: International Monetary Fund, *International Financial Statistics* (Washington, DC: various years).

A 5-percent cut in oil production early in 2001 buoyed prices that had begun to decline after a small increase in production, and few analysts expect the average for the year to drop much below $25.[25] High demand for an inadequate supply of natural gas may elevate the price of this alternate fossil fuel, prompting industrial consumers and utilities to switch to oil, helping to maintain lofty prices.[26]

The demonstrated sensitivity of fuel commodity prices to a small intentional reduction in supply may foreshadow what will happen when production of oil, a finite resource, is inevitably reduced by depletion of reserves.[27] Several estimates of the ultimately recoverable oil supply show production peaking between 2007 and 2013, as long as consumption continues to increase at current levels of 1.5–2 percent annually.[28] New estimates by the U.S. Geological Survey that incorporate a tally of oil in and around current fields, as well as undiscovered oil, see peaking being delayed beyond 2013, but only by a few additional years.[29] Financial problems lie ahead for heavy oil-importing countries like the United States, which has already exploited almost half its known reserves, unless reliance on fossil fuels is reduced.[30]

In a September 2000 speech, U.N. Secretary General Kofi Annan noted that developing countries are hit hardest by rising oil prices.[31] Leaders at the International Monetary Fund and the World Bank echoed his sentiments, stressing that the economic stability of the entire world, including oil-producing nations, is threatened by price fluctuations.[32] Such prospects serve only to reinforce governments' need to free themselves from dependence on fossil fuels and to invest in renewable systems, such as wind power.

While recent changes in oil prices have been due largely to agreements by key producers to cut output, grain price fluctuations are influenced primarily by weather. In the face of uncertain climatic change and shrinking oil supplies, the wheat/oil exchange rate will continue to tell us where the relationship between the food and energy sectors is heading.

Commodity Prices Weak

Michael Renner

World market prices for all raw materials—for fuel and nonfuel commodities, that is—have been on a downward slide for more than two decades.[1] On average, nonfuel commodities now fetch only about 46 percent as much as in the mid-1970s.[2] (See Figure 1.) Among these, prices for tropical beverage crops—coffee, tea, and cocoa—have taken the worst beating, dropping to just one sixth their peak price in 1977.[3] Food and fertilizer prices are at about one fourth their 1974 peak.[4] Metals, at half their 1974 prices, and agricultural raw materials—cotton, rubber, timber, and others—at three quarters their 1973 top value, have done better.[5] Only crude oil has seen a sustained upswing in recent years, but nevertheless remains at about half the zenith reached in 1980.[6]

Links: pp. 58, 62, 120

This trend is part of a larger, century-long decline that was only briefly reversed in the 1970s.[7] On average, nonfuel commodity prices are now at only one third their 1900 level.[8] Although crude oil prices have fared somewhat better, in real terms they are no higher today than they were in 1900.[9]

The World Bank projects prices for most commodities to continue to be weak, and in some cases volatile, in coming years.[10] While circumstances vary from one commodity market to the next, the essence is that the ability to produce these materials cheaply far outpaces demand.

An abundance of natural resources would appear to be a blessing. However, heavy dependence on primary industries more often turns out to be a curse. The extreme ups and downs in commodity prices frequently trigger distorting boom-and-bust cycles. And even when prices are strong, resource-extractive industries are not known to spawn diversified, balanced economies. In fact, once a mine, forest, or the nutrients of a tract of arable land are depleted, extractive industries move on, leaving behind a barren economic and environmental landscape.[11]

Any country or region that depends heavily on resource extraction is susceptible to low or volatile prices, but developing countries tend to be far more vulnerable. Although a good number of them have been able to diversify their economies and increase the importance of manufacturing and service industries in the last few decades, many remain highly dependent on the export of raw materials for their foreign-exchange earnings.[12]

For some countries, particularly many in sub-Saharan Africa, a single commodity accounts for the bulk of foreign-exchange revenues. In 1996, there were 23 nations that derived 80 percent or more of their total export income from one commodity; among them were many oil exporters like Saudi Arabia, Nigeria, and Angola, but also Mali (cotton) and Rwanda (coffee).[13] Another 21 countries derived 60–80 percent from one commodity; among them were Ethiopia and Uganda (coffee), Uzbekistan (cotton), and Zambia (copper).[14] Finally, 21 more nations fell into the 40–59 percent range; this list included Cambodia (timber), Côte d'Ivoire (cocoa), and the Democratic Republic of Congo (diamonds).[15]

Of course, falling export prices are less damaging for a country if the prices of its imports also decline. The "terms of trade" measure this ratio. Developing countries experienced a substantial improvement in their terms of trade during the 1970s, but saw them deteriorate in the 1980s, remain relatively unchanged during much of the 1990s, and decline again in the last two years.[16] While the terms of trade of oil exporters improved in recent years, oil-importing agricultural exporters are facing a severe squeeze: in 2000 it took more than twice as many bushels of wheat to pay for a barrel of petroleum as just two years earlier, in 1998.[17]

Despite declining world market prices, the total value of the global commodities trade continues to rise, due to sharply higher volumes of production and exports. The price for palm oil, for instance, is less than half what it was in 1970, but because the volume of production grew eightfold, the total value of output tripled.[18] For rice, price erosion and production gains cancelled each other out.[19]

For coffee, copper, cotton, and iron ore, however, the decline in price outweighed gains in production volume.[20]

From $835 billion worth (in 1999 dollars) in 1970–71, global production of 22 key commodities grew 59 percent to $1.33 trillion by 1996–97 (the most recent year for which the World Bank has compiled comparable data).[21] Trade expanded twice as fast during this period, from $203 billion (25 percent of output) to $444 billion (33 percent).[22] Some 91 percent of potash fertilizer produced worldwide is exported. Other heavily trade-dependent commodities are cocoa (72 percent), palm oil (68 percent), aluminum (61 percent), crude oil (53 percent), and copper (41 percent).[23]

Beyond the dynamics of supply and demand (and the ebb and flow of inventories), raw materials prices are influenced by the development of new technologies that may increase supplies at lower cost, deliver greater end-use efficiency, and allow the substitution of certain raw materials in industrial and other applications (such as the substitution of synthetic rubber for natural, of specialty plastics for aluminum, or of fiber glass for copper).

For a short time in the 1970s, developing countries managed to force prices up through export cartels. But divergent interests made such policy coordination short-lived. And multinational companies have considerable leverage through their control of large chunks of the raw materials trade.[24] In addition, commodity prices today are strongly influenced by rapidly expanding futures exchanges in New York, Chicago, London, Frankfurt, and Tokyo.[25]

One reason commodity prices fell during the past two decades is that many developing countries—often on the advice of the International Monetary Fund and the World Bank—are trying to export more of their resources, but end up competing head-on with each other in pursuit of the same strategy. Such export strategies were devised in order to bring in revenues to service foreign debts, but deteriorating commodity prices have made this an elusive goal.[26]

In the quest for higher export revenues, one risk is that the environment becomes a casualty of stepped-up resource exploitation. The detrimental impact of mining and logging operations is obvious enough. But other raw materials operations also carry increasing environmental costs. Coffee plantations are a case in point. The shift from small producers growing coffee plants in mixed-use, shaded plots to industrial-scale cultivation leads to increasing deforestation, loss of biodiversity, soil degradation, and water pollution (from higher fertilizer and pesticide use). Farm workers risk pesticide poisoning, and smaller-scale growers—that is, many of the 20–25 million people involved worldwide—are sometimes no longer able to compete.[27]

Low commodity prices may be good news for consumers, but they tend to weaken incentives to use materials more efficiently and sparingly. All things being equal, greater consumption translates into greater negative environmental impact.

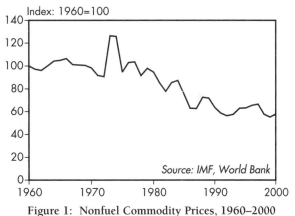

Figure 1: Nonfuel Commodity Prices, 1960–2000

Transportation Features

Urban Rail Systems Gather Steam

Gasoline Taxes Vary Widely

Urban Rail Systems Gather Steam   *Molly O. Sheehan*

Cities have long built rail lines to increase travel speeds and improve people's access to places. Today, urban rail tracks are concentrated in Europe, the former Soviet republics, and Japan, while the largest demand for urban transportation is in the developing world. Rail alone cannot meet the transport needs of all growing cities, but in many places it could play an important role as part of an integrated strategy.

Urban rail is typically classified as "heavy" or "light." Subways, elevated railways, and metros are all heavy rail, operating on rights-of-way from which all other traffic is excluded.[1] In contrast, light rail—streetcars, tramways, or trolley cars—runs along tracks at street level that may not be separated from other traffic.[2] In recent years, some cities have found ways to expand the usefulness of their tracks by allowing light rail to use heavy rail lines, and vice versa.[3]

Urban rail systems are not spread evenly among the world's regions.[4] (See Table 1.) Western Europe has some 31 percent of the world's metros and 33 percent of its trams.[5] Buses, automobiles, and subways began to displace some light rail lines in North American cities in the 1920s and in West European cities in the 1930s and 1940s.[6] But light rail systems were preserved in Eastern Europe and the former Soviet Union, so today this region is home to some 46 percent of those systems.[7]

Recent heavy rail projects have been suggested as an alternative to motor vehicle use in some of the most traffic-clogged regions. Residents of Bangkok, who endure some of the world's longest commutes, welcomed an elevated Skytrain in December 1999.[8] With one 17-station, 17-kilometer line and another 7-station, 6-kilometer line, this is not yet a complete network, however, and is attracting only 150,000–200,000 riders a day.[9] In Athens, a 14-station, 13-kilometer underground rail route that opened in January 2000 and an intersecting route that opened in November 2000 are the first links in a subway network that is now serving some 400,000 people daily.[10] The government expects that by reducing the need for people to drive pollution-belching motor vehicles, the subway system will cut by almost a third the smog that chokes Athens.[11] Heavy rail systems are costly to construct, however, and both the Bangkok and Athens projects have encountered delays.

Light rail has become increasingly popular, as it is cheaper than heavy rail yet shares the advantage of increasing land value near stations (which bus routes generally do not). In Western Europe, the resurgence of interest in light rail has reversed a decades-long decline in this form of transport.[12] (See Table 2.) In the United States, light-rail riders are the fastest-growing segment of public transportation riders.[13] And the number of Americans riding public transport in general is growing faster than those using cars, reaching its highest level in nearly four decades in 2000.[14]

Demand for urban transportation is increasing where cities are growing fastest: Latin America, Asia, and Africa. U.N. demographers project a net addition of 2 billion people by 2030, pushing world population over 8 million, but most of the growth will occur in urban areas of the developing world.[15]

Table 1: Cities with Urban Rail Systems, by Region, 2000

Region	Heavy Rail	Light Rail
	(number of systems)	
Eastern Europe/Central Asia	15	166
Western Europe[1]	29	119
United States and Canada	17	33
Japan	9	20
Other Asia-Pacific	12	8
Latin America	11	6
Australia and New Zealand	0	6
Africa	1	6
World Total	94	364

[1]The 15 members of the European Union plus Switzerland and Norway.
Source: Tony Pattison, ed., *Jane's Urban Transport Systems 2000–2001* (London: 2000), pp. 20–24.

Transit systems could help meet this demand with less damage to the environment than car-based systems. The roads and parking lots needed to accommodate motor vehicles eat up land.[16] By burning fuel, cars release gases and particles that contribute to much of the air pollution in many urban regions.[17] And road traffic is the fastest-growing contributor to climate change.[18]

Rail can move people with less space and energy than cars require. In Portland, Oregon, planners estimate that the opening of a new light rail line has saved the region from building eight new parking garages and two extra lanes on major highways.[19] In 1998, rail transit in the United States averaged 12 percent less energy per passenger-kilometer than cars did, although the energy savings of transit has likely increased as transit ridership has grown and the automobile fleet has become less efficient.[20]

While the up-front cost of rail is high, cities with effective urban transit spend less on transportation over the long run. Researchers at Australia's Institute for Sustainability and Technology Policy (ISTP), led by Peter Newman and Jeffrey Kenworthy, found that auto-dependent Australian and U.S. cities spend 12–13 percent of their per capita wealth on passenger transport, whereas rail-filled cities in Europe and Asia spend less (8 percent in the European cities and 5 percent in Tokyo, Hong Kong, and Singapore).[21] Developing countries without the means to invest in rail may achieve benefits by setting aside rights-of-way for buses, as Curitiba in Brazil has so effectively done.[22] At a later date, dedicated bus lanes might be turned over to rail lines.

To reach the areas that need it most, urban rail will need support from major lending institutions, which often give greater priority to transportation links between cities than to movement within urban regions. Between 1997 and 1999, 63 percent of the World Bank's transportation loans went to highways, while only 15 percent went to urban transport.[23] In Central and Eastern Europe, where many urban rail systems need repair, the European Union's Instrument for Structural Policies for

Table 2: Urban Light Rail Systems in 15 Nations of the European Union, 1930–2000

Year	Number
1930	438
1940	341
1950	272
1960	157
1970	108
1980	91
1990	92
2000	102

Source: 1930–90 from European Commission, Transport in Figures, <www.europa.eu.int>, viewed 8 December 2000; 2000 from Tony Pattison, ed., Jane's Urban Transport Systems 2000–2001 (London: 2000).

Pre-Accession is targeting improvements in long-distance links at the expense of urban transit.[24]

For rail lines or buses to compete with road vehicles, governments must couple investment in transit with incentives to steer new development toward transit stations. ISTP's researchers have identified a critical threshold below which urban transit is not viable: 30 people per hectare.[25] The U.S. cities studied by ISTP have, on average, 14 people per hectare, whereas the European cities have 50.[26] A city need not be as crowded as Hong Kong's 300 people per hectare to support effective urban transit; for instance, Stockholm's transit systems work well with only 53 people per hectare.[27]

A useful urban rail system must connect to other forms of transportation. One of the current shortcomings of Bangkok's new Skytrain is that it lacks adequate bicycle parking and connections to bus routes.[28] Bicycles are often not convenient for long trips, and buses and trains are limited to fixed routes. But bicycles and public transit can complement each other when people are able to carry their bikes aboard buses or trains or to park them at stations.

Gasoline Taxes Vary Widely

Molly O. Sheehan

A spike in gasoline prices in 2000 highlighted not only many societies' reliance on oil but also discrepancies in how governments tax it. The price that a driver pays for gas at the pump has two components: production costs and taxes. The cost of producing gasoline includes the price of crude oil, the cost of refining it, and the cost of distributing it. Governments typically impose a fixed excise tax plus a sales tax, which is a percentage of the full production cost plus the excise tax.[1]

Fluctuations in crude oil supply and demand influence the first component, production costs. Worldwide, there is a mismatch between the countries that produce oil and those that use it. Many industrial nations rely on oil produced elsewhere to run their vehicles, heat their buildings, and power their factories. The 11 members of the Organization of Petroleum-Exporting Countries (OPEC) produced 40 percent of the world's oil in 2000.[2] The remainder came from the United States, Canada, the North Sea, and other industrial areas (26 percent); the developing world (24 percent); and the countries of the former Soviet Union (10 percent).[3] Most of the demand, in sharp contrast, came from the United States, Japan, and Western Europe.[4]

The cost of producing gasoline rose in 2000 as crude oil demand outstripped supply.[5] While countries struggled to recover from the financial crisis that began in Asia in 1997, they used less oil, which caused prices to drop. In response, OPEC nations decided to cut back production. So as economies rebounded and demand for oil grew in 2000, supply was low.

Taxes, the other component of gasoline prices, vary widely from country to country.[6] (See Table 1.) Relatively low U.S. taxes are striking because the United States produces 12 percent of the world's crude oil, yet consumes 26 percent of the total in the

Links:
pp. 40, 68

world and uses 43 percent of the world's crude that is made into gasoline.[7] Despite growing reliance on oil from politically unstable countries and heightened awareness of the environmental harm wrought by fuel use, U.S. taxes have remained relatively constant since the 1930s.[8] (See Figure 1.)

Dr. Gerhard Metschies, who has surveyed gasoline prices in 132 countries worldwide, identifies four categories of nations.[9] The benchmarks separating the groups are the tax rates of the nations that use the most gasoline and the untaxed price of gas. Many countries that import all or most of their oil have relatively high taxes. These nations, 45 in all, include not only Japan and those in Western Europe, but also many countries in Eastern Europe, South America, Africa, and Asia. Another 46 countries, mainly oil importers in the developing world, have gasoline prices lower than in Western Europe but higher than

Table 1: Gasoline Prices, Selected Countries, Fall 2000

Country	Price[1]	Tax	Tax Share of Price
	(cents per liter)		(percent)
United Kingdom	113	85	76
Japan	102	55	54
France	96	67	69
Italy	95	61	64
Brazil[2]	92	60	65
Germany	92	61	67
Spain	73	42	58
India[2]	60	28	47
Canada	50	20	41
South Africa[2]	50	18	36
United States	41	10	25
China[2]	40	8	20
Russia[2]	33	1	3
Indonesia[2]	17	0	subsidy

[1]Unleaded "premium" gasoline pump prices in October 2000 for all countries except Japan, Canada, and the United States, which unleaded "regular" gasoline pump prices. [2]Capital city premium gasoline prices for November 2000; tax is a rough estimate determined by the pump price minus 32¢ per liter untaxed world average price for gasoline. *Sources:* See endnote 6.

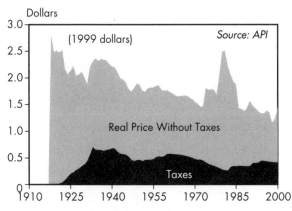

Figure 1: U.S. City Average Retail Gasoline
Prices and Taxes, 1918–2000

in the United States. India, South Africa, and Kenya are in this category. A third group (26 countries) has taxes ranging from the level of the United States to no tax at all. While some produce oil, most are net importers. This category includes Libya, Jordan, China, and Russia. Finally, some 15 nations subsidize their gasoline. This group includes net exporters such as Saudi Arabia, Nigeria, and Venezuela, as well as a few net importers such as Sudan.

Many countries could benefit from gradually phasing out subsidies and raising taxes. The gases and particles released when vehicles burn fuel are the single largest contributor to health-threatening air pollution in many urban areas.[10] And even the best pollution-control technologies do not eliminate carbon dioxide, which is a key contributor to climate change.[11] By raising gasoline taxes, governments can generate funds for public transportation, discourage excessive driving, and encourage development of alternative fuels and vehicles.

In response to rising crude oil prices, a few Asian governments decided to reduce fuel subsidies in late 2000.[12] Viet Nam announced it was removing import taxes and beginning to cut subsidies.[13] In Malaysia, where pump prices of unleaded gasoline had remained unchanged since 1983, the nation's finance minister said the subsidies should have been cut years ago.[14] A senior economics minister in

Indonesia noted that some $100 million in savings from the reduction in fuel subsidies in 2000 would allow the government to increase spending on poverty alleviation and rural infrastructure.[15]

Given society's heavy reliance on motor fuels, sudden, sharp price hikes—whether from taxes or production costs—are disruptive. In Europe, the rising price of crude oil on the world market in the fall of 2000 was compounded by a weak European currency.[16] Farmers, truckers, and taxi drivers organized protests from Norway to Italy, and from Spain to Poland.[17] Ironically, many of the protesters requesting tax cuts benefited from those tax revenues: half of the value-added tax on fuel that goes to the European Union supports agricultural programs; most of the rest funds transportation infrastructure.[18] Nonetheless, some governments caved in to pressure; the Dutch government agreed to subsidize taxi, bus, and trucking enterprises, for instance, and the Italian government agreed to fuel discounts for truckers.[19]

Dramatic price hikes are particularly distressing for people in developing countries. To appease taxi drivers hurt by the rise in oil prices, Beijing's Transportation Bureau gave them a new subsidy.[20] When high crude oil prices combined with a cut in subsidies, fuel prices surged in Indonesia in October 2000, prompting students to vandalize government offices and to take civil servants hostage in protest.[21] In Cotabato Province in the Philippines, a hike in gasoline prices reflecting the increase in crude oil prices led protesters to explode bombs at several gasoline stations.[22] Gerhard Metschies concludes that to avoid protests, no single increase in price should exceed more than 10 percent of the pump price.[23] Rather, a steady series of small price adjustments would be better.

Health Features

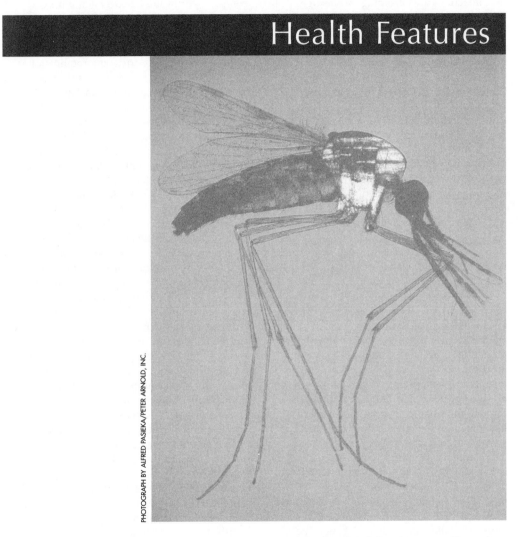

Antimicrobial Resistance Growing

Malaria's Lethal Grip Tightens

Being Overweight Now Epidemic

Health Care Spending Uneven

Antimicrobial Resistance Growing

Lisa Mastny

Microbes that cause many of the world's deadliest infections are becoming increasingly immune to the drugs used to treat them.[1] Resistance is rising among a wide range of bacteria, viruses, parasites, and fungi that are responsible for diseases from malaria to AIDS.[2] (See Table 1.) This threatens to reverse a half-century of public health improvements, which began with the introduction of the "miracle drug" penicillin in 1943.[3]

Many diseases are developing resistance not only to first-line drugs but also to second-, third-, and even last-resort treatments. Certain types of tuberculosis (TB) now evade every existing antibiotic—an arsenal of more than 100 drugs.[4] Even common hospital-acquired infections like *Staphylococcus aureus* (staph) are increasingly lethal, with strains failing to respond to vancomycin, the antibiotic of last resort.[5]

Links: pp. 106, 134, 138

Resistance spreads when an antimicrobial agent fails to kill all the germs that cause an infection, favoring the overgrowth of those that are particularly immune. These "super-bugs" acquire their initial resistance through rapid mutations in their own DNA, or from other microbes.[6] The resistant strains can then multiply and spread to new human or other hosts through the usual pathways of contagion, including infected blood, saliva, and nasal fluid.[7]

A key factor behind emerging resistance is the soaring use of antimicrobial drugs—particularly antibiotics, used to fight bacterial infections.[8] In the United States, antibiotic production increased more than 80-fold between 1950 and 1994, and hospitals now administer some 160 million doses daily.[9] Though antibiotic use does not always trigger resistance, more frequent use creates greater opportunities for the survival and spread of resistant bacteria.[10]

Studies suggest that at least half of all antibiotics used in human medicine are prescribed unnecessarily.[11] Many doctors administer these drugs before they are needed, or apply them in situations where they are ineffective, such as to fight colds and other viruses.[12] They may do this in response to patient demand, to speed patient visits, or under pressure from drug companies or health management groups.[13]

In the developing world, misuse of antibiotics is rapidly depleting the arsenal of viable treatments, worsening the tolls of many deadly diseases. In parts of Africa, chloroquine, once the cheapest and most effective anti-malarial, is now taken more frequently than aspirin to treat minor pains—an overuse that has contributed to its rising ineffectiveness on the continent.[14] With many treatments available over-the-counter, patients often purchase pills in single doses and take them only as long as their symptoms persist, enabling the hardiest microbes to survive.[15] Such self-dosage is also a large factor behind the rising failure of many anti-TB drugs, which must be taken for at least six months to be fully effective.[16]

Surging agricultural use of many of the same antibiotics used for human medicine also encourages resistance. Farmers now use up to 84 percent of all antimicrobials in the United States—some to fight animal disease and prevent bacterial growth on crops or in fish ponds, but the bulk as feed additives to boost livestock growth.[17] Such nontherapeutic livestock use has nearly doubled in the United States since 1985.[18] Any resistant infections that develop in animals or the environment can spread to humans through contact with infected creatures or water, as well as through the food chain.[19]

The booming use of antimicrobials to kill surface germs on living tissue, water, and everyday objects can also promote resistance.[20] Between 1992 and mid-1998, some 700 new "antibacterial" products were introduced in the United States, among them cleansers, cutting boards, toys, cat litter, and ballpoint pens.[21] But this sanitation revolution has its downside: in 1998, for the first time, scientists isolated strains of the bacteria *Escherichia coli* that resisted triclosan, a common antiseptic used in soaps and toothpaste.[22]

Resistant infections are typically costlier to treat than regular infections, requiring longer medication and hospitalization.[23] Treating multi-drug-resistant TB, for example, costs roughly 100 times more than regular TB—at least $2,000 per patient in the developing world.[24] The expense of second- or third-line treatments can be prohibitive in many countries, making the human toll of resistance particularly high.[25] In Senegal, for instance, the risk of malaria death to children under 10 has increased nearly sixfold since the early 1980s due to rising resistance.[26]

As antimicrobial resistance spreads, pharmaceutical companies are showing renewed interest in developing more powerful treatments.[27] Two promising antibiotics, Synercid and Zyvox, were recently approved in the United States to fight drug-resistant hospital-acquired infections.[28] Another prospect is the anti-malarial artemisinin, a variation of which has been used as a herbal remedy in China for 2,000 years.[29] But each new compound costs an estimated $500 million to research and develop, and many firms remain reluctant to invest in substances that could lose their effectiveness in a matter of years.[30]

As the world becomes increasingly integrated, the resistance problem is likely to worsen.

Rising prison populations, refugee flows, and international travel all contribute to continuous microbial exchange among people, animals, and the environment.[31] Today, roughly 1 in 40 travelers to West Africa who have not taken any preventative anti-malaria medication return home with a drug-resistant strain.[32] In the absence of a comprehensive monitoring and reporting system to assess the pathways and prevalence of resistance, however, the full global scope of the problem remains unknown.[33]

Carefully regulating the distribution and use of antimicrobials in health care and agriculture would prolong the effectiveness of many drugs.[34] In Canada, a recent campaign to raise awareness of the problem among patients and health care providers led to a sharp reduction in antibiotic use—while in Iceland, the end of government drug subsidies had a similar effect.[35] The European Union, meanwhile, has addressed the spread of antibiotics in agriculture by banning the use of four antibiotics in animal feed.[36]

Table 1: Antimicrobial Resistance Among Selected Diseases Worldwide

Disease	Prevalence of Resistance
Malaria	Resistance to quinine first encountered in the 1950s. Resistance to its replacement, chloroquine, identified in 81 of 92 malaria-endemic countries, including most of Africa. Failure of third-line mefloquine now reported in Southeast Asia, the center for malaria resistance.
Tuberculosis	At least one sixth of all known TB strains now show some degree of resistance. Multidrug resistance is highest in China, the Dominican Republic, Estonia, India, Latvia, and Russia, with more than 10 percent of new cases evading the two most powerful drugs.
Typhoid	Since 1989, 11 countries have had epidemics of multidrug-resistant typhoid—evading first-line chloramphenicol, second-line quinolones, and even third-line treatments. In the past five years, 20 percent of typhoid isolates in India have developed resistance to ciprofloxacin, a costly third-line drug.
HIV/AIDS	Resistance is reported to all marketed antiretrovirals—including zidovudine (AZT), nevirapine, and relatively new protease inhibitors. Studies in industrial countries have found resistant strains in up to half the patients undergoing drug therapy. (In the developing world, access to such treatments is generally limited.) Because HIV compromises the immune system, HIV infection may help encourage resistance among other pathogens, including malaria and TB.
Hospital-acquired infections	Resistant microbes cause as many as 60 percent of hospital infections in industrial countries, and are responsible for some 14,000 deaths annually in the United States. In many developing countries, they are now a leading cause of death. Nearly all staph strains show resistance to penicillin, up to 60 percent to second-line methicillin, and a growing number to last-line vancomycin.

Sources: See endnote 2.

Malaria's Lethal Grip Tightens

Anne Platt McGinn

Although AIDS has grabbed the headlines in recent years, malaria remains one of the world's deadliest diseases. This parasitic disease kills at least a million people each year.[1] (This figure is probably a gross underestimate, since most deaths occur at home and are never formally registered.)[2] Worldwide, nearly a half-billion people become ill each year, an average of 950 people every minute.[3] The young and poor bear the brunt of the burden.

Malaria's often fatal cycle begins when someone is bitten by an infected female *Anopheles* mosquito. This water-breeding vector transfers the *Plasmodium* parasite to human blood, where it circulates through the kidneys, liver, and brain.[4] Once infected, a person will experience various stages of high fever, convulsions, difficult breathing, and, in severe cases, coma, which can lead to sudden death.[5]

Links: pp. 106, 132, 138

Fifty years ago, about 2 million people died annually from malaria, primarily in Asia and the Pacific.[6] Following World War II, however, the United States and other industrial countries declared war on this disease. In 1955, the World Health Organization (WHO) recommended heavy DDT spraying to control *Anopheles*.[7] Combined with antimalarial drugs, this strategy brought significant improvements: in 1950, the annual global mortality rate was 48 per 100,000 people.[8] By 1970, the figure had dropped to 16 per 100,000, where it has remained, although in 1997 the global rate edged up to 18 per 100,000.[9] (See Figure 1.) Still, the annual global death rate from malaria dropped 63 percent between 1950 and 1997, saving millions of lives worldwide.

Africans, however, are losing ground in this battle.[10] Death rates from malaria on the continent declined just 10 percent between 1950 and 1997, despite early progress with insecticide spraying and therapeutic drugs.[11] In the late 1970s, drug-resistant parasites took hold, and the health sector failed to respond. By 1997, Africa's death rate from malaria stood at 165 per 100,00 people, nine times higher than the global average.[12] Since the mid-1980s, mortality rates among African children have tripled due to drug-resistant strains.[13]

Malaria also poses an enormous public health problem in tropical regions of Asia, Latin America, and the Middle East. Nearly 40 percent of the world's population is at risk, and malaria is considered endemic in 105 countries.[14] People in temperate regions are not spared either: tourists and travelers sporadically become infected and carry the parasite back home with them.[15]

Sub-Saharan Africa is ground zero for a number of reasons. Inadequate health services play a role. In Southeast Asia, for example, laboratory diagnosis is generally the rule, whereas in sub-Saharan Africa, it is the exception.[16] As a result, many cases are initially mistreated and they progress to more advanced forms that are more expensive and complicated to treat. Outpatient clinics throughout the region routinely treat more people for malaria than for any other disease.[17]

There are 60 different vector species, each with varying behaviors and habitats. On average, people in Southeast Asia and South America are infected about once a year.[18] In contrast, transmission rates exceed 100 infective bites per person annually over large swaths of Africa.[19] The average Tanzanian, for example, suffers more infective bites each night than the average Thai or Vietnamese does in a year.[20] Africa's at-risk population totals some 470 million people, more than 200 million of whom were infected in 1995.[21]

Such exposure has significant economic implications. A recent study estimated that malaria drags Africa's economy down by 1.3 percent of gross domestic product (GDP) a year—representing a loss of $2 billion in 1998 alone.[22] Over the past 35 years, this adds up to about $100 billion, or one third of Africa's current GDP.[23]

Environmental change, social upheaval, and drug resistance have all contributed to the recent upswing in malaria.[24] Weather anomalies have helped malaria gain a foothold in the highlands of Ethiopia and Kenya, areas that were previously free of this disease.[25] Global climate change promises to exacerbate the problem, as *Anopheles* will be able to spread to new areas.

Malaria is also coming back to places where it was once largely under control.[26] In Afghanistan and Sierra Leone, for example, malaria gained ground in the midst of civil wars and the flow of thousands of refugees who lacked basic sanitation.[27] In parts of South America and Southeast Asia, logging and dam- and road-building projects routinely attract laborers into frontier areas, where they are often exposed to the parasite. Between 1974 and 1991, Brazil witnessed a 10-fold increase in cases largely due to logging in the Amazon.[28]

Drug-resistant strains of the *Plasmodium* parasite first emerged in Southeast Asia in the early 1970s, and have since spread to nearly every country where the disease is found.[29] Chloroquine, which served as the treatment of choice for decades, is now useless in more than 80 countries because of resistance.[30] In recent years, health officials in Asia have fought back with artemisinins, new drugs that are derived from the Chinese herbal remedy quinhaosu.[31] Combining artemisinin with mefloquine (a cousin of chloroquine) has helped slow the spread of resistance in some areas, buying time to find new drugs or a vaccine.[32]

Controlling the *Anopheles* mosquito is also a challenge. In the mid-1990s, South African health officials banned DDT in response to its adverse health effects.[33] Safer pyrethroid insecticides were phased in, but by 1999 cases of malaria had increased in South Africa to levels not seen in decades.[34] And in KwaZulu-Natal, a mosquito species that had been wiped out reemerged, proving resistant to pyrethroids.[35] In response to this crisis, health officials have reintroduced DDT in selected areas.[36]

In December 2000, negotiators of a U.N. treaty on persistent organic pollutants recognized this dilemma; the treaty thus requires global elimination of DDT but grants temporary health exemptions to a handful of countries where it remains the cheapest and most accessi-

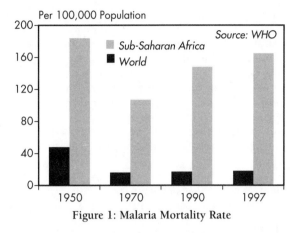

Per 100,000 Population

Figure 1: Malaria Mortality Rate

ble defense against malaria.[37] (These countries are obligated to phase in alternatives over time.)

Fortunately, several preventive measures can reduce malaria's toll. They include the selective use of safer pesticides, physical barriers such as nets and screens, improved sanitation and elimination of stagnant water to reduce mosquito breeding grounds, and public education. Now the challenge is to encourage greater use of these tools. Viet Nam offers free insecticides to people with bednets, which keep the nocturnal vector from biting people.[38] Uganda and Tanzania have reduced taxes on nets to make them more affordable.[39]

In 1998, WHO, the World Bank, and several other institutions launched the Roll Back Malaria program.[40] It combines the latest chemical and nonchemical tools with efforts to strengthen public health systems more broadly to get at the root causes of susceptibility. Such efforts can make a significant difference. In the early 1990s, for example, health officials responded to the malaria epidemic in the Brazilian Amazon by concentrating mosquito control efforts in areas of greatest risk and by detecting and treating cases earlier. As a result, they were able to reduce the mortality rate by 21 percent, the incidence rate by 38 percent, and the cost of saving a life by 85 percent between 1992 and 1996.[41]

Being Overweight Now Epidemic

Gary Gardner

More than a billion people—one in six of the human family—are now overweight by international standards, likely the highest proportion of people in this category in human history.[1] The ranks of the overweight have increased dramatically in the last few decades in rich and poor countries alike, and this group now rivals the underweight population globally. The World Health Organization (WHO) has labeled the trend "today's principal neglected public health problem."[2]

Being overweight is measured using a standard known as the body mass index (BMI), a ratio of weight to height that reflects the health risks of weight gain.[3] A BMI of 25 signals overweight, and a BMI of 30 indicates obesity. By this standard, a full 61 percent of the adult population in the United States is overweight—the highest figure in the industrial world, and an increase from 55 percent in 1994.[4]

Link: p. 138

Obesity, the extreme form of overweight that carries grave health risks, has risen rapidly as well. In the United States, 27 percent of the adult population is now obese, compared with 15 percent in 1980.[5] Obesity is blamed for 300,000 deaths annually in this country.[6] European nations have also seen rapid increases, but from lower levels: obesity among British adults climbed from 6 percent for men and 8 percent for women in 1980 to 15 and 16.5 percent, respectively, in 1995.[7]

Many developing countries are approaching and even surpassing industrial-country levels of overweight, particularly in urban areas. In Colombia and Iran, for example, overweight afflicts more than 30 percent and more than 40 percent of people, respectively.[8] Nearly 20 percent of South Africans over the age of 15 are obese.[9] And the world's highest prevalence of extreme overweight is found in the South Pacific; 77 percent of Samoan women and 58 percent of men were obese in 1991, the most recent year with data.[10] Meanwhile, less-affected countries have also seen dramatic increases in this problem: in China, the share of adults who are overweight surged from 9 to 15 percent in just three years, from 1989 to 1992.[11]

Perhaps most disturbing is the increase in overweight among children, which is especially notable in the United States. One in five American children is now overweight or obese, and being overweight has spread rapidly even among younger children.[12] In 1976–80, more than 6 percent of children aged 6 to 11 were overweight; by 1990–94, the share had grown to more than 11 percent.[13] The pattern is worrisome because overweight children tend to become overweight adults.[14]

The trend toward heavier people is the product of demographic and economic trends that are sweeping an increasingly industrialized world. Industrialization and urbanization have made more food available more cheaply to more people than ever before, even as lifestyles have become more sedentary.[15] And food companies have capitalized on the human love of sugar and fat—an evolutionary leftover of our prehistoric past, when we needed high-calorie foods to survive harsh conditions—to promote foods loaded with calories but with little additional nutritional value.[16]

Indeed, more than half of Americans' caloric intake now comes from sugar and fat.[17] Americans consume more than 53 teaspoons of added sugars each day, and children in the United States get some 10 percent of their calories from soda.[18] Meanwhile, consumption of fruits and vegetables remains below recommended levels. A 1997 survey of U.S. high school students found that 71 percent ate fewer than the recommended five daily servings of fruits and vegetables.[19]

At the same time, industrial societies are increasingly sedentary, as technology and urban lifestyles reduce the need for physical exertion. More than 60 percent of Americans, for example, are not regularly active, and 25 percent get no leisure-time exercise whatsoever.[20] Studies in the United Kingdom have shown a close correlation between obesity and proxy measures of physical activity, such as car ownership or television viewing.[21] And in the United States, children who watch five hours or more of television a day are more than five times as likely to be obese as children who watch for less than two hours a day.[22]

Societies and individuals are paying a mounting toll, especially a health toll, for the epidemic of overweight. It is a major risk factor for chronic diseases such as stroke, heart disease, cancer, and diabetes—the four leading causes of death in the industrial world.[23] In the United States, the health care costs associated with being overweight are estimated at $118 billion, which represents nearly 12 percent of U.S. spending on health care.[24] Meanwhile, WHO predicts that obesity will help make chronic diseases the major disease burden in developing countries over the next quarter-century, surpassing infectious diseases.[25]

Diabetes is of particular concern in industrial and developing countries alike. In the United States, the prevalence of diabetes rose by 33 percent in just eight years, from 1990 to 1998.[26] The increase was fastest among younger Americans, traditionally not an afflicted segment: people in their thirties saw a 76-percent increase in diabetes prevalence.[27] This condition is estimated to cost Americans some $98 billion annually.[28]

Globally, the population with adult-onset diabetes—the kind that correlates closely with being overweight—increased nearly fivefold between 1985 and 1998.[29] WHO estimates that the population affected by diabetes will nearly double to 300 million by 2025, with nearly 90 percent of this increase coming in developing countries.[30] (See Table 1.) The increase in "diseases of affluence" threatens the hungry in these countries as well, as scarce health care resources are apportioned to more prosperous groups, likely at the expense of the poor.

Because overweight is a public health issue and not simply a personal, cosmetic problem, solutions will need to extend well beyond individual dieting efforts. A 1999 campaign by the Australian government to increase cycling, for example, was promoted jointly by the transport and health ministries partly as an effort to combat overweight.[31] Another structural approach

is the proposal of a Yale University psychologist to tax foods based on their nutrient value per calorie; cookies and sodas would be taxed heavily, while fruits and vegetables might escape taxation entirely.[32] Systemic solutions such as these are the best tools for meeting ambitious national weight reduction goals, such as the U.S. objective of cutting obesity to less than 15 percent by 2010.[33]

Table 1: Population with Diabetes, by Region, 1995 and 2000, with Projections for 2025

Region	2000	2025
	(million)	
Europe	36	48
Americas	35	64
Southeast Asia	33	80
Western Pacific	30	56
Eastern Mediterranean	17	43
Africa	4	10
Industrial Countries	55	72
Developing Countries	99	228
World	154	300

Source: World Health Organization, Diabetes Database, <www.who.int/ncd/dia/databases0.htm>, viewed 19 January 2001.

Health Care Spending Uneven

Anne Platt McGinn

In 1948, spending on health care totaled 3 percent of the gross world product; by 1997, the figure reached 7.9–9.2 percent.[1] (Health care here includes preventive, curative, and palliative services.)[2] Some $3 trillion is now spent on health care around the world annually, making this one of the largest sectors in the global economy.[3]

These expenditures are heavily skewed to the wealthy and the healthy: the 84 percent of the world living in low- and middle-income countries claim just 11 percent of global health spending but bear 93 percent of the world's disease burden.[4] (Disease burden is measured by years of healthy life lost from illness combined with those lost from premature death.)[5]

Links: pp. 76, 78, 106, 134

Health care bills for Americans add up to about $1 trillion each year, fully one third of the world total.[6] In contrast, about $250 billion is spent on health care in low- and middle-income countries.[7] Hundreds of millions of people have no access to basic and affordable care, and others receive care only sporadically.[8]

On average, countries earmark 5.5 percent of their gross domestic product (GDP) for health care.[9] The United States dedicates the largest share to health, 13.7 percent of GDP annually; Somalia spends the smallest share—just 1.5 percent.[10]

In per capita terms, the disparities among rich and poor are equally stark. Worldwide, annual health expenditures during the 1990s averaged $561 per person (based on purchasing power parities).[11] Low-income countries spent $93 per person compared with $2,505 in high-income countries—a 27-fold difference.[12] At the extremes, 20 of the world's poorest countries each spend $50 or less per person on health care each year, while in the United States the figure was more than $4,100.[13] Similar variations are found across regions.[14] (See Table 1.)

Although increased spending plays an important role in providing health care services, non-health factors were the primary reasons that infant mortality rates dropped and life expectancy climbed so dramatically during the last 50 years.[15] About half of the gains between 1952 and 1992 resulted from higher levels of female education and rising income levels; the other half stemmed from advances in scientific knowledge, most notably immunizations and antibiotics.[16] The environment also plays a role in human susceptibility to and transmission of diseases, especially malaria, diarrheal diseases, and acute respiratory infections.[17] Worldwide, almost one fourth of disability can be traced back to environmental factors, which include polluted air and water, inadequate housing and shelter, and unsafe food.[18]

Nevertheless, funding for disease prevention and treatment remains a critical determinant of health, particularly among the poor. One third of the world's disease burden could be eliminated for just $12 per person by providing primary health care, basic education, and access to clean drinking water and adequate sanitation.[19] Without investments in health care systems—which includes disease surveillance, human resources, delivery mechanisms, and primary health care services—an estimated 1.2 billion people who have no access to safe drinking water will be condemned to a life of avoidable illness, poverty, and premature death.[20]

Because expenditure data are limited in scope, they should be interpreted with caution. With fewer formal health services available, for example, up to 80 percent of people in developing countries turn to traditional healers for their primary health care, a reality that is not reflected in current measures.[21]

Also hidden are details about access to care. Health care providers almost universally concentrate in urban areas. In Cambodia, for example, 85 percent of the population is rural, while 87 percent of government health workers are found in urban areas.[22] In other cases, access is determined by the patient's ability to pay. In Karachi, Pakistan, the poor typically wait several hours to be seen in a hospital, while well-to-do patients can walk right in.[23] Such disparities are not limited to developing countries: an estimated 45 million Americans—16 percent of the nation—have no health insurance, and 55 million people living in other nations in the Organisation for Economic Co-operation and Development (OECD) lack access to adequate care.[24]

In many countries, the biggest challenge is trying to contain skyrocketing health care costs that are in part driven by new technologies and prescription drugs.[25] In Denmark, France, Germany, Sweden, the United Kingdom, and the United States, per capita spending on health care and pharmaceuticals roughly doubled between 1986 and 1996.[26] Some companies now ask employees to choose between paid vacation leave and health care coverage.[27]

To meet rising costs, governments must seek additional sources of money, often turning to the private sector for assistance. Today, slightly more than half of global health care funding comes from private sources, which include households, insurers, private corporations, and charities.[28]

In many Asian countries, health care is now largely paid for out of pocket.[29] In Africa, the role of private funding is growing as governments are either unwilling or unable to provide even the most basic services for their citizens.[30]

In middle- and high-income countries, public funding for health—government money and external assistance, that is—is considerably higher than the share from private sources.[31] In most OECD countries, at least 60 percent of these expenditures comes from public coffers; in the Czech Republic and Luxembourg, the figure is 92 percent.[32]

In the years ahead, privatization promises to continue. Private health insurance is expected to soon mushroom in India, for instance.[33] But without policies to ensure equitable access, privatizing health care tends to favor those who can afford to pay. In essence, it shifts the financial burden from the healthy to the sick, often requiring people to pay costs they can ill afford at a time when they are least able to do so.[34] Moreover, a recent study in the *Journal of the American Medical Association* found that the level of care is lower in for-profit health maintenance organizations than in non-profit ones.[35]

Addressing these issues requires government oversight to ensure that health care is accessible to those most in need, is equitable in treatment and delivery, and is well managed from a financial standpoint.[36] While important and necessary, dedicating money to health care systems is only the first step in improving public health. Beyond this, the challenges include channeling resources to where they are needed, ensuring viable health systems, reducing poverty, and improving education and environmental conditions. Tackling these factors together will go a long way toward improving global public health among both rich and poor.

Table 1: Health Care Expenditures Per Capita and as Public, Private, and Total Share of Gross Domestic Product, by Region, Mid-1990s

Region	Per Capita (dollars)[1]	Public	Private	Total
		(as percent of gross domestic product)		
High-Income[2]	2,505	6.2	3.7	9.9
Latin America and the Caribbean	461	3.3	3.3	6.6
Eastern Europe and Central Asia	355	4.0	1.8	5.8
Middle East and North Africa	237	2.4	2.3	4.7
East Asia and the Pacific	154	1.7	2.4	4.1
Sub-Saharan Africa[3]	84	1.5	1.8	3.3
South Asia	69	0.8	3.7	4.5
World	561	2.5	2.9	5.5

[1]Currency conversion based on purchasing power parities. [2]Australia, Canada, Israel, Japan, New Zealand, the United States, and Western Europe. [3]All African countries except those bordering on the Mediterranean.
Source: World Bank, *World Development Indicators 2000* (Washington, DC: 2000), p. 92.

Social Features

Migrants and Refugees on the Move
World's Many Languages Disappearing
Religious Environmentalism Rises
Education Still Falling Short of Goals
Social Security Facing Challenges

Migrants and Refugees on the Move   *Danielle Nierenberg*

More than 150 million people—about 3 out of every 100 human beings—were living outside their country of origin as the new century began.[1] Add to that the number of "internal migrants," people who move mainly from rural to urban areas inside their own nations, and the total number of "people on the move" could be as high as 1 billion.[2] (See Table 1.) Though not a new phenomenon, the current movement of people both within and across borders—forced or voluntary, legal or illegal—is unprecedented in recent history, affecting the economies, cultures, and environments of both sending and receiving nations.

Links: pp. 74, 82 According to the International Organization for Migration (IOM), most migration occurs on the same continent.[3] People move from Afghanistan to Iran or Pakistan, for example, from Turkey to Germany, or from Sri Lanka to India to escape persecution or to find work.[4] More than half of all international migrants live in developing countries.[5]

China is one of the biggest source nations—a conservative estimate places the number of people who leave China each year at 400,000, including 100,000 who move legally to the United States, Australia, or Canada for work or study.[6] Estimates of China's "floating population," or internal migrants, range between 100 million and 200 million people, but the true figure is likely much higher, particularly as more and more Chinese make the transition from rural to urban life.[7]

The United States is the largest recipient of foreign-born migrants—at the end of the 1990s, more than 25 million nonnative citizens lived in this country, accounting for nearly 10 percent of the total population.[8] About 1 million legal immigrants enter the United States each year, while the number of "unauthorized" immigrants is estimated at 300,000.[9] Canada, too, has one of the world's highest intakes of legal immigrants: 200,000 a year.[10] Net legal migration into Western Europe is about 400,000 people a year.[11] Central and Eastern Europe became major recipients of migrants in the 1990s because of repatriation by former cit-

izens—more than a half-million repatriants migrated there in 1997 alone.[12] The area also hosts approximately 1.5 million refugees and 1.8 million internally displaced persons.[13]

Political persecution, war, natural disasters, employment, family reunification, and rural poverty are among the incentives for people to move. The "real motivator of migration," says security expert Thomas Homer-Dixon, "is the gap between the potential migrants' current level of satisfaction and the level they expect to attain in a new land. The larger the gap, the greater the incentive to migrate."[14]

War can be an important motivator to move. In Guinea—one of the poorest but once one of the most peaceful African nations—more than a half-million refugees from Sierra Leone and Rwanda flooded the region in the past decade to escape violence.[15] War has followed the refugees, turning Guinea into a "free fire zone" between rebel groups and the armies of the three nations.[16]

Refugees—migrants who do not leave by choice but who are forced out of their homes by armed conflict, political persecution, or environmental disaster—are particularly compelled to cross international boundaries, although it is typically only into a neighboring country.[17] As of January 2000 (the latest date for which figures are available), more than 22.3 million people were considered refugees, asylum seekers, returned refugees, or internally displaced persons by the U.N. High Commissioner for Refugees—almost a million more than a year earlier.[18] Not included in that figure are 4 million Palestinian refugees, and the more than 21 million civilians who are "internally displaced" because of armed conflict or persecution in their own countries.[19]

Roughly half of the world's migrants are women, creating a "feminization of migration."[20] As these women work in factories—the *maquiladoras, zonas francas,* and other foreign-owned textile and assembly plants that dot Mexico, Central America, and the Caribbean—or as domestic servants, their specific needs have received little attention. They are particularly vulnerable to discrimination and physical or sexual abuse by employers or family members. Paid less than men in the workplace and without the same rights as native workers, some of these mostly very young women are forced into prostitution and other illicit activities in order to survive.[21]

Many countries are tightening migration rules, boosting the illegal trafficking of desperate human beings. Worldwide, between 700,000 and 2 million women and children each year are brought illegally into other nations for sexual exploitation.[22] Migrant smuggling has become a highly professional segment of organized crime, netting $7 billion annually.[23] Smugglers provide such services as transportation, documentation, and sometimes employment in a new country. No one knows how many migrants pay smugglers to get them from Iraq, northern Africa, China, or other nations to Europe or North America. Nor is it officially known how many people are smuggled without their consent from Southeast Asia,

Indonesia, and other developing regions as part of the human slavery trade. But in both cases the number is believed to be increasing.[24]

Economically, migration can help raise the standard of living not only for the migrants themselves but for the family members they leave behind. Remittances—the earnings that migrant workers send to their families back home—are an increasingly important part of the economies of developing nations.[25] In Senegal, as much as 80 percent of household budgets comes from remittances, and in the Dominican Republic, remittances exceed the value of the country's exports by 50 percent.[26]

Despite these economic benefits, countries that migrants leave experience a "brain drain" as their most talented members seek education or employment outside their country of origin. The World Bank estimates that during the 1990s, some 23,000 academics from Africa alone emigrated each year in search of better working conditions elsewhere.[27]

Table 1: Selected Examples of People on the Move

Country/Region	Migrant or Refugee Situation
Afghanistan	Approximately 2.5 million Afghanis are considered refugees, and 500,000–750,000 are internally displaced.
Africa	Some 5.9 million Africans are internally displaced in Sudan, Rwanda, Sierra Leone, Somalia, Kenya, and Liberia because of civil war and ethnic conflict.
Central and Eastern Europe	Hundreds of thousands of illegally trafficked migrants enter and leave Bosnia, Croatia, and Yugoslavia each year.
China	More than 400,000 people leave every year for another country, and the rural-to-urban "floating population" is estimated at 100–200 million.
India	Some 50,000 Indians leave annually to live, work, or study in the United States, Canada, Australia, or the United Kingdom.
Middle East	Palestinians make up the single largest group of refugees, totaling about 4 million individuals.
Southeast Asia	Fewer than half of the 250,000 East Timorese who fled their nation in 1999 because of political turmoil have been able to return home.
United States and Canada	Approximately 1.2 million new and documented immigrants—and thousands of illegal, undocumented people—enter North America annually.

Sources: U.S. Committee for Refugees, *World Refugee Survey 2000* (Washington, DC: 2000); International Organization for Migration, *World Migration Report 2000* (New York: IOM and United Nations: 2000).

World's Many Languages Disappearing   *Payal Sampat*

At least half of the 6,800 languages spoken around the world today are expected to become extinct by the end of this century.[1] (See Table 1.) Bleaker projections suggest the loss may be as high as 90 percent.[2] An estimated 4,000–9,000 languages have already disappeared in the last 500 years as a result of wars, genocide, bans on regional languages, and the cultural assimilation of ethnic minorities.[3]

Only 250 languages—4 percent of the total—are spoken by more than 1 million people each.[4] A handful of these now dominate the world's speech, with half the planet conversing in the 15 most spoken languages.[5] (See Figure 1.) Mandarin Chinese leads, with 885 million speakers.[6] Half of the top 10 languages are European, although the continent has produced just 4 percent of all languages.[7] As English spreads through global media and markets, it is now spoken by more people as a second language (350 million) than as a native tongue (322 million).[8]

Some 6,000 languages are spoken by just a tenth of the world.[9] Indeed, nearly half of all languages have fewer than 2,500 speakers.[10]

A mere eight countries are home to half the world's languages.[11] Papua New Guinea, with 832 languages, and Indonesia, with 731, are the planet's linguistic heavyweights, followed by Nigeria with 515 languages; India with 398; Mexico, Cameroon, and Australia with just under 300 each; and Brazil with 234.[12]

Thus some of the most biologically diverse regions are also the most linguistically rich. Islands, for instance, have spawned unique speeches as well as species because of their physical isolation from larger land masses.[13] Amazingly, 110 different languages are spoken on the tiny Pacific archipelego of Vanuatu.[14] Large countries with varied terrain, ecosystems, and climate—India, Brazil, and the United States, for instance—are also hotbeds of both kinds of diversity.[15]

Just 600 of the world's languages are considered "safe" from extinction, meaning they are still being learned by children.[16] About 90 percent of Australia's 250 Aboriginal languages are near extinction.[17] In the United States and Canada, 80 percent of native tongues are no longer being learned by younger generations.[18] Only 6 out of 300 native languages spoken in what is now the United States when Columbus arrived in 1492 are still spoken by more than 10,000 people.[19] Alaska's Eyak has just one remaining speaker, while Idaho's Coeur D'Alene has five; Catawba and Iowa both disappeared in 1996.[20]

Although hundreds of South American languages were wiped out following the Spanish conquest, the continent's remaining 640 languages are derived from a rich diversity of language stocks—93, compared with 6 stocks for Europe and 20 for Africa.[21] About 27 percent of South America's languages are near extinction, and four out of five are spoken by fewer than 10,000 people.[22] Smallpox, migration, and cultural assimilation have displaced all but five speakers of Chamicuro, spoken in the Peruvian Amazon.[23]

Table 1: Status of World's Languages, by Region

Region	World's Languages		Share at Risk[1]
	(number)	(percent of total)	(percent)
Asia	2,197	32	53
Africa	2,058	30	33
Australia and Pacific	1,311	19	93
Americas	1,013	15	
North America			78
South America			77
Central America			36
Europe	230	4	30
World	6,809	100	59

[1] Languages with fewer than 10,000 speakers.
Sources: Distribution from Barbara F. Grimes, ed., *Ethnologue: Languages of the World,* 14th ed. (Dallas, TX: Summer Institute of Linguistics, 2000); share at risk from Daniel Nettle and Suzanne Romaine, *Vanishing Voices: The Extinction of the World's Languages* (New York: Oxford University Press, 2000), p. 40.

In Africa, 54 languages are believed dead; another 116 are near extinction.[24] And in Asia, despite 3 billion inhabitants, more than half the languages are spoken by fewer than 10,000 people.[25] For example, Brokskat in Kashmir has 3,000 speakers; Burmeso, native to Irian Jaya, has 250 speakers; and Arta in the Philippines is now spoken by just three families.[26] Roads, schools, and missionaries have left just 100 speakers of Taiap, an isolate spoken in the remote Papua New Guinean village of Gupan; younger generations speak pidgin English.[27]

Even as some European languages gain global dominance, many others are in decline. Manx, once spoken on the Isle of Man, became extinct in the late 20th century, as did Ubykh, a Caucasian language with more consonants than any other—and with over 50,000 speakers just a century ago.[28] In Russia, where 90 percent of the population now speaks Russian, 70 percent of native languages are near extinction.[29]

Fewer than 4 percent of languages have any official status in their countries of origin.[30] Governments often advocate a single language as a way to foster national identity in ethnically diverse places—often disparate villages unified under colonial rule.[31] East African governments have actively promoted Swahili, for instance, overpowering languages such as Zalamo in Tanzania and Alagwa in Kenya.[32] Education in the dominant language often means fewer children will learn their native tongue. Until recently, the United States, for example, made it a policy to run Native American reservation schools in English.[33]

Although the disappearance of diverse languages is most devastating for communities that are losing their unique voices and cultural identities, it also has global significance. Languages hold important clues to human history, helping to explain, for instance, ancient migration routes between continents.[34] Experts believe Igo, a language with just 6,000 speakers in southern Togo, may hold clues to West African migration.[35] And linguists lament the

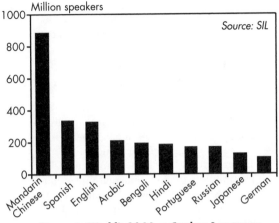

Figure 1: World's 10 Most Spoken Languages

fading opportunity to analyze the astounding variations in grammar and speech structures.[36] As in the case of species extinction, we may not even know what we are losing: perhaps a dozen of Papua New Guinea's 830 languages—many of which are unrelated to any other—have been studied in any detail, for instance.[37]

Loss of linguistic diversity also diminishes our understanding of biological diversity. Most of the world's languages are spoken in tropical forests or islands, and have elaborate vocabularies to describe the natural world. Native Hawaiians named fish species for their breeding seasons, medicinal uses, and methods of capture.[38] And in Papua New Guinea, native languages have hundreds of unique names for the many bird species on the island, whereas pidgin English has just two.[39]

Despite this discouraging picture, a few languages are slowly making a comeback following efforts by nonprofits, communities, and governments. In 1999, four students in Hawaii graduated from high school educated exclusively in Hawaiian—the first to do so in the 100 years since U.S. annexation.[40] The Celtic language, Cornish, has been revived since its last speaker died in 1777, and now has 2,000 speakers.[41] And in the last century, Hebrew has grown from a purely written form to Israel's national language, with 5 million speakers.[42]

Religious Environmentalism Rises

Lisa Mastny

Over the past two decades, the global religious community has become a powerful new force for environmental change. The U.K.-based Alliance of Religions and Conservation—a group that promotes conservation efforts among the world's faiths—estimates that some 200,000 religious communities worldwide are now involved in some form of environmental activity.[1] This ranges from advocating sustainable resource use to raising awareness of issues like biodiversity loss, deforestation, and climate change.

Religious groups have also strengthened their commitment to environmental protection at the international level. Since the mid-1980s, representatives of diverse faiths have issued numerous calls for unified action toward achieving a more sustainable relationship between humans and the planet.[2] (See Table 1.)

Many top religious leaders have become staunch defenders of the natural world. Pope John Paul II, considered the first "environmental pope," has urged Catholics to reduce resource consumption and warned farmers to use ethical caution when embracing biotechnology.[3] And Ecumenical Patriarch Bartholomew—the spiritual leader of some 200 million Orthodox Christians—has launched an official crusade against pollution, calling it a "sin against creation."[4] His efforts to green the church have included establishing an annual day of prayer and action for the planet and launching environmental training for priests.[5]

As a whole, the world's religious communities have a significant stake in the planet's future. They include roughly five sixths of the world's population—some 2 billion Christians, 1.4 billion Muslims, 750 million Hindus, 700 million Buddhists, 16 million Sikhs, 13 million Jews, and smaller groups like the Jains, Bahá'ís, Shintos, and Zoroastrians.[6] They also own or oversee an estimated 5 percent of Earth's landmass, including most green spaces in large cities like Hong Kong, Istanbul, and Tokyo.[7]

Many of the world's faiths are stepping up efforts to protect this rich biological heritage. Hindus in India, Jews in Israel, and Buddhists in China and Thailand are expanding their traditional roles in managing green spaces, planting trees, or caring for sacred groves or animals.[8] Other groups have adopted new activities in light of changing environmental realities. The Chinese Taoist Association, for instance, has called on its 40 million members to stop using endangered wildlife in traditional medicines.[9] And India's 300,000-strong Zoroastrian community is launching a captive breeding program to boost populations of griffon vultures, needed for ritual disposal of the dead.[10]

Faith-based groups also play a valuable role in spurring green markets and industry. The United Methodist Church has been at the forefront of this in the United States, pledging to phase out use of chlorine-free paper products and investing some $22 billion of church assets in ethical companies.[11] The world's Jain community, meanwhile, presents an annual award to environmentally sound Jain businesses.[12] And in Japan, the Shinto community has agreed to purchase only sustainably grown wood for its more than 80,000 shrines.[13]

The world's religions are also taking action on global warming. In November 2000, leaders from nine major faiths pledged to reduce their collective greenhouse gas emissions by 15 percent by conserving energy in places of worship, schools, and elsewhere.[14] Meanwhile, in an effort to promote energy alternatives, the Church of Germany has installed solar power in some 300 churches—while the U.S. Episcopal Church recently held one of the first major conventions powered by wind energy alone.[15]

Rising environmentalism among many people of faith stems from a desire to restore balance to human-Earth relations and to counter the moral and spiritual emptiness of a world increasingly dominated by technology and consumerism.[16] At a more practical level, religious institutions recognize that to remain relevant, they need to harness some of the ethical or moral energy that many people now devote to environmental or social causes.[17] This new thrust appears to be working: in the United States, attendance at environmentally focused churches reportedly tripled in the mid-1990s.[18]

The world's faiths are also uniquely positioned to expand environmental awareness through their vast educational and media networks.[19] In many developing countries, religious institutions provide up to 80 percent of schooling.[20] The Kenyan Council of Churches has used this clout to integrate environmental messages into all levels of national Christian classes.[21] And the Bahá'í faith incorporates the environment into all its educational and developmental work—including special programming on its radio stations in Latin America and elsewhere.[22]

Despite its new activist incarnation, religious environmentalism is firmly rooted in age-old rituals, texts, and teachings.[23] Many of the world's faiths share common views of the interdependence of humans, the divine, and nature, and lay out an ethic of harmony with the natural world.[24] In practice, however, this relationship has not always benefited the environment—Biblical references to human "dominion" over nature, for instance, have justified calls for manipulation as well as for benign stewardship.[25] In contrast, Eastern religions like Buddhism or Hinduism have tended to highlight the spiritual "oneness" of humans and nature, encouraging respect for sacred places and beings.[26]

Table 1: Rising Environmental Commitment Among the World's Religions

1986	World Wide Fund for Nature's (WWF) 25th Anniversary, Assisi, Italy
	At the first major meeting on religion and environment, WWF invited leaders from five major world faiths to establish a common platform on the need to protect the planet.
1992	U.N. Conference on Environment and Development, Rio de Janeiro, Brazil
	Religious representatives and other participants began efforts to frame an Earth Charter that sets forth fundamental shared values and ethical principles for a sustainable way of life. The Charter was revised throughout the 1990s for presentation at a Rio +10 Conference in 2002.
1993	Parliament of the World's Religions, Chicago, United States
	Nearly 200 religious and spiritual leaders signed "Towards a Global Ethic," a groundbreaking document stating shared ethical principles, including respect for life and the need for sustainability.
1995	Summit of Religions and Conservation, Windsor Castle, United Kingdom
	Building on WWF's earlier work, Prince Philip launched the Alliance of Religions and Conservation (ARC) to work with nine major world faiths on developing practical conservation projects.
1996–98	Religions of the World and Ecology Conference Series, Harvard University, United States
	During three years of discussions, more than 1,000 world scholars, religious leaders, and environmentalists explored how diverse religions view the natural world. In 1998, Harvard set up a Forum on Religion and Ecology to further this work in public policy and education.
1999	Parliament of the World's Religions, Cape Town, South Africa
	Participants issued "A Call to Our Guiding Institutions," an interfaith document urging key institutions—including governments, industries, and civil society—to embrace "Towards a Global Ethic."
2000	Sacred Gifts for a Living Planet Conference, Bhaktapur, Nepal
	WWF and ARC brought together more than 500 delegates from 56 countries—representing 11 world faiths—to jointly reaffirm their commitment to the environment, at the largest multinational and multireligions forum ever. Many participants pledged to take specific actions dedicated to protecting the planet.

Sources: See endnote 2.

Education Still Falling Short of Goals   *Gary Gardner*

The share of the world's adults who cannot read or write has fallen nearly in half since 1970, which is welcome news, yet the number of illiterate adults is now slightly higher than it was then. (See Figure 1).[1] Despite a commitment by the international community in 1990 to expand access to education and eliminate illiteracy by 2000, nearly one in six adults today cannot read or write.[2]

Some 99 percent of illiterate people are found in the developing world, with the remainder in the poorest regions of the industrial world.[3] Africa has the highest illiteracy rate of any region—about 40 percent of adults.[4] But Asia has the largest illiterate population, 641 million people—nearly three quarters of the global total.[5] In the least developed countries, nearly half of adults cannot read or write.[6]

In all regions, women are more likely than men to be illiterate.[7] The adult illiteracy rate for women in developing countries is almost twice as high as that of men.[8] (See Table 1.) In industrial countries, women account for 60 percent of the small population who cannot read.[9] Globally, since 1970 the number of illiterate women has increased slightly, while the number of illiterate men has declined a bit.[10]

Education is important in global efforts to achieve sustainable development for several reasons. It has a strong link to improved health: each additional year spent by mothers in primary school has been shown to lower the risk of premature child death by some 8 percent.[11] It is also a powerful tool against poverty: education raises productivity, innovation, and output—important ingredients for economic prosperity—and it tends to reduce economic inequality.[12] Education is an important strategy for population stabilization as well, since educated women tend to marry later and bear fewer children.[13] And in an increasingly industrial world, where people are often disconnected from nature, education is indispensable for under-

standing the vital need to care for the natural world.

A concerted effort to improve education globally was launched by 155 nations in 1990 at the World Conference on Education for All in Jontien, Thailand.[14] In contrast to previous meetings on education, which had focused on levels of school enrollment, the Jontien conference emphasized quality of education, especially the importance of preschool, basic primary education, and continuing education for adults. Among its goals for 2000 was to achieve universal access to primary education and to halve the global adult illiteracy rate.[15]

While the conference fell short of many of its objectives, it is credited with advancing global education on several fronts. The number of children not enrolled in school dropped from 127 million in 1990 to 113 million in 1998.[16] The average share of national government budgets devoted to primary education increased in every region of the world except Central Asia and Central and Western Africa.[17] The number of students per teacher declined slightly in most regions between 1990 and 1996.[18] And adult illiteracy rates fell, even in regions of greatest concern: India, for example, brought its rate down by 10 percentage points between 1991 and 1997.[19]

Still, much work remains to be done in pro-

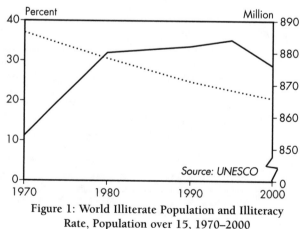

Figure 1: World Illiterate Population and Illiteracy Rate, Population over 15, 1970–2000

Table 1: Adult Illiteracy, 2000

Region	Illiterate Population	Illiteracy Rate		
		Total	Male	Female
	(million)	(percent)		
Industrial countries	11	1.1	0.9	1.3
Developing countries	865	26	19	34
World	876	21	15	26

Source: Based on UNESCO, *Statistical Yearbook 1999 Database*, <unescostat.unesco.org/en/stats/stats0.htm>, viewed 26 February 2001.

viding education for all. In Latin America, for example, a quarter of children entering primary school do not continue past the fifth grade.[20] And in nearly half of Latin American countries, 10 percent or more of children in primary school are repeating grades.[21] These high rates of dropout and repetition suggest that educational quality is lacking. And this can be expensive: in the 1980s, children in Latin America required 1.7 years, on average, to be promoted to the next grade, a delay that cost primary and secondary schools $5.2 billion.[22]

The challenge of getting children to school and keeping them there is compounded in Africa by the HIV/AIDS epidemic. Some 12 million children have been orphaned by the disease—a figure projected to balloon to 42 million by 2010—and many of these children lose access to schooling.[23] The school enrollment rate among orphans in the Central African Republic is 39 percent, for instance, compared with 60 percent nationwide.[24] And AIDS is ravaging the teaching corps as well. The disease is responsible for 70 percent of the deaths of teachers in Côte d'Ivoire, for example.[25] In the Central African Republic, between 1996 and 1998 as many teachers died of AIDS as retired.[26] And in Zambia, 1,300 teachers died of AIDS in the first 10 months of 1998—equal to about two thirds of all teachers trained annually.[27]

Despite the challenges, the formula for educational success is increasingly understood. In a study of several nations and of the Indian state of Kerala, UNICEF found that countries with strong educational systems typically achieved universal primary enrollment early in their development process, gave emphasis to primary education without tuition or fees, and improved educational quality while minimizing costs per student, dropout rates, and repetition of grades.[28] The study also highlighted the benefits for girls' enrollment of having female teachers, and the advantages of instruction in a child's mother language.

UNICEF estimates that achieving its goal of Education for All would require some $7 billion over the next decade.[29] Many countries demonstrated a willingness to increase education funding in recent years, but this is not true across the board. Real public spending on education has fallen by a third in Russia and by more than 75 percent in Azerbaijan, Bulgaria, Georgia, and Kyrgystan, for example, as these countries face tough economic challenges.[30] Given the many benefits of a well-designed educational system, such belt-tightening could well strangle the economic life it is trying to save.

Social Security Facing Challenges

Gary Gardner

As nations seek affordable ways to care for their elderly and poorest citizens, many are turning to social security programs. Still, more than half of the world's people are not covered by any formal social security protection today.[1] In the industrial world, roughly 20 percent of the work force is not covered.[2] In the developing world, 50–90 percent of workers are not covered, and even that figure is declining in some regions, such as South Asia and sub-Saharan Africa.[3]

Social security is one of the ways societies attempt to support people who face individual, social, or economic distress.[4] Such aid is as old as human communities, and civil statutes related to social security go back at least to the European Poor Laws of the sixteenth century.[5] With the rise of industrial societies, governments began to establish formal programs to insure individuals against economic upheaval caused by debilitating sickness, old age, pregnancy, and other life events, and for the maintenance of children.[6] While varying greatly in quality and coverage, social security systems are now found on all continents.

Formal social security programs—in contrast to informal family or community care—take many forms. The most common is social insurance, which is funded by workers, employers, and sometimes government, using a broad base of contributions to fund cases of need as they arise.[7] Social assistance, in contrast, consists of cash or in-kind benefits, usually funded by the government and provided on a means-test basis, that help bring people's income up to a specified minimum level.[8] And social allowances are uniform benefits given to particular categories of people, such as the blind or disabled.[9] Other programs include mandated private savings, employer liability, and health coverage.[10]

A 1999 study of 172 national social security systems evaluated 860 program design features against International Labour Organization minimum standards for social security, and then ranked the national systems.[11] (See Table 1.) Evaluated design features included extent of coverage, eligibility requirements, benefit lev-

els, and how well supplementary social security strategies complemented a country's principal strategy.[12] Not surprisingly, wealthy countries generally ranked higher than poor ones, but there were several notable exceptions. Nicaragua, a low-income country, made it into the second tier of nations, with a design score about the same as the United Kingdom's.[13] The United States finished in the third tier, tied with Ecuador, because U.S. policy generally leaves social security needs to employers and individuals.[14] And Kuwait, although rich in oil wealth, has a very restrictive system and ends up in the bottom tier.[15]

A country's approach to social security reflects its values. Most industrial countries constructed safety nets in the twentieth century primarily to protect their middle classes from being thrown into poverty by disruptive life events. In this they have been very successful. Seniors, for example, once a very poor segment in many industrial countries, now have a poverty rate no greater than younger groups in these societies.[16] But social security systems in most countries have largely ignored the neediest, such as the chronically unemployed or those who work in the informal sector.[17]

Many social security programs are funded or administered through the workplace. Globally, the social security contributions from workers and their employers in 1995 was 22 percent of payroll, up from 17 percent 10 years earlier.[18] Contributions ranged from 8 percent of payroll in the Pacific Islands to 39 percent in Eastern Europe.[19] Of the total contributions, employers were responsible for nearly three quarters in 1995, and employees for just over one quarter.[20]

Several demographic and economic trends will boost the cost of funding retirement programs in coming decades. The share of the population over 65 years of age in industrial countries is expected to increase from 14 percent in 2000 to nearly 26 percent by 2050.[21] In developing nations, the equivalent figure is projected to triple by then, to 15 percent.[22] Meanwhile, working-age populations are expected to grow more slowly, so the burden on workers to provide for seniors will steadily increase.[23] The number of workers per retiree will fall by half in industrial nations over the next 50 years—from 4.7 to 2.3—while in developing countries it is expected to fall by two thirds—from 12.2 to 4.3.[24]

Moreover, retirement periods are becoming longer as life expectancies increase and as people stop working at a younger age. In industrial countries, the average length of retirement in 1950 was 11 years for men and 14 years for women, but by 1990 this had reached 17 and 23 years, respectively.[25] Partly as a consequence, pension outlays in these nations grew at twice the rate of gross national product in the second half of the century. The pressure on government budgets led 22 countries—half of them wealthy nations, including Germany, Japan, and the United States—to raise their retirement ages between 1985 and 1995.[26]

Changing economies will also pose challenges for social security systems. Planners in many governments have long assumed that all workers would eventually work in large companies, or at least in the formal sector.[27] But in rich and poor countries alike, more and more workers are self-employed, work casually or in the home, or have other insecure forms of employment.[28] To expand social security coverage will require looking beyond formal sector employment to mutual aid societies, cooperatives, indigenous customs, and other non-state sponsored social institutions.[29]

The growing pressures on social security have led many governments to experiment with privately based systems, which require workers to invest a share of their salary in individual retirement accounts. Chile adopted such a system 20 years ago, and other Latin American nations have embraced variants of the Chilean system.[30] Proponents claim that private investments will yield greater returns for workers, increase domestic savings, and avoid the prospect of excessive burdens on the next generation of workers.[31] Opponents note that the plans abandon the principle of risk pooling, a staple of social insurance over the past century under which risks are shared through redistribution of retirement income across recipients.[32] Without risk pooling, privatized plans become more an economic and social tool than a means to achieve social security.[33]

Table 1: Ranking of Social Security System Designs

Ranking, Based on Design Score	Number of Countries	Countries	Share of the 172 Surveyed Social Security Systems (percent)
Top 10 percent (first tier)	19	9 West European, 3 East European, Israel, Armenia	11
Second 10 percent (second tier)	38	12 East European, 8 West European, 3 Latin American, 5 Asian, 4 African, Canada, Iran	22
Third 10 percent (third tier)	49	18 African, 16 Latin American, 5 Asian, 3 Middle Eastern, 2 East European, United States	28
Bottom 70 percent (fourth tier)	66	More than half of Asia and the Middle East, nearly half of Africa, one third of Latin America, all Pacific Island nations	38

Source: Derived from John Dixon, *Social Security in Global Perspective* (London: Praeger, 1999), pp. 217–31.

Notes

WORLD GRAIN HARVEST DROPS
(pages 28–29)

1. U.S. Department of Agriculture (USDA), *Production, Supply, and Distribution*, electronic database, Washington, DC, updated December 2000.
2. Ibid.
3. Ibid.
4. Ibid.
5. Erik Eckholm, "In China's Heartland, the Fertile Fields Lie Fallow," *New York Times,* 24 December 2000; Ted Plafker, "China Struggles with Water Shortage," *Washington Post*, 7 September 2000.
6. USDA, op. cit. note 1.
7. Ibid.
8. Ibid.
9. Ibid.
10. Ibid.
11. Ibid.
12. Ibid.; U.S. Bureau of the Census, *International Data Base*, electronic database, Suitland, MD, updated 10 May 2000.
13. USDA, op. cit. note 1.
14. Ibid.
15. Ibid.
16. Ibid.
17. Ibid.
18. Role of rice in India from U.N. Food and Agriculture Organization, "The Outlook for Water Resources in 2020: Challenges for Research on Water Management in Rice Production," *International Rice Commission Newsletter*, <www.fao.org/docrep/x7164t/x7164t00.htm>, viewed 23 January 2001; rates of consumption from USDA, op. cit. note 1.
19. USDA, op. cit. note 1.
20. Ibid.
21. Ibid.
22. Ibid.
23. Ibid.
24. USDA, Foreign Agricultural Service, *Grain: World Markets and Trade* (Washington, DC: December 2000).
25. Ibid.
26. USDA, op. cit. note 1.
27. USDA, op. cit. note 24.
28. Ibid.
29. Ibid.
30. Ibid.; water shortage from Sandra Postel, *Pillar of Sand* (New York: W.W. Norton & Company, 1999), p. 42.
31. USDA, op. cit. note 24. Days of consumption are calculated by dividing annual global grain consumption by 365 and then dividing the result by world carryover stocks.
32. Lester R. Brown, "The Future of Growth," in Lester R. Brown et al., *State of the World 1998* (New York: W.W. Norton & Company, 1998), p. 16.

SOYBEAN HARVEST SETS RECORD
(pages 30–31)

1. U.S. Department of Agriculture (USDA), *Production, Supply, and Distribution*, electronic database, Washington, DC, updated December 2000.
2. Ibid.
3. Ibid.
4. Ibid.
5. Ibid.
6. Ibid.
7. Ibid.
8. Ibid.
9. Ibid.
10. China's share of soybean harvest from USDA, Foreign Agricultural Service, *Oilseeds: World Markets and Trade* (Washington, DC: December 2000).
11. Ibid.
12. Ibid.
13. USDA, op. cit. note 1.
14. Ibid.
15. M. Prud'homme and K.G. Soh, *Short Term Prospects for World Agriculture and Fertilizer Use*

Notes

(Paris: International Fertilizer Industry Association, November 2000), p. 14.

16. USDA, op. cit. note 1.

17. USDA, Economic Research Service, "Cropping Patterns of Major Field Crops and Associated Chemical Use," *AREI Updates* (Updates on Agricultural Resources and Environmental Indicators), December 1996, p. 1.

18. Council for Agricultural Science and Technology, "Animal Production Systems and Resource Use," *Animal Agriculture and Global Food Supply* (Ames, IA: July 1999), p. 72.

19. USDA, op. cit. note 1.

20. Ibid.

21. Vegetable oil demand from USDA, op. cit. note 10.

22. Ibid.

23. Ibid.

24. Ibid.

25. Ibid.

26. Ibid.

FERTILIZER USE RISES (pages 32–33)

1. Kim Gay Soh and Michel Prud'homme, *Fertilizer Consumption Report: World and Regional Overview and Country Reports* (Paris: International Fertilizer Industry Association (IFA), December 2000).

2. Ibid.

3. M. Prud'homme and K.G. Soh, *Short Term Prospects for World Agriculture and Fertilizer Use* (Paris: International Fertilizer Industry Association, November 2000), p. 24.

4. Ibid.

5. Economic growth from International Monetary Fund, *World Economic Outlook* (Washington, DC: October 2000), p. 3.

6. Ibid.

7. Prud'homme and Soh, op. cit. note 3, p. 1.

8. Ibid.

9. Ibid.

10. Ibid., p. 9.

11. Ibid.

12. Soh and Prud'homme, op. cit. note 1.

13. Ibid.

14. Ibid.

15. Ibid.

16. Ibid.

17. Population estimates from Population Reference Bureau, *2000 World Population Data Sheet*, wall chart (Washington, DC: June 2000); fertilizer data from Soh and Prud'homme, op. cit. note 1.

18. IFA, "The Soil Fertility Initiative for Africa," *Fertilizers & Agriculture*, December 2000, p. 2.

19. Ibid.

20. Ibid.

21. Prud'homme and Soh, op. cit. note 3, p. 14.

22. Ibid.

23. Soh and Prud'homme. op. cit. note 1.

24. Grain stock information in U.S. Department of Agriculture, *Production, Supply, and Distribution*, electronic database, Washington, DC, updated December 2000.

MILK PRODUCTION MAINTAINS MOMENTUM (pages 34–35)

1. U.N. Food and Agriculture Organization (FAO), *Food Outlook*, no. 5 (Rome: November 2000), pp. 25–27.

2. Ibid.; U.S. Bureau of the Census, *International Data Base*, electronic database, Suitland, MD, updated 10 May 2000.

3. FAO, op. cit. note 1.

4. Ibid.

5. Ibid.

6. Michael Griffin, *Overview of Developments in the World Dairy Market*, presented at the Fifth Holstein Congress of the Americas, FAO, Rome, 12–16 April 1999.

7. FAO, *FAOSTAT Statistics Database*, <apps.fao. org>, updated 27 October 2000.

8. Ibid.

9. Ibid.

10. Ibid.; proportion of India's livestock from Surinder Sud, "India is Now World's Largest Milk Producer," *India Perspectives*, May 1999, p. 26; milk yield reliability from Jim Miller, milk analyst, U.S. Department of Agriculture (USDA), Washington, DC, discussion with author, 2 January 2001.

11. "India to Remain Global Leader in Milk Production," *The Financial Express*, 17 May 1999.

12. S.C. Dhall and Meena Dhall, "Dairy Industry—India's Strength is in its Livestock," *Business Line*, Internet edition of *Financial Daily*, <www.india server.com/businessline/1997/11/07/stories/ 03070311.htm>, 7 November 1997.

13. Council for Agricultural Science and Technology (CAST), "Animal Production Systems and Resource Use," *Animal Agriculture and Global Food Supply* (Ames, IA: July 1999), p. 34.

14. Frederick W. Crook, "China's Dairy Economy: Production, Marketing, Consumption, and Foreign Trade," *International Agricultural and Trade Reports: China* (Washington, DC: USDA, Economic Research Service, July 1998), pp. 51–54.

15. FAO, op. cit. note 7.

16. CAST, op. cit. note 13, p. 4.
17. Robin Marks and Rebecca Knuffke, *America's Animal Factories: How States Fail to Prevent Pollution from Livestock Waste* (Washington, DC: Natural Resources Defense Council, December 1998); 30 million tons of manure from "Dairy Farmers Welcome Environmental Inspections," *Associated Press*, 27 December 2000.
18. CAST, op. cit. note 13, p. 4.
19. World Resources Institute, *World Resources 2000–01* (Washington, DC: World Resources Institute, 2000), p. 125.
20. Kazimuddin Ahmed, "The Milk That Ate the Grass," *Down to Earth*, 15 April 1999.
21. Griffin, op. cit. note 6.
22. CAST, op. cit. note 13, p. 1.

COFFEE PRODUCTION HITS NEW HIGH
(pages 36–37)

1. U.N. Food and Agriculture Organization (FAO), *FAOSTAT Statistics Database,* <apps.fao.org>, updated 27 October 2000.
2. Ibid
3. Ibid.
4. David Griswald, Sustainable Harvest, Berkeley, CA, discussion with author, 27 December 2000; Guy Taylor, New York Board of Trade, e-mail to author, 8 January 2001.
5. Ibid.
6. Ibid.
7. FAO, op. cit. note 1.
8. Ibid.
9. Ibid.
10. Ibid.
11. Griswald, op. cit. note 4.
12. Share of global acreage from Robert A. Rice, Smithsonian Migratory Birds Center, Washington, DC, discussion with author, 14 December 2000.
13. Griswald, op. cit. note 4.
14. Rice, op. cit. note 12.
15. FAO, op. cit. note 1; Howard LaFranchi, "Made in the Shade: Java That Saves Forests," Christian Science Monitor, 2 March 2000.
16. FAO, op. cit. note 1.
17. Ibid.
18. Ibid.
19. Ibid.
20. Ibid.
21. Ibid.; Robert A. Rice and Justin R. Ward, *Coffee, Conservation, and Commerce in the Western Hemisphere* (Washington, DC: National Resources Defense Council and Smithsonian Migratory Birds Center, June 1996).
22. Rice and Ward, op. cit. note 21, p. 15.
23. Ibid., p. 38.
24. FAO, op. cit. note 1.
25. Matt Quinlan, Coffee Program, Conservation International, Washington, DC, discussion with author, 5 January 2001.
26. Rice and Ward, op. cit. note 21, p. 17.
27. Griswald, op. cit. note 4.
28. Robert A. Rice, *Noble Goals and Challenging Terrain: Organic and Fair Trade Coffee Movements in the Global Marketplace* (draft) (Washington, DC: Smithsonian Migratory Birds Center, 22 December 2000), p. 7.
29. Ibid., p. 4.

FOSSIL FUEL USE FALLS AGAIN
(pages 40–41)

1. Data for 1950–99 data based on United Nations, *World Energy Supplies 1950–74* (New York: 1976), p. 3, and on BP Amoco, *Statistical Review of World Energy June 2000* (London: Group Media & Publicationas, June 2000), pp. 9, 25, 33; Worldwatch preliminary estimate for 2000 based on ibid., on U.S. Department of Energy (DOE), Energy Information Administration (EIA), *Monthly Energy Review, December 2000* (Washington, DC: 2000), p. 7, on David Fridley, Lawrence Berkeley National Laboratory (LBL), e-mail to author, 24 January 2001, on International Energy Agency (IEA), *Oil, Gas, Coal and Electricity Quarterly Statistics*, Second Quarter (Paris: Organisation for Economic Co-operation and Development (OECD)/IEA, 2000), pp. 400–01, 446–47, on idem, *Monthly Oil Market Report* (Paris: OECD/IEA, 11 December 2000), pp. 4–14, and on International Gas Union (IGU), "World Gas Review," IGU Council Meeting, Japan, October 2000, p. 3.
2. BP Amoco, op. cit. note 1.
3. Ibid.
4. Based on United Nations, op. cit. note 1, p. 3, on BP Amoco, op. cit. note 1, on DOE, op. cit. note 1, on LBL, op. cit. note 1, on IEA, *Oil, Gas, Coal*, op. cit. note 1, on idem, *Monthly Oil*, op. cit. note 1, and on IGU, op. cit. note 1.
5. DOE, op. cit. note 1.
6. BP Amoco, op. cit. note 1, p. 33; Fridley, op. cit. note 1.
7. BP Amoco, op. cit. note 1, p. 33; Fridley, op. cit. note 1.
8. IEA, *Oil, Gas, Coal and Electricity*, op. cit. note 1, p. 446.

9. BP Amoco, op. cit. note 1, p. 9; IEA, *Monthly Oil Market Report*, op. cit. note 1, p. 4.

10. BP Amoco, op. cit. note 1, p. 9; DOE, op. cit. note 1.

11. BP Amoco, op. cit. note 1, p. 9; IEA, *Monthly Oil Market Report*, op. cit. note 1, p. 4.

12. BP Amoco, op. cit. note 1, p. 9; IEA, *Monthly Oil Market Report*, op. cit. note 1, p. 4.

13. BP Amoco, op. cit. note 1, p. 25; IGU, op. cit. note 1.

14. BP Amoco, op. cit. note 1, p. 9; DOE, op. cit. note 1.

15. IGU, op. cit. note 1, p. 2.

16. Ibid.

17. International Monetary Fund, *The Impact of Higher Oil Prices on the Global* Economy (Washington, DC: 8 December 2000); "Worldwide Look at Reserves and Production," *Oil & Gas Journal*, 18 December 2000, p. 123; BP Amoco, op. cit. note 1, p. 14; DOE, op. cit. note 1, p. 115.

18. Neela Banerjee, "As Oil Prices Decline, Natural Gas Threatens to Upset the Trend," *New York Times*, 18 December 2000.

19. John Varoli, "Energy On Ice," *New York Times*, 3 October 2000.

20. DOE, EIA, *Potential Oil Production from the Coastal Plain of the Arctic National Wildlife Refuge: Updated Assessment* (Washington, DC: 2000), p. 2; Worldwatch estimate based on ibid. and on BP Amoco, op. cit. note 1, p. 9.

21. IEA, *World Energy Outlook 2000* (Paris: OECD/IEA, 2000), p. 22.

22. Ibid.

23. Ibid., p. 23.

24. Ibid., p. 22.

25. Ibid., pp. 22–23.

26. Ibid., p. 21.

NUCLEAR POWER INCHES UP (pages 42–43)

1. Installed nuclear capacity is defined as reactors connected to the grid as of 31 December 2000, and is based on Worldwatch Institute database compiled from statistics from the International Atomic Energy Agency and press reports primarily from *Associated Press, Reuters, Agence FrancePresse, Uranium Institute News Briefing*, and Web sites.

2. Worldwatch Institute database, op. cit. note 1.

3. Ibid.

4. Ibid.

5. Ibid.

6. Ibid.

7. See, for example, "FERC OKs Millstone Nuclear Plant Sale to Dominion," *Reuters*, 24 January 2001.

8. "Germany Renounces Nuclear Power," *BBC News*, <news.bbc.co.uk>, viewed 15 June 2000.

9. "UK," *Uranium Institute News Briefing*, 17–23 May 2000.

10. "Sweden," *Uranium Institute News Briefing*, 27 September–3 October 2000.

11. "France," *Uranium Institute News Briefing*, 22–28 November 2000.

12. "Chernobyl Reactor Restarts Before Final Shutdown," *Agence Press de France*, 1 December 2000.

13. "Fuel Extracted from Mothballed Kazakh Nuclear Reactor," *BBC Monitoring Former Soviet Union*, via EnergyCentral <energycentral.com>, viewed 21 November 2000.

14. Vladimir Slivyak, Socio-Ecological Union, Moscow, e-mail to author, 25 January 2001.

15. CEZ, s.a., "Temporary Tripping of the Turbine," press release, <cez.cz/jete/tednes/NewsEN>, viewed 4 January 2001.

16. "Austrians Blockade Border to Protest Czech Nuclear Plant," *Agence Press de France*, 2 September 2000.

17. "Japan," *Uranium Institute News Briefing*, 19–25 April 2000.

18. Department of Atomic Energy (India), "Nuclear Power in India," <dae.gov.in/power.htm>, viewed 4 January 2001.

19. Ibid.

20. Emma Davies, "The Nuclear Industry Learns Its Market Value," *Nuclear Engineering International*, 30 June 2000.

21. "Cuba," *Uranium Institute News Briefing*, 13–19 December 2000.

22. "Update 3 Turkey Puts Nuke Power Plans on Indefinite Hold," *Reuters*, 25 July 2000.

23. "Taiwan Scraps Fourth Nuclear Power Plant," *Power Engineering International*, December 2000.

24. "Operation of Taiwan's Nuclear Power Plant to be Delayed," *Xinhua News Agency*, 14 February 2001, via EnergyCentral <energycentral.com>, viewed 15 February 2001.

25. "Final Agreement Between Framatome and Siemens," *Nuclear Notes from France*, August-September 2000.

26. ABB, "ABB's Sale of Nuclear Business to BNFL Closes," press release, 2 May 2000.

27. "The Shaw Group Inc. Submits Bid for Assets of Stone & Webster, Inc.," *Business Wire*, <businesswire.com>, viewed 6 July 2000.

WIND ENERGY GROWTH CONTINUES
(pages 44–45)

1. Worldwatch Institute preliminary estimate based on figures from Birger Madsen, BTM Consult, e-mail to author, 16 February 2001, on "Windicator," *Windpower Monthly*, January 2001, p. 46, on Andreas Wagner, European Wind Energy Association, e-mail to author, 29 January 2001, on "Another Year of Records—Wind Power Growth in 2000," *New Energy*, February 2001, p. 44, and on American Wind Energy Association (AWEA), *Global Wind Energy Market Report* (Washington, DC: January 2001); historical data in Figures 1 and 2 from BTM Consult, *International Wind Energy Development: World Market Update, 1999* (Ringkobing, Denmark: March 2000).
2. BTM Consult, op. cit. note 1.
3. AWEA, *Wind Energy Press Background Information* (Washington, DC: February 2001).
4. Christian Hinsch, "Wind Power Flying Even Higher," *New Energy*, February 2001, pp. 14–20.
5. Worldwatch estimate based on Madsen, op. cit. note 1, on "Windicator," op. cit. note 1, on Wagner, op. cit. note 1, on "Another Year of Records," op. cit. note 1, and on AWEA, op. cit. note 1. Annual capacity additions are not additive to determine total capacity since the latter figures are adjusted to reflect turbine retirements.
6. AWEA, op. cit. note 1. Estimates of U.S. installations in 2000 range from AWEA's 53 megawatts to BTM's 175 megawatts. The wide difference reflects the fact that some turbines shipped or delivered in December 2000 may not have begun generating electricity until January 2001.
7. AWEA, op. cit. note 1; Executive Office of the President of the United States, *A Blueprint for New Beginnings: A Responsible Budget for America's Priorities* (Washington, DC: 28 February 2001).
8. Hinsch, op. cit. note 4.
9. Ibid.
10. Ibid.
11. According to Andreas Wagner, vice president of the European Wind Energy Association, cited in Claire-Louise Isted, "German Offshore Wind Power Key to European Target," *Reuters*, 23 January 2001.
12. Estimate based on Madsen, op. cit. note 1.
13. Torgny Møller, "The End of the Beginning," *Windpower Monthly*, September 2000, pp. 43–44.
14. Ibid.
15. Estimate based on Madsen, op. cit. note 1.
16. "Spain Status Report," *Wind Directions*, March 2001, pp. 13–17.
17. "Another Year of Records," op. cit. note 1.
18. "Government Backs 3,000 MW Target," *Wind Directions*, November 2000, p. 3.
19. Karl Royce and Michael McGovern, "Problems Ahead for Argentina Ambitions," *Windpower Monthly*, February 2001, pp. 21–22.
20. "Danes Open Shop," *Windpower Monthly*, January 2001, p. 10.
21. Frank Sieren, "A Fit of the Doldrums," *New Energy*, February 2001, pp. 32–34.
22. David Milborrow, "Looking More Competitive than Ever," *Windpower Monthly*, January 2001, pp. 32–33; AWEA, "Wind Energy's Costs Hit New Low," press release (Washington, DC: 6 March 2001).
23. Milborrow, op. cit. note 22; Jim Carlton, "As Demands for Energy Multiply, Windmill Farms Stage a Comeback," *Wall Street Journal*, 26 January 2001; Rebecca Smith and John R. Emshwiller, "California Agrees to Spend $40 Billion to Buy Power Under 10-Year Agreements," *Wall Street Journal*, 6 March 2001.

SOLAR POWER MARKET SURGES
(pages 46–47)

1. Paul Maycock, *PV News*, letter to author, 28 February 2001.
2. Ibid.
3. Ibid.
4. "World Cell/Module Production Grows 38% to 277.90 MW," *PV News*, February 2001, p. 1.
5. "Sharp Increases PV Production," *PV News*, February 2001, p. 5.
6. Ibid.
7. Ibid.
8. Ibid.
9. "World Cell/Module Production Grows," op. cit. note 4.
10. Ibid.
11. U.S. Department of Energy, "Million Solar Roofs," <www.eren.doe.gov/millionroofs>, viewed on 27 February 2001.
12. Stella Danker, "Sunshine States," *The BP Magazine*, Issue Three 2000, pp. 37–38.
13. "European PV Production in 2000 Gains 46% Over 1999," *PV News*, February 2001, p. 4.
14. Paul Maycock, "The World PV Market 2000: Shifting from Subsidy to 'Fully Economic'?" *Renewable Energy World*, July–August 2000, pp. 59–74.
15. Ibid.
16. Ibid.

Notes

17. Eric Martinot, "Renewable Energy Markets and the Global Environment Facility," *Renewable Energy Report*, February 2000, pp. 18–22.
18. "Revised Forecast," *PV News*, November 2000, p. 1.
19. Rene Karottki and Douglas Banks, "PV Power and Profit? Electrifying Rural South Africa," *Renewable Energy World*, January–February 2000, pp. 50–59.
20. Ibid.

GLOBAL TEMPERATURE STEADY
(pages 50–51)

1. J. Hansen, "Global Land-Ocean Temperature Index in .01 C," <www.giss.nasa.gov/data/update/gistemp>, viewed 20 January 2001.
2. Ibid.
3. J. Hansen, "Global Temperature Anomalies in .01 C," <www.giss.nasa.gov/data/update/gistemp>, viewed 20 January 2001.
4. Ibid.; Hansen, op. cit. note 1.
5. National Climatic Data Center, "Climate of 2000—Annual Review," 12 January 2001, <www.ncdc.noaa.gov/ol/climate/research>, viewed 23 January 2001.
6. Ibid.
7. Ibid.
8. Ibid.
9. Ibid.
10. Ibid.
11. Ibid.
12. Ibid.
13. Ibid.
14. Intergovernmental Panel on Climate Change, *Climate Change 2001: The Scientific Basis*, Summary for Policymakers, <www.ipcc.ch>, viewed 22 January 2001.
15. Ibid., p. 8.
16. Ibid.
17. Ibid.
18. Ibid.
19. Ibid, p. 10.
20. Ibid, p. 9.
21. Ibid.
22. Ibid.
23. Ibid., p. 8.
24. National Assessment Synthesis Team, U.S. Global Change Research Program, *Climate Change Impacts on the United States* (New York: Cambridge University Press, 2000), p. 6.
25. Ibid.

CARBON EMISSIONS CONTINUE DECLINE
(pages 52–53)

1. Historical trends and preliminary 2000 estimate based on G. Marland, T.A. Boden, and R.J. Andres, "Global, Regional, and National CO_2 Estimates from Fossil Fuel Burning, Cement Production, and Gas Flaring: 1751–1997 (Revised August 2000)," Carbon Dioxide Information Analysis Center, Oak Ridge National Laboratory, Oak Ridge, TN, 22 August 2000, on BP Amoco, *Statistical Review of World Energy 2000* (London: Group Media & Publications, June 2000), pp. 9, 25, 33, on U.S. Department of Energy (DOE), Energy Information Administration (EIA), *Monthly Energy Review, December 2000* (Washington, DC), p. 7, on David Fridley, Lawrence Berkeley National Laboratory, e-mail to author, 24 January 2001, on International Energy Agency (IEA), *Oil, Gas, Coal and Electricity Quarterly Statistics*, Second Quarter (Paris: Organisation for Economic Co-operation and Development (OECD)/IEA, 2000), pp. 400–01, 446–447, on idem, *Monthly Oil Market Report* (Paris: OECD/IEA, 11 December 2000), pp. 4–14, and on International Gas Union (IGU), "World Gas Review," IGU Council Meeting, Japan, October 2000, p. 3.
2. Worldwatch estimate based on Marland, Boden, and Andres, op. cit. note 1, on BP Amoco, op. cit. note 1, on DOE, op. cit. note 1, on Fridley, op. cit. note 1, on IEA, *Oil, Gas, Coal and Electricity*, op. cit. note 1, on idem, *Monthly Oil Market Report*, op. cit. note 1, and on IGU, op. cit. note 1.
3. Historical trends and 2000 estimate based on Marland, Boden, and Andres, op. cit. note 1, on BP Amoco, op. cit. note 1, on DOE, op. cit. note 1, p. 7, on Fridley, op. cit. note 1, on IEA, *Oil, Gas, Coal and Electricity*, op. cit. note 1, on idem, *Monthly Oil Market Report*, op. cit. note 1, on IGU, op. cit. note 1, and on International Monetary Fund (IMF), *World Economic Outlook* (Washington, DC: October 2000), p. 197.
4. Worldwatch estimate based on Marland, Boden, and Andres, op. cit. note 1, on BP Amoco, op. cit. note 1, on DOE, op. cit. note 1, on Fridley, op. cit. note 1, on IEA, *Oil, Gas, Coal and Electricity*, op. cit. note 1, on idem, *Monthly Oil Market Report*, op. cit. note 1, on IGU, op. cit. note 1, on Angus Maddison, *Monitoring the World Economy, 1820–1992* (Paris: OECD, 1995), and on IMF, op. cit. note 3.
5. Earth Negotiations Bulletin (ENB), "Summary of the Sixth Conference of the Parties to the Framework Convention on Climate Change: 13–25

November 2000," <www.iisd.ca/climate/cop6>, viewed 10 January 2001, p. 2.

6. Worldwatch estimate based on IEA, *CO₂ Emissions from Fossil Fuel Combustion (2000 Edition)* (Paris: OECD/IEA, 2000), p. xix, and on BP Amoco, op. cit. note 1.

7. Worldwatch estimate based on IEA, op. cit. note 6, and on BP Amoco, op. cit. note 1.

8. Worldwatch estimate based on IEA, op. cit. note 6, and on BP Amoco, op. cit. note 1.

9. Worldwatch estimate based on IEA, op. cit. note 6, and on BP Amoco, op. cit. note 1.

10. Worldwatch estimate based on IEA, op. cit. note 6, and on BP Amoco, op. cit. note 1.

11. Worldwatch estimate based on IEA, op. cit. note 6, and on BP Amoco, op. cit. note 1.

12. Worldwatch estimate based on Marland, Boden, and Andres, op. cit. note 1, on BP Amoco, op. cit. note 1, on Maddison, op. cit. note 4, and on IMF, op. cit. note 3.

13. C.D. Keeling and T.P. Whorf, "Atmospheric CO_2 Concentrations (ppmv) Derived From In Situ Air Samples Collected at Mauna Loa Observatory, Hawaii," Scripps Institution of Oceanography, La Jolla, CA, 16 August 2000; Timothy Whorf and C.D. Keeling, Scripps Institution of Oceanography, e-mail to author, 6 February 2001.

14. Intergovernmental Panel on Climate Change (IPCC), *Climate Change 2001: The Scientific Basis,* Summary for Policymakers, <www.ipcc.ch>, viewed 22 January 2001, p. 4.

15. Ibid.

16. James Hansen et al., "Global Warming in the Twenty-First Century: An Alternative Scenario," *Proceedings of the National Academy of Sciences,* 16 June 2000, p. 1.

17. Ibid., p. 2.

18. Ibid., p. 1.

19. IPCC, *Special Report on Emissions Scenarios,* Summary for Policymakers, <www.ipcc.ch>, viewed 12 January 2001.

20. Ibid.

21. ENB, op. cit. note 5, p. 1.

22. Ibid.

23. Ibid.

24. Ibid.

25. Ibid.

26. Ibid, p. 19.

WORLD ECONOMY EXPANDS (pages 56–57)

1. Worldwatch update of Angus Maddison, *Monitoring the World Economy 1820–1992* (Paris: Organisa-

tion for Economic Co-operation and Development, 1995), using deflators and recent growth rates from International Monetary Fund (IMF), *World Economic Outlook* (Washington, DC: October 2000).

2. IMF, op. cit. note 1; U.S. Bureau of the Census, *International Data Base,* electronic database, Suitland, MD, updated 10 May 2000.

3. IMF, op. cit. note 1.

4. Ibid.

5. Ibid.

6. Ibid.

7. Ibid.

8. Ibid.

9. Ibid.

10. Ibid.

11. Ibid.

12. Ibid.

13. World Bank, *World Development Report 2000/2001* (New York: Oxford University Press, 2000), pp. 21–23.

14. Crop data from U.S. Department of Agriculture, *Production, Supply, and Distribution,* electronic database, Washington, DC, updated December 2000.

15. IMF, op. cit. note 1.

16. Ibid.

17. Ibid.

18. Ibid.

19. Oil and gas commodity prices from IMF, *International Financial Statistics Yearbook* (Washington, DC: various years).

20. IMF, op. cit. note 1.

21. Ibid.

22. Ibid.

23. Ibid.

24. Ibid.

25. Ibid.

26. Ibid.; U.N. Office for the Coordination of Humanitarian Affairs, "Iran: Drought Threatens Devastating Consequences," Integrated Regional Information Networks, on-line news brief, <www.reliefweb.int/IRIN/asia/countrystories/iran/20000823.phtml>, 23 August 2000.

27. IMF, op. cit. note 1.

28. Ibid.

29. Ibid.; United Nations, op. cit. note 2.

30. IMF, op. cit. note 1.

31. Ibid.

32. Ibid.

FOREIGN DEBT UNCHANGED (pages 58–59)

1. World Bank, *Global Development Finance 2000,*

Notes

electronic database, Washington, DC, 2000; idem, *Global Development Finance 2001* (advance release), electronic database, Washington, DC, 2001.

2. World Bank, *Global Development Finance 2001*, op. cit. note 1.
3. Ibid.
4. Ibid.
5. Ibid.
6. Ibid.
7. Ibid.
8. Ibid.
9. Ibid.
10. Mahn-Je Kim, "The Republic of Korea's Successful Economic Development and the World Bank," in Devesh Kapur, John P. Lewis, and Richard Webb, eds., *The World Bank: Its First Half Century*, vol. 2 (Washington, DC: Brookings Institution Press, 1997), p. 25; Susan M. Collins and Won-Am Park, "External Debt and Macroeconomic Performance in South Korea," in Jeffrey D. Sachs, ed., *Developing Country Debt and the World Economy* (Chicago: University of Chicago Press, 1989), pp. 129–30.
11. Karin Lissakers, *Banks, Borrowers, and the Establishment: A Revisionist Account of the International Debt Crisis* (New York: BasicBooks, 1991), pp. 60–83.
12. Edward F. Buffie and Allen Sangines Krause, "Mexico 1968–86: From Stabilizing Development to the Debt Crisis," in Sachs, op. cit. note 10, p. 156.
13. Wilfredo Cruz and Robert Repetto, *The Environmental Effects of Stabilization and Structural Adjustment Programs: The Philippines Case* (Washington, DC: World Resources Institute, 1992), p. 50.
14. World Bank, *Global Development Finance 2000*, op. cit. note 1; idem, *Global Development Finance 2001*, op. cit. note 1.
15. Ibid. These figures somewhat overstate the region's debt burden since they treat concessional loans from aid agencies—which often charge almost no interest—the same as they treat more-burdensome commercial loans.
16. World Bank, *Global Development Finance 2000*, vol. 1 (Washington, DC: 2000), p. 156.
17. Figure of 45 percent is a Worldwatch estimate based on World Bank, Debt Initiative for Heavily Indebted Poor Countries, <www.worldbank.org/hipc>, viewed 24 October 2000, on idem, *Global Development Finance 2001*, op. cit. note 1, and on idem, *Global Development Finance 2000*, vol. 1 (Washington, DC: 2000), pp. 144–46.

18. David Malin Roodman, *Still Waiting for the Jubilee: Pragmatic Solutions for the Third World Debt Crisis*, Worldwatch Paper 155 (Washington, DC: Worldwatch Institute, April 2001).

U.N. FUNDS STAY ON ROLLER COASTER
(pages 60–61)

1. Compiled by author from current-dollar data provided in Klaus Hüfner, "Assessments of Specialized Agencies 1971–2001," "Expenditures of UN Specialized Agencies' Voluntarily-Financed Activities: 1971–1999," and "Voluntary Contributions: 1971–1999," all at Global Policy Forum, <www.globalpolicy.org/finance/tables>, viewed 16 February 2001; in U.N. General Assembly, "Budgetary and Financial Situation of Organizations of the United Nations System," A/55/525, 26 October 2000, Tables 7 and 8; and in Executive Board of the U.N. Development Programme and the U.N. Population Fund, "Annual Report of the Administrator for 1999 and Related Matters. Statistical Annex," DP/2000/23/Add.2, 15 May 2000.
2. U.N. General Assembly, op. cit. note 1, Table 1.
3. Klaus Hüfner, "Assessed Payments to the Regular Budget and Specialized Agencies: 1971–2001," Global Policy Forum, <www.globalpolicy.org/finance/tables/fintab.htm>, viewed 16 February 2001; idem, "Expenditures of UN Specialized Agencies' Voluntarily-Financed Activities," and "Voluntary Contributions," op. cit. note 1.
4. Author's calculation based on Hüfner, op. cit. note 1.
5. Ibid.
6. Calculated from Hüfner, "Voluntary Contributions," op. cit. note 1.
7. Author's calculation based on Hüfner, op. cit. note 1, on U.N. General Assembly, op. cit. note 1, and on Executive Board, op. cit. note 1.
8. Klaus Hüfner, "List of Members Paying Promptly and Fully 1991–1999," Global Policy Forum, <www.globalpolicy.org/finance/tables/honroll.htm>, viewed 27 September 2000.
9. United Nations, Office of the Spokesman for the Secretary-General, "Payments to the UN Regular Budget for 2001," <www.un.org/News/ossg/hon2001.htm>, viewed 20 February 2001.
10. Hüfner, op. cit. note 8; United Nations, op. cit. note 9.
11. U.N. General Assembly (26 October 2000, 6 November 1998, 18 October 1996), op. cit. note 1, Table 5.
12. Calculated by author from data in Klaus Hüfner,

"Specialized Agencies: Collection of Assessed Contributions 1971–1999," Global Policy Forum, <www.globalpolicy.org/finance/tables/collect. htm>, viewed 17 February 2001.

13. Ibid.

14. These numbers include arrears for current and past years, at the end of the calendar year; Klaus Hüfner, "Outstanding Debts to the UN Regular Budget 1971–1999," Global Policy Forum, <www.globalpolicy.org/finance/tables/tab5.htm>, viewed 31 January 2001; "US vs. Total Debt to the UN: 2000," Global Policy Forum, <www. globalpolicy.org/finance/tables/dbttab00.htm>, viewed 31 January 2001.

15. Calculated by author from U.N. General Assembly (26 October 2000, 6 November 1998, 18 October 1996), op. cit. note 1, Table 5.

16. Amb. Richard Holbrooke, U.S. Permanent Representative to the United Nations, "Remarks at UN Headquarters on Reform of the UN Scales of Assessment," 22 December 2000.

17. U.S. Department of State, "U.S. Plan for Paying UN Arrears," fact sheet (Washington, DC: Bureau of International Organization Affairs, 24 October 2000).

FOOD TRADE SLUMPS (pages 62–63)

1. U.N. Food and Agriculture Organization (FAO), *FAOSTAT Statistics Database*, <apps.fao.org>, updated 27 October 2000.

2. Ibid.

3. Peter Uvin, *The International Organization of Hunger* (London: Kegan Paul International, 1994), pp. 92–128.

4. Ibid.

5. FAO, op. cit. note 1.

6. World Trade Organization (WTO), *WTO Annual Report 1998—Special Topic: Globalization and Trade* (Geneva: 1998).

7. WTO, *International Trade Statistics 2000* (Geneva: 2000).

8. FAO, op. cit. note 1.

9. Hilary French, *Vanishing Borders* (New York: W.W. Norton & Company, 2000), p. 51.

10. FAO, op. cit. note 1.

11. Ibid.

12. Ibid.

13. U.S. Bureau of Transportation Statistics and U.S. Bureau of the Census, *1997 Commodity Flow Survey Report on Exports* (Washington, DC: April 2000).

14. FAO, op. cit. note 1.

15. Ibid.

16. Ibid.

17. Ibid.

18. Ibid.

19. Fileman Torres et al., *Agriculture in the Early XXI Century: Agrodiversity and Pluralism as a Contribution to Address Issues on Food Security, Poverty, and Natural Resource Conservation* (draft) (Rome: Global Forum on Agricultural Research, April 2000), p. 14.

20. Ibid.

21. Uvin, op. cit. note 3; FAO, "Issues and Options in the Forthcoming WTO Negotiations from the Perspective of Developing Countries, Paper No 3: Synthesis of Country Case Studies," FAO Symposium on Agriculture, Trade and Food Security, Geneva, 23–24 September 1999.

22. *Food Miles—Still on the Road to Ruin?* (London: Sustain—The Alliance for Better Food and Farming, October 1999), p. 6.

23. Ibid.

ALUMINUM PRODUCTION KEEPS GROWING (pages 64–65)

1. Aluminum and bauxite production from U.S. Geological Survey (USGS), *Mineral Commodity Summaries 2001* (Washington, DC: Government Printing Office, 2001), pp. 18–19, and from Patricia A. Plunkert, commodity specialist, USGS, Reston, VA, e-mail to author, 15 November 2000.

2. USGS, op. cit. note 1.

3. Ibid.; U.S. Bureau of the Census, *International Data Base*, electronic database, updated 10 May 2000.

4. USGS, op. cit. note 1; it takes two to three tons of bauxite to produce one ton of alumina, and two tons of alumina to produce one ton of aluminum; International Aluminium Institute (IAI), "Aluminium Production," <www.world-aluminium. org/production/index.html>, viewed 13 February 2001.

5. USGS, op. cit. note 1.

6. U.S. share of world aluminum production from USGS, op. cit. note 1; the United States accounted for about 40 percent of world primary aluminum production in the mid-1960s, according to Plunkert, op. cit. note 1, and idem, *Aluminum Statistical Compendium* (Reston, VA: USGS, 5 September 1998).

7. USGS, op. cit. note 1; Plunkert, op. cit. note 1.

8. Worldwatch Institute estimate, based on USGS, op. cit. note 1, and on Patricia A. Plunkert, commodity specialist, USGS, Reston, VA, discussion

with author, 1 February 2001.

9. USGS, op. cit. note 1.

10. Wayne Wagner, "Aluminum," *Canadian Minerals Yearbook, 1999* (Ottawa, ON, Canada: Natural Resources Canada, 2000), p. 8.16.

11. Ibid.

12. Ibid.

13. Patricia A. Plunkert, "Aluminum," *Engineering & Mining Journal*, April 2000, p. 39.

14. European Aluminum Association, *Aluminum Industry in Europe—Key Statistics for 1999* (Brussels: June 2000).

15. Plunkert, op. cit. note 13.

16. IAI, "Energy Use," <www.world-aluminium.org/environment/challenges/energy.html>, viewed 13 February 2001; the average U.S. household used 10,210 kilowatt-hours in 1997, according to U.S. Department of Energy (DOE), Energy Information Administration, *A Look at Residential Energy Consumption in 1997* (Washington, DC: 1999), p. 113.

17. Smelter energy use is a Worldwatch estimate, based on production data from USGS, op. cit. note 1, and on electricity consumption per ton of aluminum production from IAI, op. cit. note 16.

18. IAI, "Electrical Power Used in Primary Aluminium Production—Form ES002," <world-aluminium. org/iai/stats/es002.html>, viewed 20 December 2000.

19. Intergovernmental Panel on Climate Change, *IPCC Special Report on Emissions Scenarios* (Geneva: 2000), p. 3.6.6.

20. IAI, op. cit. note 16.

21. Worldwatch estimates of annual electricity use in aluminum production based on IAI, op. cit. note 16, on USGS, op. cit. note 1, and on Plunkert, op. cit. note 1.

22. Wagner, op. cit. note 10, p. 8.13.

23. U.S. Environmental Protection Agency, *Characterization of Municipal Solid Waste in the United States: Source Data on the 1999 Update* (Washington, DC: May 2000).

24. Energy savings is a Worldwatch estimate, based on IAI, op. cit. note 16, on Wagner, op. cit. note 10, on DOE, op. cit. note 16, and on U.S. Bureau of the Census, *1990 Census Lookup*, electronic database, updated 12 February 2001.

VEHICLE PRODUCTION SETS NEW
RECORD (pages 68–69)

1. Standard and Poor's DRI, *World Car Industry Forecast Report, December 2000* (London: 2000); earlier data from idem, *World Car Industry Forecast*

Report, December 1999 (London: 1999), and from American Automobile Manufacturers Association (AAMA), *World Motor Vehicle Facts and Figures 1998* (Washington, DC: 1998).

2. DRI, *December 2000*, op. cit. note 1. Light trucks are vehicles up to 6 tons in weight and include the increasingly popular "sports utility vehicles."

3. Colin Couchman, Global Automotive Group, Standard and Poor's DRI, London, e-mail to author, 13 February 2001.

4. Ward's Communications, *Ward's World Motor Vehicle Data 2000* (Southfield, MI: 2000); DRI, *December 2000*, op. cit. note 1.

5. Ward's Communications, op. cit. note 4; DRI, *December 2000*, op. cit. note 1.

6. Ward's Communications, op. cit. note 4, various tables; DRI, *December 2000*, op. cit. note 1.

7. According to forecasts to 2005, Brazil, China, and India will increase their passenger car production by 78 percent, from 2.6 million in 2000 to 4.6 million in 2005. DRI, *December 2000*, op. cit. note 1.

8. DRI, *December 2000*, op. cit. note 1.

9. Ibid.

10. Ibid.

11. Ibid.

12. Pricewaterhouse Coopers, "Autofacts World Summary," 2000, <www.autofacts.com>, viewed 28 December 2000.

13. Ibid.

14. Automobile industry merger data from Carrie Smith, Thomson Financial Securities Data, Newark, NJ, e-mail to author, 20 December 2000.

15. Keith Bradsher, "Gentlemen, Merge Your Manufacturers," *New York Times*, 23 March 2000; Stephanie Strom, "DaimlerChrysler Buying a Third of Mitsubishi for $2.1 Billion," *New York Times*, 28 March 2000.

16. Worldwatch calculations based on Ward's Communications, op. cit. note 4, on Pricewaterhouse Coopers, op. cit. note 12, and on newspaper reports cited throughout the notes.

17. This calculation counts the portion of a company owned by another firm as part of the acquiring firm's market share. For instance, it counts 20 percent of Fiat's production under General Motors, in accord with the latter's 20-percent stake in Fiat; Keith Bradsher with Andrew Ross Sorkin, "Fiat Weighs Sale to G.M. of a Stake in Auto Line," *New York Times*, 13 March 2000.

18. U.S. General Accounting Office (GAO), *Automobile Fuel Economy: Potential Effects of Increasing the Corporate Average Fuel Economy Standards* (Washington, DC: August 2000), p. 10.

19. "Auto Firms' CO_2 Pact With EU Lacks Teeth," *Environment News Service*, 12 January 2001.

20. U.S. Department of Energy (DOE) forecast reported in Michael T. Klare, "Resource Competition and World Politics in the Twenty-First Century," *Current History*, December 2000, p. 404.

21. U.S. Federal Highway Administration, "Highway Statistics Summary to 1995" and "Highway Statistics 1999," <www.fhwa.dot.gov/>, viewed 2 February 2001; projection to 2020 from DOE, *Annual Energy Outlook 2001* (Washington, DC: 2001).

22. U.K. Government, "Achieving a Better Quality of Life," *Annual Report 2000*, <www.sustainable-development.gov.uk/ann_rep/ch3/h11.htm>, viewed 30 January 2001.

23. GAO, op. cit. note 18, p. 7.

24. DOE, op. cit. note 21.

25. Ibid.

BICYCLE PRODUCTION RECOVERS
(pages 70–71)

1. Estimate for 1999 based on data from "World Market Report," in Bicycle Retailer and Industry News, *Industry Directory 2001* (Santa Fe, NM: Bill Communications, 2001), pp. 6, 10, and from United Nations, *Industrial Commodity Statistics Yearbook 1998* (New York: 1999).

2. "World Market Report," op. cit. note 1; United Nations, op. cit. note 1.

3. "World Market Report," op. cit. note 1, p. 6.

4. Ibid.

5. Ibid.

6. Ibid.

7. Worldwatch calculation based on ibid., and on United Nations, op. cit. note 1.

8. "World Market Report," op. cit. note 1, p. 6.

9. Ibid.

10. Ibid.

11. Ibid., pp. 6, 18.

12. Ibid., p. 18.

13. Ibid., p. 6.

14. Frank Jamerson, Electric Battery Bicycle Company, e-mail to author, 2 February 2001.

15. Ed Benjamin, Electric Cycle Association, e-mail to author, 1 February 2001.

16. Ford from Think Mobility, <www.thinkmobility.com>, viewed 1 February 2001.

17. Jay Townley, Jay Townley and Associates, untitled newsletter, <www.jaytownley.com/jaytown/hmtl/news2.htm>, viewed 2 February 2001.

18. "World Market Report," op. cit. note 1, p. 18; population from United Nations, *World Population*

Prospects, 1998 Update (New York: 1998).

19. "Europe Tests Car Bans, Fights Smog and Noise," *Bicycle Retailer and Industry News*, need date.

20. Lou Mazzante, "Make Marin the Model," *Bicycle Retailer and Industry News*, 1 August 2000; Lou Mazzante, "The Delft Experiment Gives Ideas to Marin Model Planners," *Bicycle Retailer and Industry News*, 1 August 2000.

21. "Chinese Bike Crash Fatalities Approach 35,000," *Bicycle Retailer and Industry News*, 15 July 2000.

22. Nate Jackson, "Millions Still Available for Bike Projects," *Bicycle Retailer and Industry News*, 1 August 2000.

23. Lou Mazzante, "Pedals for Progress Spurs Economic Development," *Bicycle Retailer and Industry News*, 1 December 2000.

24. Ibid.

POPULATION INCREASES STEADILY
(pages 74–75)

1. U.S. Bureau of the Census, *International Data Base*, electronic database, Suitland, MD, updated 10 May 2000.

2. Tokyo from United Nations, *World Urbanization Prospects: The 1999 Revision, Key Findings* (New York: 1999), p. 9.

3. U.S. Bureau of the Census, "IDB Summary Demographic Data for the United States," <www.census.gov/cgi-bin/ipc/idbsum?cty=US>, viewed 17 February 2001.

4. Census Bureau, op. cit. note 1.

5. Worldwatch calculation based on ibid.

6. Ibid.

7. Ibid.

8. United Nations, "World Population Prospects: The 2000 Revision—Highlights" (New York: 2001), p. v.

9. United Nations, *World Urbanization Prospects: The 1998 Revision* (New York: United Nations, 1998); drop in 2000 from Census Bureau, op. cit. note 1.

10. Census Bureau, op. cit. note 1.

11. United Nations Population Fund (UNFPA), *Population Issues Briefing Kit 2000* (New York: 2000), p. 3.

12. Ibid.

13. Jean-Claude Chesnais, "Determinants of Below-Replacement Fertility," in United Nations, *Below Replacement Fertility* (New York: 2000), p. 127.

14. Ibid., p. 130.

15. UNFPA, op. cit. note 11.

16. Growth rate in 1986 from Abubakar Dungas, "Iran's Other Revolution," *Populi*, September

2000, p. 8; growth rate in 2000 from Census Bureau, op. cit. note 1.

17. Dungas, op. cit. note 16.

18. Joint United Nations Programme on HIV/AIDS, *AIDS Epidemic Update: December 2000* (Geneva: 2000), p. 24.

19. United Nations, op. cit. note 8, p. 9.

20. "AIDS Will Kill One Third of 15 Year Olds in Worst-Affected States," *Populi,* September 2000, p. 7.

21. U.N. Development Programme, "Levels and Trends of Contraceptive Use as Assessed in 1998," <www.undp.org/popin/wdtrends/contraceptives 1998.htm>, viewed 17 February 2001.

22. UNFPA, op. cit. note 11, p. 23.

CIGARETTE PRODUCTION REMAINS HIGH (pages 76–77)

1. Arnella Trent, Tobacco Analyst, Foreign Agriculture Service (FAS), U.S. Department of Agriculture (USDA), Washington, DC, letter to author, 7 February 2001, and e-mail to author, 9 February 2001.

2. Based on production from ibid., and on population from U.S. Bureau of the Census, *International Data Base,* electronic database, Suitland, MD, updated 10 May 2000.

3. Based on production from Trent, op. cit. note 1, and on population from Census Bureau, op. cit. note 2.

4. Trent, op. cit. note 1.

5. Ibid.

6. USDA, FAS, "China, People's Republic of: Tobacco and Products, Tobacco Update 2000," *Global Agriculture Information Network (GAIN) Report No. CH0044* (Washington, DC: 11 December 2000), p. 1; population from Census Bureau, op. cit. note 2.

7. USDA, Economic Research Service (ERS), *Tobacco: Situation and Outlook Yearbook* (Washington, DC: December 2000), p. 17; population from Census Bureau, op. cit. note 2.

8. USDA, ERS, "Tobacco: Summary," 20 April 2000, <www.ers.usda.gov/Briefing/Tobacco/trade.htm>, viewed 25 January 2001; share from USDA, FAS, "World Cigarette Exports by Country," *Tobacco: World Markets and Trade,* August 1999, <www.fas.usda.gov/tobacco/circular/1999/9908/tablec.pdf>, viewed 7 February 2001.

9. Trent, op. cit. note 1.

10. USDA, FAS, "Russian Federation: Tobacco and Products, Annual 2000," *GAIN Report No. RS0022* (Washington, DC: 26 April 2000) p. 2.

11. Ibid.

12. Trent, op. cit. note 1; USDA, FAS, "Japan: Tobacco Annual—Revised 2000," *GAIN Report, No. JA0058* (Washington, DC: 15 May 2000), p. 23.

13. Trent, op. cit. note 1.

14. World Bank, "Tobacco Control Can Prevent Millions of Deaths Worldwide," press release (Washington, DC: 18 May 1999).

15. World Health Organization (WHO), *The World Health Report 1999* (Geneva: 1999), p. 65.

16. Marlo Ann Corrao et al., "Building the Evidence Base for Global Tobacco Control," *Bulletin of the World Health Organization,* July 2000, p. 887.

17. George Mwangi, "Groups Meet About Africa Tobacco Use," *Associated Press,* 23 October 2000.

18. Allyn L. Taylor and Douglas W. Bettcher, "WHO Framework Convention on Tobacco Control: A Global 'Good' for Public Health, *Bulletin of the World Health Organization,* July 2000, p. 923.

19. World Bank, op. cit. note 14.

20. Africa from ibid.; 3 percent rate from WHO, op. cit. note 15, p. 67.

21. World Bank, op. cit. note 14.

22. USDA, FAS, "China, People's Republic of, Tobacco and Products, Annual Report, Part I 2000," *GAIN Report No. CH0021* (Washington, DC: 1 June 2000), p. 15.

23. Dan Bilefsky and Jean Eaglesham, "Brussels Raises the Stakes Against Big Tobacco," *Financial Times,* 8 November 2000.

24. Canada and United Kingdom from USDA, FAS, "European Union: Tobacco and Products Annual 2000," *GAIN Report No. E20156* (Washington, DC: 22 December 2000), p. 11; Ukraine from USDA, op. cit. note 10, p. 6.

25. Warren Giles, "Tobacco Sector Accused of 'Invisible' Anti-WHO Campaign," *Financial Times,* 3 August 2000.

26. Taylor and Bettcher, op. cit. note 18, pp. 920–29.

27. Ibid.

AIDS ERODES DECADES OF PROGRESS (pages 78–79)

1. Joint United Nations Programme on HIV/AIDS (UNAIDS), *AIDS Epidemic Update: December 2000* (Geneva: 2000), p. 3; data for 1980–99 from Neff Walker, UNAIDS, Geneva, e-mail to Brian Halweil, Worldwatch Institute, 20 March 2000.

2. UNAIDS, op. cit. note 1, p. 5.

3. Ibid., p. 3; 1999 estimate from U.S. Census Bureau, Population Estimates Program, "Metropolitian Area Population Estimates," 20 October 1999, <www.census.gov/population/estimates/

metro-city/ma99-01.txt>.

4. UNAIDS, op. cit. note 1, p. 4.

5. Botswana from UNAIDS, *Report on the Global HIV/AIDS Epidemic: June 2000* (Geneva: 2000), p. 124; UNAIDS, op. cit. note 1, p. 4.

6. International Labour Organization, *HIV/AIDS in Africa: The Impact on the World of Work* (Geneva: 2000), pp. 2–3.

7. Ibid., pp. 4–5.

8. UNAIDS, op. cit. note 5, pp. 29–30.

9. UNAIDS, op. cit. note 1, p. 5.

10. Ibid.

11. Ibid.

12. "High Risk Sex Common Among Young Gay, Bisexual Men," *Yahoo Daily News*, 26 December 2000.

13. Maxine Frith, "Sexually-Transmitted Diseases Reach 10-Year High," *Press Association News*, 15 December 2000.

14. L.A. Valleroy et al., "HIV Prevalence and Associated Risks in Young Men Who Have Sex with Men: Young Men's Survey Study Group," *Journal of the American Medical Association,* 12 July 2000, pp. 198–204.

15. G.A. Bennett et al., "Gender Differences in Sharing Injecting Equipment by Drug Users in England," *AIDS Care*, February 2000, pp. 77–87.

16. UNAIDS, op. cit. note 1, p. 9.

17. Ibid., p. 3.

18. Barton Gellman, "A Turning Point That Left Millions Behind," *Washington Post*, 28 December 2000.

19. Ibid.

20. Donald G. McNeil, Jr., "Indian Company Offers to Supply AIDS Drugs at Low Cost in Africa," *New York Times*, 7 February 2001.

21. Patrice M. Jones, "Brazil's Free AIDS-Drug Program Slashes Cases, Earns Global Interest," *Chicago Tribune*, 24 December 2000; see also Stephen Buckley, "U.S., Brazil Clash Over AIDS Drugs," *Washington Post*, 6 February 2001.

22. UNAIDS, op. cit. note 1, p. 20.

23. Ed Susman, "Economist: Rich Should Spend Billions on AIDS," *UPI Science News*, 4 February 2001.

24. General Accounting Office, "B-2 Bomber: Cost to Complete 20 Aircraft Is Uncertain," 8 September 1994, <www.fas.org/man/gao/gao94217.htm>.

WAR TRENDS MIXED (pages 82–83)

1. Number of wars from Arbeitsgemeinschaft Kriegsursachenforschung (AKUF), "Das Kriegsgeschehen des Jahres 2000," press release (Hamburg, Germany: Institute for Political Science, University of Hamburg), December 2000, from Klaus Jürgen Gantzel and Torsten Schwinghammer, *Die Kriege nach dem Zweiten Weltkrieg 1945 bis 1992* (Münster and Hamburg: Lit Verlag, 1995), from Dietrich Jung, Klaus Schlichte, and Jens Siegelberg, *Das Kriegsgeschehen 1995* (Bonn: Stiftung Entwicklung und Frieden, 1996), from Thomas Rabehl, AKUF, e-mail to author, 8 January 1998, from AKUF, "Kriegesbilanz 1998," press release, 11 January 1999, from AKUF, "Weltweit 35 Kriege in 1999," press release, 20 December 1999, and from Wolfgang Schreiber, AKUF, e-mail to author, 21 January 2001. AKUF defines a "war" as a mass conflict in which regular armed forces are involved on at least one side, where there is at least a minimal degree of central organization, and where there is a continuity of military operations rather than a series of spontaneous, occasional clashes. "Armed conflicts" are those cases where its definition of "war," particularly the criterion of a continuity of armed operations, is not fully met or where a lack of information does not justify including a violent conflict in the "war" category.

2. AKUF, "Das Kriegsgeschehen des Jahres 2000," op. cit. note 1.

3. Ibid.; "Fuelling Africa's Wars," *The Economist*, 13 January 2001.

4. AKUF, "Das Kriegsgeschehen des Jahres 2000," op. cit. note 1.

5. Ibid.

6. Margareta Sollenberg, ed., *States in Armed Conflict 1999*, Report No. 55 (Uppsala, Sweden: Uppsala University, Department of Peace and Conflict Research, 2000), p. 8.

7. Project Ploughshares, "Armed Conflicts Report 2000," foldout map (Waterloo, ON, Canada: Institute of Peace and Conflict Studies, Conrad Grebel College, 2000).

8. Interdisciplinary Research Programme on Causes of Human Rights Violations (PIOOM), "World Conflict & Human Rights Map 2000," foldout map (Leiden, Netherlands: 2000).

9. Heidelberger Institut für Internationale Konfliktforschung (HIIK), *Konfliktbarometer 2000* (Heidelberg, Germany: Institute for Political Science, University of Heidelberg, 2000), p. 3; idem, *Konfliktbarometer 1999* (Heidelberg, Germany: Institute for Political Science, University of Heidelberg, 1999), p. 1.

10. Developing-country share of more than 90 percent from AKUF, "Das Kriegsgeschehen des Jahres

Notes

2000," op. cit. note 1.

11. AKUF, "Das Kriegsgeschehen des Jahres 2000," op. cit. note 1. AKUF uses a geographical delimitation that includes Afghanistan, the former Central Asian republics of the Soviet Union, and Chechnya in the Middle East. By contrast, the Uppsala group includes Afghanistan under Asia, but Chechnya and other areas of the Caucasus under Europe.

12. Tobias Debiel, Norbert Ropers, and Elisabeth Wollefs, "Krieg und Frieden," in Ingomar Hauchler, Dirk Messner, and Franz Nuscheler, eds., *Globale Trends 1998* (Frankfurt, Germany: Fischer Taschenbuch Verlag, November 1997), p. 350.

13. PIOOM, op. cit. note 8.

14. A.J. Jongman, "Mapping Dimensions of Contemporary Conflicts and Human Rights Violations," in PIOOM, op. cit. note 8.

15. Sollenberg, op. cit. note 6, p. 10.

16. Ibid.

17. Thomas Rabehl, "Daten und Tendenzen des Kriegsgeschehens," in Thomas Rabehl, ed., *Das Kriegsgeschehen 1999* (Opladen, Germany: Leske + Budrich, 2000), pp. 30–31.

18. "Central African Republic: Annan Warns Of Growing Tensions," *UN Wire*, 17 January 2001.

19. Rabehl, "Daten und Tendenzen des Kriegsgeschehens," op. cit. note 17, pp. 22–23; HIIK, *Konfliktbarometer 2000*, op. cit. note 9, pp. 14–16.

20. Larry Rohter, "Ecuador Is Fearful As Colombia's War Spills Over Border," *New York Times*, 8 January 2001.

21. Patrick Gilkes and Martin Plaut, "War Between Ethiopia and Eritrea," *Foreign Policy in Focus*, <www.foreignpolicy-infocus.org/briefs/vol5/v5n25eritethiop.html>.

22. International Rescue Committee, "Mortality in Eastern DRC" (New York: May 2000).

23. Norimitsu Onishi, "Congo Leader Reportedly Dead After Being Shot by Bodyguard," *New York Times*, 17 January 2001.

24. Silja Teege, "Angola (UNITA)," in Rabehl, *Das Kriegsgeschehen 1999*, op. cit. note 17, p. 74.

PEACEKEEPING EXPENDITURES REBOUND (pages 84–85)

1. Figure of $2.4 billion reflects appropriations for the individual missions, with the exception of those in Kosovo and East Timor (proposed budgets), and the Democratic Republic of Congo (so-called commitment authority only, with full budget proposal pending); U.N. Department of Public Information (UNDPI), "United Nations Peacekeeping Operations. Background Note," New York, 1 March 2001; idem, "United Nations Peacekeeping from 1991 to 2000. Statistical Data and Charts," December 2000, p. 9. (Beginning with July 1997, the United Nations switched its peacekeeping accounts from calendar years to July–June reporting periods.)

2. Share of world military expenditures from Andrew Mack, "The Brahimi Report—A Cogent Analysis of UN Peace Operations," *BICC Bulletin* (Bonn International Center for Conversion, Germany), 1 October 2000.

3. Number of missions from UNDPI, "Background Note," op. cit. note 1; cumulative spending is a Worldwatch estimate.

4. UNDPI, "Background Note," op. cit. note 1; "Monthly Summary of Contributors," <www.un.org/Depts/dpko/dpko/contributors>, viewed 18 January 2001.

5. UNDPI, "Background Note," op. cit. note 1.

6. Author's calculation, based on data from Global Policy Forum, <www.globalpolicy.org/security/peacekpg/data/pkomctab.htm>, viewed 3 January 2001, and from U.N. Department of Peacekeeping Operations, <www.un.org/Depts/dpko/dpko/contributors>, viewed 16 January 2001.

7. Ibid.

8. Ibid.

9. UNDPI, "Statistical Data and Charts," op. cit. note 1, p. 1.

10. UNDPI, "Background Note," op. cit. note 1; U.N. Department of Peacekeeping Operations, "Current Peacekeeping Operations," <www.un.org/Depts/DPKO/c_miss.htm>, viewed 2 January 2001.

11. Additional personnel calculated from UNDPI, "Background Note," op. cit. note 1.

12. Barbara Crossette, "U.N. Peacekeeping Mission to Congo Is Revived," *New York Times*, 15 December 2000.

13. United Nations, "Report of the Panel on United Nations Peace Operations," A/55/305—S/2000/809, 21 August 2000.

14. Ibid. In response to the Brahimi report's suggestion, U.N. Secretary-General Kofi Annan called for emergency funding of $22 million in 2001 in order to add 250 staff to the peacekeeping department; "Funding: Annan Calls For Beefed Up Peacekeeping Budget," *UN Wire*, 28 November 2000.

15. United Nations, op. cit. note 13.

16. Ibid. In mid-2000, there were just 32 officers providing military planning and guidance to 27,000

troops in the field and nine civilian police staff to provide guidance for 8,600 police personnel.

17. Cash in hand from Joseph Connor, "Statement to the Fifth Committee on the U.N. Financial Situation," press release (New York: United Nations, 17 October 2000).

18. Money owed by all members was $1.989 billion ($1.958 in 1999 dollars); "Status of Contributions to the Regular Budget, International Tribunals and Peacekeeping Operations as at 31 December 2000," Office of the Spokesman for the Secretary-General, United Nations, New York.

19. Ibid.

20. Michael Renner, "UN Peacekeeping: An Uncertain Future," *Foreign Policy in Focus* (Albuquerque, NM, and Washington, DC: Interhemispheric Resource Center and Institute for Policy Studies), September 2000.

21. Barbara Crossette, "After Long Fight, U.N. Agrees to Cut Dues Paid by U.S.," *New York Times*, 23 December 2000.

22. Christopher Marquis, "Satisfied with U.N. Reforms, Helms Relents on Back Dues," *New York Times*, 10 January 2001.

23. Ibid.

LIMITED PROGRESS ON NUCLEAR ARSENALS (pages 86–87)

1. Robert S. Norris and William M. Arkin, "Global Nuclear Stockpiles, 1945–2000," Nuclear Notebook, *Bulletin of the Atomic Scientists*, March/April 2000, p. 79. These figures are slightly revised from those reported in earlier editions of *Vital Signs*. Nuclear warhead data are estimates because much information about these arsenals remains a government secret. The most reliable data are for the U.S. stockpile.

2. These numbers include warheads that are deployed, held in reserve, and awaiting dismantlement. Norris and Arkin, op. cit. note 1. Strategic warheads are those intended to be fired over long distances, traversing an entire continent or ocean; tactical warheads are intended for shorter-distances.

3. Norris and Arkin, op. cit. note 1.

4. Ibid.; Robert S. Norris and William M. Arkin, "French and British Nuclear Forces," Nuclear Notebook, *Bulletin of the Atomic Scientists*, September/October 2000, pp. 69–71; idem, "Chinese Nuclear Forces," Nuclear Notebook, *Bulletin of the Atomic Scientists*, November/December 2000, pp. 78–79.

5. Norris and Arkin, op. cit. note 1; "The Nuclear Numbers," *Science for Democratic Action* (Institute for Energy and Environmental Research (IEER), Takoma Park, MD), October 1998, p. 20.

6. Norris and Arkin, op. cit. note 1.

7. "World Plutonium Inventories, 1999," Nuclear Notebook, *Bulletin of the Atomic Scientists*, September/October 1999, p. 71.

8. Megatons from Carnegie Endowment for International Peace, Non-Proliferation Project, "Nuclear Numbers," <www.ceip.org/files/npp/Nuclear Numbers/index.htm>, viewed 21 November 2000.

9. Warheads on hair-trigger alert from ibid.; Arjun Makhijani, "The Nature of Post-Cold War Nuclear Dangers," *Science for Democratic Action* (IEER, Takoma Park, MD), October 1998, p. 3.

10. Total estimated at 2,054 by Institute for Defense and Disarmament Studies (IDDS), *Arms Control Reporter on CD 2000*, July 2000 edition, 608aCTB00.doc, p. 12; estimate of 2,078 in "The Nuclear Numbers," op. cit. note 5.

11. The Soviet Union initiated a moratorium in 1991; the United States and Britain, in 1992. France permanently ended testing in 1996, and China announced a suspension of tests the same year. Following their 1998 tests, India and Pakistan announced moratoria; IDDS, op. cit. note 10, p. 6.

12. Preparatory Commission for the Comprehensive Nuclear Test Ban Treaty Organization, "Status of Signatures and Ratifications," <www.ctbto.org/cgi-bin/ctbto_states.cgi?StatusReport>, viewed 27 December 2000.

13. Preparatory Commission for the Comprehensive Nuclear Test Ban Treaty Organization, "Status of the 44 States Whose Ratification is Required for the Treaty to Enter Into Force (Article XIV)," <www.ctbto.org/cgi-bin/ctbto_states.cgi?List=Required>, viewed 27 December 2000.

14. Eric Schmitt, "Senate Kills Test Ban Treaty in Crushing Loss for Clinton; Evokes Versailles Pact Defeat," *New York Times*, 14 October 1999.

15. IDDS, op. cit. note 10, pp. 9–12. Subcritical experiments involve both plutonium and conventional explosives; the plutonium does not reach criticality. See Hisham Zerriffi and Arjun Makhijani, "Pure Fusion Weapons?" *Science for Democratic Action* (IEER, Takoma Park, MD), October 1998, p. 23.

16. Leaders in the Clinton administration and in the U.S. Congress have pressed Russia to agree to amending the Anti-Ballistic Missile Treaty to allow the deployment of a U.S. anti-ballistic missile system, threatening that the United States might

Notes

withdraw from the treaty if Russia were to reject an amendment; Shannon Kile, "Nuclear Arms Control and Non-Proliferation," in Stockholm International Peace Research Institute, *SIPRI Yearbook 2000: Armaments, Disarmament, and International Security* (New York: Oxford University Press, 2000), pp. 448–52; IDDS, op. cit. note 10, p. 12.

17. Erik Eckholm, "China Says U.S. Missile Shield Could Force a Nuclear Buildup," *New York Times*, 11 May 2000.

18. Huma Siddiqui, "Is South Asia Headed for a Post-Cold War Nuclear Race?" *BASIC Reports*, 10 November 2000, p. 15.

19. Kile, op. cit. note 16, pp. 456–57; Eric Schmitt, "Pentagon Feels Pressure to Cut Out More Warheads," *New York Times*, 11 May 2000.

20. Barbara Crossette, "5 Nuclear Powers Agree on Stronger Pledge to Scrap Arsenals," *New York Times*, 22 May 2000.

WORLD'S CORAL REEFS DYING OFF
(pages 92–93)

1. Clive Wilkinson, *Status of Coral Reefs of the World: 2000* (Townsville, Australia: Global Coral Reef Monitoring Network, 2000), p. 1.

2. Ibid.

3. Table 1 derived from the following sources: share of total reef area from Reef Relief, "Map of the World's Coral Reefs," <www.reefrelief.org>, viewed 12 December 2000, and from Peter Weber, "Coral Reefs in Decline," in Lester R. Brown, Hal Kane, and David Malin Roodman, *Vital Signs 1994* (New York: W.W. Norton & Company, 1994), p. 123; Indonesia from Daniel Cooney, "Half of Indonesia's Coral Reefs Dead," *Associated Press*, 24 October 2000; Great Barrier Reef from Reef Check, "Reef Check 1998 Summary Results," <www.ust.hk/~webrc/ReefCheck/press.html>, viewed 1 December 2000; Fiji from Margot Higgins, "Fiji Fouled By Coral Reef Bleaching," *Environmental News Network*, 26 April 2000; 80–90 percent in Indian Ocean from Jamie K. Reaser, Rafe Pomerance, and Peter O. Thomas, "Coral Bleaching and Global Climate Change: Scientific Findings and Policy Recommendations," *Conservation Biology*, 5 October 2000, p. 1503; recovery in Maldives, Lakshadweep, and Palau from Dennis Normile, "Some Coral Bouncing Back From El Niño," *Science*, 12 May 2000, p. 941; disease from "Reefs Plagued by African Dust," *Washington Post*, 2 October 2000; Florida Keys from "Satellite

Images Bring Coral Reefs' Decline Into Focus," *Environment News Service*, 27 October 2000; Belize bleaching from Richard B. Aronson et al., "Coral Bleach-Out in Belize," *Nature*, 4 May 2000, p. 36; rest of table from Wilkinson, op. cit. note 1, and from idem, "Status of Coral Reefs of the World: 2000 Executive Summary" <www.nova.edu/ocean/9icrs/liveweb/1024_3.html>, viewed 12 December 2000.

4. Number of countries from Reef Relief, op. cit. note 3; $375 billion from Robert Costanza et al., "The Value of the World's Ecosystem Services and Natural Capital," *Nature*, 15 May 1997, p. 256.

5. Protection from Reaser, Pomerance, and Thomas, op. cit. note 3, p. 1502; half-billion from Dirk Bryant et al., *Reefs at Risk* (Washington, DC: World Resources Institute, 1998), p. 10.

6. One tenth from The Nature Conservancy, Rescue the Reef Initiative, "Coral Reef Facts," <www.tnc.org/international/specialinitiatives/rescuereef/resources/art938.html>, viewed 12 December 2000; one quarter from Bryant et al., op. cit. note 5, p. 9.

7. Ove Hoegh-Guldberg, *Climate Change: Coral Bleaching and the Future of the World's Coral Reefs* (Amsterdam: Greenpeace International, 1999), p. 2.

8. Area covered from Bryant et al., op. cit. note 5, p. 9; complex and productive from Reaser, Pomerance, and Thomas, op. cit. note 3, p. 1501.

9. Reaser, Pomerance, and Thomas, op. cit. note 3, p. 1501.

10. "Scientists to Explore Newly Discovered Oman Reef," *Reuters*, 27 October 1999; HIV from Paul Majendie, "Great Barrier Reef Needs Saving From Fame," *Reuters*, 14 September 2000.

11. Wilkinson, op. cit. note 1.

12. Magnus Nyström, Carl Folke, and Fredrik Moberg, "Coral Reef Disturbance and Resilience in a Human-Dominated Environment," *Trends in Ecology and Evolution*, 10 October 2000, p. 413; "Grounded Ship Damages Part of Australian Coral Reef," *Reuters*, 6 November 2000.

13. Estimate of 60 percent from Bryant et al., op. cit. note 5, p. 6; impacts from Wilkinson, op. cit. note 1.

14. Andrew W. Bruckner, "New Threat to Coral Reefs: Trade in Coral Organisms," *Issues in Science and Technology*, fall 2000.

15. TRAFFIC, *Fishing for Solutions: Can the Live Trade in Wild Groupers and Wrasses from Southeast Asia Be Managed?* (Cambridge, U.K.: 1999).

16. Reef Check, op. cit. note 3.

17. John Ryan, "Blast Fishing Competes With Reef Conference," *Environmental News Network*, 28

Notes

October 2000; 20 square meters from "What Price Coral?" *The Economist*, 4 November 2000, p. 88.

18. Ryan, op. cit. note 17.

19. Bryant et al., op. cit. note 5, p. 15.

20. Andrew Darby, "Great Barrier Reef Crisis Growing," *Environment News Service*, 14 January 1999.

21. Wilkinson, op. cit. note 1.

22. Temperature tolerance from Hoegh-Guldberg, op. cit. note 7, p. 1; good indicators from Luitzen Bijlsma, "Coastal Zones and Small Islands," in Robert T. Watson et al., eds., *Climate Change 1995. Impacts, Adaptations and Mitigation of Climate Change: Scientific-Technical Analyses* (New York: Cambridge University Press, 1996), pp. 303–04.

23. Hoegh-Guldberg, op. cit. note 7, p. 1.

24. Ibid., p. 5.

25. Reaser, Pomerance, and Thomas, op. cit. note 3.

26. Worst on record from Hoegh-Guldberg, op. cit. note 7, p. 6; 16 percent from Wilkinson, op. cit. note 1; 60 countries from Reaser, Pomerance, and Thomas, op. cit. note 3.

27. Reaser, Pomerance, and Thomas, op. cit. note 3, p. 1508.

28. Age of corals and 40 meters from University of California–Los Angeles (UCLA), "New Global Research Shows Coral Reefs Remain in Jeopardy; UCLA Scientist Announces Southern California Marine Ecology Health Study," press release (Los Angeles: 20 April 2000); 90 percent from Wilkinson, op. cit. note 1, p. 3.

29. One third from UCLA, op. cit. note 28.

30. Wilkinson, op. cit. note 1, pp. 1–2.

31. Ibid, p. 4.

32. Hoegh-Guldberg, op. cit. note 7, p. 24.

33. Capacity to adapt from ibid., p. 18; "Increasing Carbon Dioxide Threatens Coral Reefs; Major Discovery at Columbia University's Biosphere 2 Center," press release (Tucson, AZ: Columbia University's Biosphere 2 Center, 16 May 2000).

34. International Coral Reef Initiative, <www.environnement.gouv.fr/icri/index.html>, viewed 12 December 2000; International Coral Reef Action Network, "ICRAN: A Programme for the World's Coral Reefs," <www.unep.ch/earthw/icrandes.htm>, viewed 12 December 2000; Coral Reef Alliance, "The Coral Reef Alliance," <www.coral.org>, viewed 12 December 2000.

35. Reef Check, <www.reefcheck.org>, viewed 1 December 2000.

36. Cooney, op. cit. note 3.

37. Tax from "Uncertain Future of Coral Reefs Focus of Bali Conference," *Environment News Service*, 23 October 2000; revenue from "What Price Coral?"

op. cit. note 17, p. 89.

38. Reef patrol from John Ryan, "Blast Fishing Ring Busted in Indonesia," *Environmental News Network*, 7 November 2000.

39. U.S. National Oceanic and Atmospheric Administration, Coral Reef Task Force, "U.S. Coral Reef Task Force Unveils Groundbreaking Plan," press release (Washington, DC: 2 March 2000).

HYDROLOGICAL POVERTY WORSENING (pages 94–95)

1. World Health Organization (WHO) and UNICEF, *Global Water Supply and Sanitation Assessment 2000 Report* (New York: 2000), p. 8.

2. Ibid.

3. Ibid.

4. Ibid.

5. Ibid.

6. Ibid.

7. Ibid.

8. Ibid.

9. Ibid.

10. Ibid.

11. World Resources Institute, *World Resources 2000–01* (Washington, DC: World Resources Institute, 2000), p. 110.

12. Ibid.

13. Ibid.

14. Charles J. Vorosmarty et al., "Global Water Resources: Vulnerability from Climate Change and Population Growth," *Science*, 14 July 2000, pp. 284–88.

15. Andrew Keller, R. Sakthivadivel, and David Seckler, *Water Scarcity and the Role of Storage in Development* (Colombo, Sri Lanka: International Water Management Institute, 2000), pp. 1–2.

16. Seth Cook, Li Fengrui, and Wei Huilan, "Rainwater Harvesting Agriculture in Gansu Province, People's Republic of China," *Journal of Soil and Water Conservation*, second quarter 2000, p. 112.

17. Groundwater for drinking from Payal Sampat, "Uncovering Groundwater Pollution," in Lester R. Brown et al., *State of the World 2001* (New York: W. W. Norton & Company, 2001), p. 23.

18. World Commission on Water for the 21st Century, *A Water Secure World: Vision for Water, Life, and the Environment*, World Water Vision Commission Report (Cairo: World Water Council, February 2000), p. 13; Keller, Sakthivadivel, and Seckler, op. cit. note 15, p. 5.

19. World Water Vision, "World's Rivers in Crisis: Some are Dying; Others Could Die," press release

Notes

(Washington, DC: World Water Council, 29 November 1999).

20. Payal Sampat, *Deep Trouble: The Hidden Threat of Groundwater Pollution*, Worldwatch Paper 154 (Washington, DC: Worldwatch Institute, December 2000), p. 17.

21. World Bank, *World Development Report 2000/2001* (New York: Oxford University Press, 2000), pp. 21–23.

22. WHO and UNICEF, op. cit. note 1.

23. World Water Vision, "The Poor Pay Much More for Water," press release (Washington, DC: World Water Council, 4 August 1999).

24. Ibid.

25. Ibid.

26. Peter H. Gleick, "Making Every Drop Count," *Scientific American*, February 2001, p. 43; WHO, "Sustainability and Optimization of Water Supply and Sanitation Services," <www.who.int/water_sanitation_health/wss/sustoptim.html>, viewed 22 January 2001.

27. John Thompson et al., "Waiting at the Tap: Changes in Urban Water Use in East Africa Over Three Decades," *Environment and Urbanization*, October 2000, pp. 37–52.

28. Ibid., pp. 48–49.

29. World Water Vision, op. cit. note 19.

30. WHO and UNICEF, op. cit. note 1, p. 2.

31. Kris Christen, "Global Freshwater Scarcity: Is Privatization a Solution?" *Environmental Science and Technology*, 1 August 2000, p. 342.

32. Ibid.

33. Sandra Postel, *Pillar of Sand* (New York: W.W. Norton & Company, 1999), pp. 112–14.

WETLANDS DECLINE (pages 96–97)

1. Michael Moser, Crawford Prentice, and Scott Frazier, "A Global Overview of Wetland Loss and Degradation," *Proceedings to the 6th Meeting of the Conference of Contracting Parties of the Ramsar Convention*, vol. 10, March 1996.

2. Table 1 based on Thomas E. Dahl, *Status and Trends of Wetlands in the Conterminous United States 1986 to 1997* (Washington, DC: U.S. Fish and Wildlife Service, 2000), pp. 9–12, on A.J. Hails, *Wetlands, Biodiversity, and the Ramsar Convention* (Gland, Switzerland: Ramsar Convention Bureau, 1997), and on Moser, Prentice, and Frazier, op. cit. note 1.

3. Ramsar Convention Bureau, "What Are Wetlands," Ramsar Information Paper No. 1, *The Ramsar Information Pack*, <www.ramsar.org/index_about_ramsar.htm>, updated 5 February 2000.

4. C.M. Finlayson and N.C. Davidson, "Global Review of Wetland Resources and Priorities for Wetland Inventory," *Report to the Ramsar Bureau from Wetlands International and the Environmental Research Institute of the Supervising Scientist* (Wageningen, the Netherlands, and Jabiru, Australia: 1999).

5. Virginia Carter, "Wetland Hydrology, Water Quality, and Associated Functions," *National Water Summary on Wetland Resources, United States Geological Survey Water Supply Paper 2425* (Washington, DC: 9 February 1999).

6. C.J. Woltemade, "Ability of Restored Wetlands to Reduce Nitrogen and Phosphorus Concentrations in Agricultural Drainage Water," *Journal of Soil and Water Conservation*, third quarter 2000, pp. 303–09.

7. S. Darras, M. Michou, and C. Sarrat, "IGBP-DIS Wetland Data Initiative: A First Step Towards Identifying a Global Delineation of Wetlands," IGBP-DIS Working Paper No. 19 (Toulouse, France: International Geosphere-Biosphere Programme–Data and Information System, February 1999).

8. World Resources Institute, *World Resources 2000–01* (Washington, DC: 2000), p. 107.

9. Hails, op. cit. note 2; Moser, Prentice, and Frazier, op. cit. note 1.

10. Dahl, op. cit. note 2.

11. Hails, op. cit. note 2.

12. Ibid.

13. Ibid.

14. Ibid.

15. Moser, Prentice, and Frazier, op. cit. note 1.

16. Johan F. Gottens et al., "The Case of the Paraguay-Paraná Waterway ("Hidrovía") and Its Impact on the Patanal of Brazil," *Wetlands Bulletin*, 1998, pp. 12–18.

17. World Commission on Water for the 21st Century, "World's Rivers in Crisis: Some are Dying; Others Could Die," press release (Cairo: World Water Vision, 29 November 1999).

18. Dwight Peck, "Water Policy and Wetland Management: The Experience of Spain," Ramsar COP 7, Document 16.3, 7th Meeting of the Conference of the Contracting Parties to the Convention on Wetlands, San José, Costa Rica, 10–18 May 1999.

19. Ramsar Convention Bureau and World Wide Fund for Nature International, "Wetlands Events Send Another Wake-up Call for World's Fresh Water," press release (Washington, DC: 29 Janu-

ary 2001).

20. "Mozambique Floods Worsened by Wetland Loss," *Reuters*, 15 March 2000.

21. Wade Roush, "Putting a Price Tag on Nature's Bounty," *Science*, 16 May 1997, p. 1029.

22. Property damage from David R. Easterling et al., "Climate Extremes: Observations, Modeling, and Impacts," *Science*, 22 September 2000, pp. 2068–74; threatened area from Lawrence Wells, "Saving the Bayou," *E Magazine*, November/December 2000, p. 8.

23. Roush, op. cit. note 21; International Monetary Fund (IMF), *The World Economic Outlook Database*, <www.imf.org/external/pubs/ft/weo/2000/02/data/index.htm>, September 2000.

24. Todd Litman, *Land Use Impact Cost of Transportation* (Victoria, BC, Canada: Victoria Transport Policy Institute, 28 November 1999), p. 14.

25. Joy B. Zelder, "Progress in Wetland Restoration Ecology," *Trends in Ecology and Evolution*, October 2000, pp. 402–07.

26. David Malakoff, "Restored Wetlands Flunk Real World Test," *Science*, 17 April 1998, p. 371; Mark Schrope, "Save Our Swamp," *Nature*, 11 January 2001, pp. 128–30.

27. Cited in Don Hinrichsen, "The Oceans are Coming Ashore," *World Watch*, November/December 2000, pp. 26–35.

28. Moser, Prentice, and Frazier, op. cit. note 1.

BIRD SPECIES THREATENED (pages 98–99)

1. World Conservation Union–IUCN, Species Survival Commission, *2000 IUCN Red List of Threatened Species* (Gland, Switzerland: 2000), p. 1.

2. The figure for the total number of bird species varies slightly, depending on the global taxonomy followed—IUCN, op. cit. note 1, p. 8, states that there are a total of 9,946 species; 12 percent from BirdLife International (BI), *Threatened Birds of the World* (Barcelona, Spain, and Cambridge, U.K.: Lynx Edicions and BirdLife International, 2000), p. 2. IUCN, op. cit. note 1, pp. 49–56, provides the following definitions for risk categories: critical means extremely high risk of extinction in the wild in the immediate future; endangered means very high risk of extinction in the wild in the near future; vulnerable means high risk of extinction in the wild in the medium-term future; conservation-dependent means would be threatened if current conservation measures were discontinued; and near-threatened means close to qualifying as threatened.

3. IUCN, op. cit. note 1, p. 8.

4. BI, op. cit. note 2, p. 2.

5. Ibid.; Michael J. Crosby et al., "Predicting Avian Extinction Rates," *Biodiversity Letters* (1994), pp. 182–85.

6. BI, op. cit. note 2, p. 2.

7. IUCN, op. cit. note 1, p. 10; taxonomic revision from Alison Stattersfield, BI, Cambridge, U.K., e-mail to author, 8 February 2001.

8. Impact of fishing on albatross, from BI, op. cit. note 2, pp. 45–53.

9. IUCN, op. cit. note 1, p. 10.

10. P. Dee Boersma and David L. Stokes, "Conservation: Threats to Penguin Populations," in Tony D. Williams, *The Penguins: Spheniscidae* (New York: Oxford University Press, 1995) pp. 127–39; Malcolm W. Browne, "Oil and Fishing Force Penguins to Hunt Afar as Chicks Starve," *New York Times*, 10 June 1997; Colin Woodard, "For Some Penguins, Less Ice Means Stark Choices," *Christian Science Monitor*, 10 December 1998.

11. BI, op. cit. note 2, p. 4.

12. IUCN, op. cit. note 1, p. 18.

13. BI, op. cit. note 2, p. 2.

14. Ibid., p. 8.

15. Ibid., p. 6.

16. U.N. Food and Agriculture Organization, *State of the World's Forests 1999* (Rome: 1999), p. 1; Emily Matthews et al., *Pilot Analysis of Global Ecosystems: Forest Ecosystems* (Washington, DC: World Resources Institute, 2000), pp. 16–19.

17. Marjorie Castelletta, Navjot S. Sodhi, and R. Subaraj, "Heavy Extinctions of Forest Avifauna in Singapore: Lessons for Biodiversity Conservation in Southeast Asia," *Conservation Biology*, December 2000, pp. 1870–80.

18. BI, op. cit. note 2, p. 8.

19. Ibid., p. 32.

20. Craig Hoover, senior program officer, TRAFFIC North America, e-mail to author, 14 February 2001.

21. BI, op. cit. note 2, p. 257; Spix's from ibid., p. 258; "The Last Spix's Macaw—The World's Rarest Parrot—Disappears From the Wild," <worldtwitch.virtualave.net/cyanopsitta.htm>, viewed 12 February 2001.

22. BI, op. cit. note 2, p. 257; Richard Hartley, "Pet Trade Blues," *International Wildlife*, March/April 2000, p. 46.

23. Chris Bright, *Life Out of Bounds* (New York: W.W. Norton & Company, 1998), p. 114; Julie A. Savidge, "Extinction of an Island Forest Avifauna by an Introduced Snake," *Ecology*, June 1987, pp. 660–68; Gordon H. Rodda, Thomas H. Fritts,

Notes

and David Chiszar, "The Disappearance of Guam's Wildlife," *BioScience*, October 1997, pp. 565–72.

24. Bright, op. cit. note 23, pp. 111–12; Elizabeth Royte, "On the Brink: Hawaii's Vanishing Species," *National Geographic*, September 1995, pp. 27, 29, 32–33.

25. Original native species and number extinct from Bright, op. cit. note 23, p. 111; number threatened from James D. Jacobi and Carter T. Atkinson, "Hawaii's Endemic Birds," National Biological Service, U.S. Geological Survey, <biology.usgs.gov/s+t/frame/t018. htm>, viewed 23 January 2001.

26. George W. Cox, *Alien Species in North America and Hawaii: Impacts on Natural Ecosystems* (Washington, DC: Island Press, 1999), p. 221.

27. Robert J. Marquis and Christopher J. Whelan, "Insectivorous Birds Increase Growth of White Oak Through Consumption of Leaf-Chewing Insects," *Ecology*, October 1994, pp. 2007–14.

28. Paul Alan Cox and Thomas Elmqvist, "Pollinator Extinction in the Pacific Islands," *Conservation Biology*, October 2000, p. 1238.

29. Jose Maria Cardoso da Silva and Marcelo Tabarelli, "Tree Species Impoverishment and the Future Flora of the Atlantic Forest of Northeast Brazil," *Nature*, 2 March 2000, pp. 72–74.

30. Tony Reichhardt, "Peregrine Leads Flight from Endangered List," *Nature*, 3 September 1998, p. 3.

31. BI, "Back on Track," <www.wing-sbsj.or.jp/birdlife/improving.htm>, viewed 30 January 2001.

FARM ANIMAL POPULATIONS SOAR
(pages 100–01)

1. U.N. Food and Agriculture Organization (FAO), *FAOSTAT Statistics Database*, <apps.fao.org>, updated 27 October 2000.
2. Ibid.
3. Ibid.
4. Ibid.
5. Ibid.
6. Ibid.
7. Ibid.
8. Ibid.; Population Reference Bureau (PRB), "2000 World Population Datasheet," wall chart (Washington, DC: June 2000).
9. FAO, op. cit. note 1.
10. Ibid.
11. Cees de Haan et al., "Livestock & the Environment: Finding a Balance," report of a study coordinated by FAO, U.S. Agency for International Development, and World Bank (Brussels: 1997), p. 39.
12. Ibid.
13. Ibid., p. 53.
14. Janice Cox and Sari Varpama, *The "Livestock Revolution": Development or Destruction?* (Hants, U.K.: Compassion in World Farming, September 2000).
15. De Haan et al., op. cit. note 11, p. 17. This figure includes only animals raised exclusively on pasture and receiving no grain or hay. Even in nations like the United States that depend heavily on feedlots, however, most ruminants spend part of their lives on the range. For example, an estimated half of weight gain for the typical American beef cow occurs on the range.
16. De Haan et al. op. cit. note 11, p. 24.
17. Ibid., p. 8.
18. Ibid., p. 27.
19. FAO, "One Third of Farm Animal Breeds Face Extinction," press release (Rome: 5 December 2000).
20. De Haan et al., op. cit. note 11, pp. 42–43.
21. Ibid., p. 8.
22. Ibid., p. 43.
23. Ibid., pp. 42–43.
24. Ibid., p. 8.
25. Ibid., pp. 66–67; U.S. Department of Agriculture, *Production, Supply, and Distribution*, electronic database, Washington, DC, updated December 2000. Virtually all of the world's soybeans are crushed to produce high-protein meal, which makes up 80 percent of the bean by weight. (The remaining 20 percent of the bean is soy oil, widely used in cooking and processed foods.) Farm animals generally do not consume whole soybeans, but just the high-protein meal.
26. Council for Agricultural Science and Technology, *Animal Agriculture and Global Food Supply* (Ames, IA: July 1999), p. 4.
27. De Haan et al., op. cit. note 11.
28. Christopher Delgado et al., *Livestock to 2020: The Next Food Revolution* (Washington, DC: International Food Policy Research Institute, May 1999), p. 45.
29. De Haan et al., op. cit. note 11, p. 32; Delgado et al., op. cit. note 28, p. 46.
30. U.S. Senate Committee on Agriculture, Nutrition, & Forestry, "Animal Waste Pollution in America: An Emerging National Problem," report compiled for Senator Tom Harkin, December 1997, p. 11.
31. Peter S. Goodman, "An Unsavory Byproduct," *Washington Post*, 1 August 1999; Netherlands based on FAO, op. cit. note 1.
32. De Haan et al., op. cit. note 11, p. 79.

33. FAO, op. cit. note 19.
34. Ibid.
35. De Haan et al., op. cit. note 11, p. 73; Mark Derr, "Vanishing Livestock Breeds Leave Diversity Gap," *New York Times*, 14 November 2000.
36. FAO, op. cit. note 1.
37. Ibid.
38. Ibid.; PRB, op. cit. note 8.

GROWTH IN TRANSGENIC AREA SLOWS
(pages 102–03)

1. Clive James, *Global Review of Commercialized Transgenic Crops: 2000 (Preview)*, ISAAA Brief No. 21 (Ithaca, NY: International Service for the Acquisition of Agri-Biotech Applications, 2000).
2. Ibid.
3. Ibid.
4. Martin Teitel et al., *Genetically Engineered Plants: Changing the Nature of Nature* (Rochester, VT: Inner Traditions International, November 1999).
5. James, op. cit. note 1.
6. Ibid.
7. Ibid.
8. Ibid.
9. Ibid.
10. U.S. Department of Agriculture, National Agricultural Statistics Service, *Prospective Plantings* (Washington, DC: March 2000), p. 23.
11. James, op. cit. note 1.
12. Ibid.
13. Ibid.
14. Ibid.
15. Ibid.
16. Ibid.
17. Ibid.
18. Ibid.
19. Ibid.
20. Ibid.
21. Ibid.
22. Ibid.
23. Rural Advancement Foundation International (RAFI), *GM Seed 2000 Summary, Speed Bump or Blow-Out for GM Seeds? Stalling Markets, Taco Debacle & Biotech Bail Outs* (Winnipeg, MN, Canada: 21 December 2000).
24. Marc Kaufman, "Biotech Critics Cite Unapproved Corn in Taco Shells," *Washington Post*, 18 September 2000.
25. Scott Kilman, "Aventis Halts Seed Sales of Genetically Engineered Corn," *Wall Street Journal*, 27 September 2000; Marc Kaufman, "Biotech Corn Fuels a Recall," *Washington Post*, 23 September

2000; idem, "Biotech Corn May Be in Various Foods," *Washington Post*, 19 October 2000; William Claiborne, "Biotech Corn Traces Dilute Bumper Crop," *Washington Post*, 25 October 2000.
26. Andrew Pollack, "Group Reports Genetic Corn in European Food," *New York Times*, 7 November 2000.
27. RAFI, op. cit. note 23.
28. Ibid.
29. Ibid.
30. Ibid.
31. Henry A. Wallace Center for Agricultural and Environmental Policy at Winrock International, *Transgenic Crops: An Environmental Assessment* (Morrilton, AR: November 2000).
32. Leonard P. Gianessi and Janet E. Carpenter, *Agricultural Biotechnology: Benefits of Transgenic Soybeans* (Washington, DC: National Center for Food and Agricultural Policy, April 2000), p. 87.
33. Wallace Center, op. cit. note 31, pp. 15–20.
34. L.L. Wolfenbarger and P.R. Phifer, "The Ecological Risks and Benefits of Genetically Engineered Plants," *Science*, 15 December 2000, pp. 2088–93; Carol Kaesuk Yoon, "What's Next for Biotech Crops? Questions," *New York Times*, 19 December 2000.
35. Andrew Pollack, "First Complete Plant Genetic Sequence is Determined," *New York Times*, 14 December 2000.
36. Ibid.

PHARMACEUTICAL SALES THRIVING
(pages 106–07)

1. IMS Health, *Pharmaceutical World Review* (London: various years).
2. Ibid.; most profitable industry from "Fortune 500," *Fortune Magazine*, April 2000.
3. Population Reference Bureau (PRB), "2000 World Population Data Sheet," wall chart (Washington, DC: June 2000); IMS Health, *Pharmaceutical World Review* (London: 2000).
4. PRB, op. cit. note 3; IMS Health, op. cit. note 3.
5. IMS Health, op. cit. note 3.
6. Laurie Garrett, *Betrayal of Trust: The Collapse of Global Public Health* (New York: Hyperion, 2000), pp. 566–68.
7. Ibid.
8. IMS Health, op. cit. note 3.
9. Ibid.
10. Ibid.
11. Ibid.
12. Ibid.

Notes

13. Donald G. McNeil Jr., "Selling Cheap 'Generic' Drugs, India's Copycats Irk Industry," *New York Times*, 1 December 2000.
14. Amy Barrett, "Pfizer: How Big is Too Big?" *Business Week*, 28 August 2000, p. 216; health budgets from World Bank, *World Development Indicators 2000* (Washington, DC: 2000), pp. 90–93.
15. Elisabeth Rosenthal, "West's Medicine Is Raising Bills for China's Sick," *New York Times*, 19 November 1998.
16. Doubling from *Factors Affecting the Growth of Presciption Drug Expenditures* (Washington, DC: National Institute for Health Care Management, July 1999) p. 6; Robert Pear, "Marketing Tied to Increase in Prescription Drug Sales," *New York Times*, 20 September 2000.
17. IMS Health, op. cit. note 3.
18. Ibid.
19. World Health Organization (WHO) figure (for 1997 market) from Shara Rosen, *Vaccine Trends and Developments Worldwide* (New York: Theta Reports, June 1998).
20. Michael R. Reich, "The Global Drug Gap," *Science*, 17 March 2000.
21. Joint U.N. Programme on HIV/AIDS, *Patent Situation of HIV/AIDS-Related Drugs in 80 Countries* (Geneva: January 2000).
22. WHO page on Essential Drugs and Medicines, <www.who.in/medicines/edm-concept.htm>, viewed 3 December 2000.
23. Reich, op. cit. note 20; WHO, op. cit. note 22; $2 from Daphne A. Fresle, Essential Drugs and Medicines Policy, WHO, Geneva, e-mail to author, 1 December 2000.
24. Global Alliance for Vaccines and Immunizations, <www.gavi.org>, viewed 3 December 2000.
25. Reich, op. cit. note 20.
26. Ibid.
27. Tina Rosenberg, "Look at Brazil," *New York Times Magazine*, 28 January 2001.
28. Stephen M. Fried, *Bitter Pills: Inside the Hazardous World of Legal Drugs* (New York: Bantam Books, 1998).
29. Sheryl Gay Stolberg and Jeff Gerth, "High-Tech Stealth Being Used to Sway Doctor Prescriptions," *New York Times*, 16 November 2000.
30. Robert Pear, "Marketing Tied to Increase in Prescription Drug Sales," *New York Times*, 20 September 2000.
31. Sheryl Gay Stolberg, "The Boom in Medications Brings Rise in Fatal Risks," *New York Times*, 3 June 1999.
32. J. Lazarou et al., "Incidence of Adverse Drug Reactions in Hospitalized Patients: A Meta-analysis of Prospective Studies," *Journal of the American Medical Association*, April 1998, pp. 1200–05.
33. Jane Brody, "As Prescriptions Pile Up, Risks Do, Too," *New York Times*, 5 September 2000; Fried, op. cit. 28, p. 26.

PVC PLASTIC PERVADES ECONOMY
(pages 108–09)

1. Figure of 250 million tons based on Wytze van der Naald and Beverly Thorpe, *PVC Plastic: A Looming Waste Crisis* (Amsterdam: Greenpeace International, 1998), p. 5; 100 million tons based on rates from Robert U. Ayres, "The Life Cycle of Chlorine, Part III: Accounting for Final Use," *Journal of Industrial Ecology*, vol. 2, no. 1 (1998), pp. 105–06.
2. Aida M. Jebens, "Polyvinyl Chloride (PVC) Resins," *CEH [Chemical Economics Handbook] Marketing Research Report* (Zurich: SRI International, 1997), pp. 580.1880D–80H.
3. Vinyl Institute, <www.vinylinfo.org/materialvinyl/servingmoretour/4monomertopolymer.html>, viewed 13 June 2000.
4. Chemical Market Associates Inc. (CMAI), "Polyvinyl Chloride," *PVC Insight*, vol. 8, issue 15 (2000), p. 1.
5. Data for 1992 from John F. Auchter, Mario Jaeckel, and Yasuhiko Sakuma, "Polyvinyl Chloride (PVC) Resins," *CEH Marketing Research Report* (Zurich: SRI International, 1993), p. 580.1880D; 1999 from CMAI, op. cit. note 4.
6. Early 1990s from Auchter, Jaeckel, and Sakuma, op. cit. note 5, p. 580.1880E; future rate from "Chemical Market Associates Inc.'s Industry Report," *PVC Insight*, vol. 8, issue 19 (2000), p. 1.
7. Estimate based on "Chemical Market Associates Inc.'s Industry Report," op. cit. note 6.
8. "Production: Gains Beat Losses," *Chemical & Engineering News*, 26 June 2000, p. 55.
9. CMAI, op. cit. note 4.
10. Ibid.
11. Jebens, op. cit. note 2, p. 580.1880G.
12. Shin-Etsu from "Japan, PVC Output Falls 3.5% in May," *PVC Insight*, vol. 8, issue 21 (2000), p. 1; Formosa Plastics from CMAI, op. cit. note 4.
13. "Production: Gains Beat Losses," op. cit. note 8, p. 86.
14. Ibid., pp. 88, 89.
15. Sinopec, "China Struggles to Meet Growing Resin Demand," *PVC Insight*, vol. 8, issue 23 (2000), p. 3.
16. Joe Thornton, *Pandora's Poison: Chlorine, Health,*

and a New Environmental Strategy (Cambridge, MA: The MIT Press, 2000), pp. 306–12.

17. U.N. Environment Programme (UNEP), "Governments Finalize Persistent Organic Pollutants Treaty," press release (Johannesburg: 10 December 2000).

18. Principia Partners, "Post-Industrial and Post-Consumer Vinyl Reclaim: Material Flow and Uses in North America," final report to Chlor-Vinyl Steering Group (Exton, PA: Principia Partners, July 1999).

19. Share that is chlorine from Vinyl Institute, op. cit. note 3; UNEP, Chemicals Division, *Dioxin and Furan Inventories: National and Regional Emissions of PCDD/PCDF* (Geneva: Inter-Organization Programme for the Sound Management of Chemicals, May 1999), pp. 13–15.

20. ARGUS et al., *The Behaviour of PVC in Landfill*, Final Report, DGXI.E.3 (Brussels: European Commission, February 2000).

21. Eckhard Plinke et al., *Mechanical Recycling of PVC Wastes*, Study for DG XI of the European Commission (Basel, Switzerland: Prognos Institute, January 2000).

22. Alexander H. Tullo, "Plastics Additives' Steady Evolution," *Chemical & Engineering News*, 4 December 2000, p. 21.

23. Ted Schettler et al., *Generations at Risk: Reproductive Health and the Environment* (Cambridge, MA: The MIT Press, 1999), pp. 181–82.

24. Thornton, op. cit. note 16, p. 313.

25. Stephen D. Pearson and Lawrence A. Trissel, "Leaching of Diethylhexyl Phthalate from Polyvinyl Chloride Containers by Selected Drugs and Formulation Components," *American Journal of Hospital Pharmacology,* July 1993, pp. 1405–09.

26. Schettler et al., op. cit. note 23, pp. 181–82, 335.

27. Benjamin C. Blount et al., "Levels of Seven Urinary Phthalate Metabolites in a Human Reference Population," *Environmental Health Perspectives*, October 2000, pp. 979–82.

28. Jouni J.K. Jaakkola et al., "Interior Surface Materials in the Home and the Development of Bronchial Obstruction in Young Children in Oslo, Norway," *American Journal of Public Health*, February 1999, pp. 188–92.

29. European Commission, Directorate General III, "Ban of Phthalates in Childcare Articles and Toys," press release (Brussels: 10 November 1999).

30. Samer Iskander and Emma Tucker, "France Bans 'Toxic' Toys," *Financial Times*, 8 July 1999.

31. Danish Ministry of Environment and Energy, *Action Plan for Reducing and Phasing Out Phthalates in Soft Plastics* (Copenhagen: June 1999); "Denmark Plans to Cut Phthalates," *Chemical Market Reporter*, 6 July 1999.

32. Greenpeace International, *Chlorine and PVC Restrictions and PVC-Free Policies: A List Compiled by Greenpeace International*, 3rd ed. (Amsterdam: August 1999).

33. "By the Numbers: 3-PVC," *Plastics Recycling Update*, March 2000, p. 4.

34. CHEMinfo Services, Inc., "PVC Products and Markets," in *A Technical & Socio-Economic Comparion of Options, Part 2—Polyvinyl Chloride*, report prepared for Environment Canada (Toronto: November 1997).

35. Institute for Local Self-Reliance, "Biochemical Substitutions in the Polymer Industry," Pollution Solution Fact Sheet No. 4 (Minneapolis: 1995).

36. Allison Schelesinger, "Perfecting Planet-Friendly Plastics," *IT: Inventing Tomorrow* (University of Minnesota, Institute of Technology), spring 1999, pp. 30–35.

MICROCREDIT EXPANDING RAPIDLY
(pages 110–11)

1. Microcredit Summit, "Empowering Women with Microcredit: 2000 Microcredit Summit Campaign Report," <www.microcreditsummit.org/campaigns/report00.html>, viewed 26 February 2001.

2. Ibid.

3. Ibid.

4. Ibid.

5. Ibid.

6. Loans of $50 from Consultative Group to Assist the Poorest, "About & History," <www.cgap.org/html/mi_about_history.html>, viewed 5 March 2001; 3 billion from World Bank, *World Development Report 2000/2001* (New York: Oxford University Press, 2001), p. 3.

7. Consultative Group to Assist the Poorest, op. cit. note 6.

8. Microcredit Summit, "CRECER: Promoting Credit and Education in Bolivia," in *Countdown 2005: The Newsletter of the Microcredit Summit Campaign*, May/June 1999.

9. Figure of 70 percent from U.N. Development Programme, *Human Development Report 1995* (New York: Oxford University Press, 1995), p. 4.

10. Grameen Bank, <www.grameen-info.org/bank/cds.html>, viewed 4 March 2001.

11. Ibid.

12. Grameen Bank, *Annual Report 1999* (Dhaka, Bangladesh: 2000), p. 39.
13. Ibid.
14. Ibid.
15. Grameen Bank, op. cit. note 10.
16. FINCA International, *The Case for Village Banking* (Washington, DC: 1997), p. 6.
17. Ibid.
18. Jacqueline Bass and Katrena Henderson, "Leasing: A New Option for Microfinance Institutions," *Bamako 2000: Innovations in Microfinance*, Technical Note No. 6, USAID Microenterprise Best Practices Project, <www.mip.org/pubs/MBP/Leasing—A_New_Option.htm>, viewed 5 March 2001.
19. "FINCA Uganda Launches Pilot Health Program," *Village Bank Notes* (newsletter of FINCA International), fall 2000.
20. Manohar Sharma, "Impact of Microfinance on Poverty Alleviation: What Does Emerging Evidence Indicate?" in *Rural Financial Policies for Food Security of the Poor,* Policy Brief No. 2 (Washington, DC: International Food Policy Research Institute, March 2000), p. 2.
21. Ibid.
22. Freedom from Hunger, *Credit with Education Strategy for Improving Nutrition Security: Impact Evaluation Results from Ghana* (Davis, CA: 1998).
23. Ibid.
24. Craig F. Churchill, "Bulletin Highlights," *MicroBanking Bulletin*, September 2000, p. 30.
25. Ibid.
26. Consultative Group to Assist the Poorest, "When is Microfinance NOT an Appropriate Tool?" <www.cgap.org/html/mi_faq.html>, viewed 5 March 2001.
27. Ibid.
28. Goal for 2005 from David S. Gibbons and Jennifer W. Meehan, CASHPOR Financial and Technical Services, "The Microcredit Summit's Challenge: Working Towards Institutional Financial Self-Sufficiency While Maintaining a Commitment to Serving the Poorest Families," unpublished draft, June 2000, pp. 3–4; 1.2 billion from World Bank, op. cit. note 6.

STOCK MARKETS FOLLOW A ROCKY ROAD (pages 112–13)

1. London Stock Exchange from James Trager, *The People's Chronology* (New York: Henry Holt and Co., 1994), p. 270.
2. "Stocks in Trade," *The Economist*, 13 November 1999, p. 85; trading volume on stock exchanges calculated from data reported by Global Financial Data, <www.globalfindata.com>, viewed 6 December 2000.
3. Alex Berenson, "Market Paying Price for Valuing New-Economy Hope Over Profits," *New York Times*, 21 December 2000; Alex Berenson, "The End of the Party, Or Is It?" *New York Times*, 24 December 2000.
4. William Greider, *One World, Ready Or Not* (New York: Touchstone, 1997), pp. 23, 25; Robert Kuttner, *Everything for Sale: The Virtues and Limits of Markets* (Chicago: University of Chicago Press, 1996), p. 160.
5. Dean Baker, *The Costs of the Stock Market Bubble* (Washington, DC: Center for Economic and Policy Research, 27 November 2000); Floyd Norris, "During 2000, the Bursting Bubble Did Not Hurt All Stocks," *New York Times*, 29 December 2000.
6. Robert J. Shiller, *Irrational Exuberance* (Princeton, NJ: Princeton University Press, 2000), p. xii.
7. International Federation of Stock Exchanges (FIBV), <www.fibv.com>.
8. Changes since 1980 are calculated in inflation-adjusted U.S. dollar terms. Data on a current-dollar basis from Global Financial Data, op. cit. note 2, and from Morgan Stanley Capital International, <www.mscidata.com>.
9. S&P 500 values and 1980–2000 trend calculation based on inflation-adjusted data computed by Robert J. Shiller, Professor of Economics, Yale University, "Online Data," <www.econ.yale.edu/~shiller/data.htm>, viewed 18 November 2000.
10. The data are expressed in 1999 dollars; the current dollar figure for 1990 is $9.4 trillion; 1990 data from World Bank, *World Development Indicators 2000*, CD-ROM (Washington, DC: 2000); 1999 value calculated from FIBV, op. cit. note 7.
11. Leading-country shares calculated from FIBV, op. cit. note 7; developing-country share calculated from World Bank, op. cit. note 10.
12. Data in 1999 dollars; current dollar figure for 1990 is $485 billion; World Bank, op. cit. note 10; FIBV, op. cit. note 7.
13. Merrill Lynch and Gemini Consulting, *World Wealth Report 2000* (London: 2000).
14. Ibid.
15. Ibid.
16. The share of U.S. households owning stocks directly or indirectly rose from 32 percent in 1989 to 40 percent in 1995; Chuck Collins, Betsy Leondar-Wright, and Holly Sklar, *Shifting Fortunes: The*

Perils of the Growing American Wealth Gap (Boston, MA: United for a Fair Economy, 1999), pp. 12–13.

17. "Who Has Benefited from Recent Stock Market Gains," *Economic Snapshots* (Economic Policy Institute, Washington, DC), 17 March 1999.

18. Doug Henwood, "The Boom Years," *The Nation*, 29 March 1999, p. 10.

19. Edward N. Wolff, *Top Heavy: The Increasing Inequality of Wealth in America and What Can Be Done About It* (New York: The New Press, 1996), pp. 2, 7, 11; idem, *Recent Trends in Wealth Ownership, 1983–1998*, Working Paper No. 300 (Blithewood, NY: Jerome Levy Economics Institute, Bard College, April 2000), Table 2.

20. Dean Baker, "Economic Reporting Review," 6 March 2000 and 17 July 2000 editions, distributed by the Center for Economic and Policy Research, Washington, DC, <www.cepr.net>; "Profits Soar, Investment Still Lags," *Economic Snapshots* (Economic Policy Institute, Washington, DC), 26 March 1998; Dean Baker, "Too Much Bubbly on Wall Street?" Center for Economic and Policy Research, <www.cepr.net/too_much_bubbly.htm>, viewed 28 December 2000.

21. The term "irrational exuberance" was used by U.S. Federal Reserve Chairman Alan Greenspan in a speech on 5 December 1996. Robert Shiller discusses a number of underlying factors, including economics, psychology, geopolitics, demographics, and the role of the news media; Shiller, op. cit. note 6.

22. Calculated in inflation-adjusted terms from data made available online by Global Financial Data, op. cit. note 2, using the Japanese consumer price index as provided by the U.S. Bureau of Labor Statistics, "Consumer Price Indexes, Sixteen Countries, 1950–1999," 7 June 2000.

23. Shiller, op. cit. note 9.

24. The ratios reported here were calculated by Robert J. Shiller, Professor of Economics, Yale University. He divided an inflation-adjusted S&P 500 price index by a 10-year moving average of real earnings of companies included in the index, designed to smooth out temporary boosts and slumps in earnings; see Shiller, op. cit. note 9. Other analysts typically use 5-year, 3-year, or 1-year averages to calculate the P-E ratio, but these different methodologies do not change the fundamental picture of an overvalued stock market.

25. As a rough rule of thumb, every dollar in stock market growth generates about 3–4¢ worth of additional consumption; Baker, op. cit. note 5.

26. Dean Baker, "After the Fall," *In These Times*, 12 December 1999, pp. 14–15.

27. "Slowing Down, to What?" *The Economist*, 9 December 2000.

SOCIALLY RESPONSIBLE INVESTING SURGES (pages 114–15)

1. Figures for 1984 and 1999 based on Social Investment Forum, *1999 Report on Socially Responsible Investing Trends in the United States* (Washington, DC: 4 November 1999), pp. 3, 6; 1995 number based on idem, *1995 Trends Report, After South Africa: The State of Socially Responsible Investing in the United States* (Washington, DC: 1995). These figures are in 1999 dollars, and thus differ from the current dollar sums provided in the Social Investment Forum report. For the 1995 number, portfolios that were both screened and involved shareholder advocacy are included in the screened category. For presentational reasons, Figure 1 excludes community investing, which amounted to $5.4 billion in 1999.

2. Social Investment Forum, *1999 Report*, op. cit. note 1, p. 5.

3. Based on ibid., p. 3.

4. Social Investment Organization, *Canadian Social Investment Review 2000* (Toronto: December 2000), p. 4.

5. Ibid.

6. Current number is an Avanzi estimate cited in ibid., p. 16; number for mid-1980s from Avanzi et al., *Green and Ethical Funds in Europe, 1999* (city unknown: Global Partners for Corporate Responsibility Research, date unknown).

7. Avanzi et al., op. cit. note 6.

8. Number of funds and assets under management supplied by Karen Eldridge, Ethical Investment Research Service, e-mail to Maya Brennan, Worldwatch Institute, 13 March 2001.

9. Avanzi et al., op. cit. note 6.

10. For details of the screens employed by U.S.-based funds, see <www.socialinvest.org/areas/sriguide/mfscdetails.htm>.

11. Social Investment Forum, *1999 Report*, op. cit. note 1, p. 10.

12. Ibid.

13. Ibid.

14. Alios Flatz, "Looking Forward—Sustainability and SRI," *Environmental Finance*, November 2000, p. 21.

15. Dow Jones Sustainability Group Index, "Dow Jones Indexes and SAM Sustainability Group Launch Sustainability Indexes," press release

Notes

(Zurich: 8 September 1999); idem, *Key Facts*, <www.sustainability-index.com/description/key_facts.html>, viewed 28 February 2001.

16. "Europe Tops Business Sustainability Index," *Environment News Service*, 20 September 1999.

17. Dow Jones Sustainability Group Index, *Current Licensees*, <www.sustainability-index.com/licensees/current.html>, viewed 28 February 2001.

18. Social Investment Forum, *1999 Report*, op. cit. note 1, p. 15.

19. Ibid.; "Forest Stewardship Council Applauds Home Depot Leadership in Forest Conservation," press release (Washington, DC: 30 August 1999).

20. Shareholder Action Network, "IRRC's Review of Shareholder Actions in 2000," <www.shareholderaction.org/victory.cgi?id=2>, viewed 16 February 2001.

21. "Domini 400 Social Index Trails in 2000, Outperforms S & P in 7 of Last 10 Years," KLD & Co. Inc., <www.kld.com/sitenews.cgi?id=7>, viewed 16 February 2001.

22. Danny Hakim, "On Wall Street, More Investors Push Social Goals," *New York Times*, 11 February 2001.

TOLL OF NATURAL DISASTERS GROWS
(pages 116–17)

1. Economic losses from Munich Reinsurance Company (Munich Re), *Topics: Annual Review of Natural Catastrophes 1999* (Munich: June 2000).

2. Ibid., p. 19.

3. Munich Re, *Topics 2000: Natural Catastrophes— The Current Position* (Munich: December 1999), p. 14.

4. Seth Dunn, "Weather-Related Losses Hit New High," in Lester R. Brown, Michael Renner, and Brian Halweil, *Vital Signs 1999* (New York: W.W. Norton & Company), pp. 74–75, based on data from Munich Re.

5. Munich Re, op. cit. note 1.

6. Munich Re, op. cit. note 3, pp. 64–65.

7. Ibid.

8. Ibid.; homeless from Worldwatch analysis of data from the Centre for Research on the Epidemiology of Disasters (CRED), *EM-DAT Database* (Brussels, Belgium), <www.md.ucl.ac.be/cred/emdat/intro.html>, obtained June 2000.

9. Munich Re, op. cit. note 1, p. 24. "Richest countries" are defined as having a per capita annual income greater than $9,361, while "poorest" are defined as those with less than $760.

10. Munich Re, op. cit. note 1.

11. Ibid.

12. Munich Re, *World Map of Natural Hazards* (Munich: 1998), p. 19.

13. Munich Re, op. cit. note 3, pp. 64–65.

14. Ibid.

15. Ibid.

16. Ibid.

17. Ibid., p. 123; number affected from Red Cross, *World Disasters Report 2000* (Geneva: 2000).

18. Red Cross, *World Disasters Report 1999* (Geneva: 1999), p. 34.

19. Janet N. Abramovitz, "Averting Unnatural Disasters," in Lester R. Brown et al., *State of the World 2001* (New York: W.W. Norton & Company, 2001), pp. 129–30.

20. Joel E. Cohen et al., "Estimates of Coastal Populations," *Science*, 14 November 1997, p. 1209c.

21. Molly O. Sheehan, "Urban Population Continues to Rise," in Lester R. Brown, Michael Renner, and Brian Halweil, *Vital Signs 2000* (New York: W.W. Norton & Company, 2000), pp. 104–05.

22. U.N. Population Division, *World Urbanization Prospects: The 1999 Revision* (New York: 1999).

23. Red Cross, op. cit. note 18, p. 19.

24. Intergovernmental Panel on Climate Change, *Climate Change 2001: The Scientific Basis, Summary for Policymakers*, <www.ipcc.ch>, viewed 23 January 2001.

25. "Impact of Climate Change to Cost World $US 300 Billion a Year," press release (Nairobi: U.N. Environment Programme, 2 February 2001).

26. World Bank/U.S. Geological Survey cited in John Twigg, ed., *Developments at Risk: Natural Disasters and the Third World* (Oxford, U.K.: Oxford Centre for Disaster Studies, UK Coordinated Committee for the IDNDR, May 1998).

WHEAT/OIL EXCHANGE RATE SKYROCKETS (pages 120–21)

1. Wheat and oil prices from International Monetary Fund (IMF), *International Financial Statistics Yearbook* (Washington, DC: various years). The figures for oil do not match data in "Fossil Fuel Use Falls Again" as different sources were used; IMF data were used here so they could be compared with IMF data on wheat prices.

2. Calculated by Worldwatch Institute from IMF, op. cit. note 1.

3. IMF, op. cit. note 1.

4. U.N. Food and Agriculture Organization (FAO), *The State of Food and Agriculture 2000* (Rome: 2000), p. 138.

5. IMF, op. cit. note 1.
6. James J. MacKenzie, "Oil as a Finite Resource: When is Global Production Likely to Peak?" World Resources Institute, <www.wri.org/climate/jm_oil_000.html>, updated March 2000.
7. U.S. Department of Agriculture (USDA), Foreign Agricultural Service, Grain: World Markets and Trade (Washington, DC: December 2000).
8. FAO, op. cit. note 4, p. 140.
9. Production quotient from BP Amoco, BP Amoco Statistical Review of World Energy 2000 (London: Group and Media Publications, June 2000); grain import information in USDA, Production, Supply, and Distribution, electronic database, Washington, DC, updated 12 December 2000.
10. BP Amoco, op. cit. note 9; USDA, op. cit. note 7.
11. IMF, op. cit. note 1.
12. Ibid.
13. USDA, op. cit. note 7.
14. FAO, Food Outlook (Rome: November 2000), p. 3; USDA, op. cit. note 7.
15. BP Amoco, op. cit. note 9.
16. Production cut from U.S. Department of Energy, Energy Information Administration, Monthly Energy Chronology—1999, <www.eia.doe.gov/emeu/cabs/monchron.html>, January 2000; output and price declines from BP Amoco, op. cit. note 9.
17. BP Amoco, op. cit. note 9.
18. Neela Banerjee, "As Oil Prices Decline, Natural Gas Threatens to Upset the Trend," New York Times, 18 December 2000.
19. Neela Banerjee, "As Prices Rise, Nations Ask for More Oil," New York Times, 9 September 2000; John J. Fialka, "Clinton Seeks Saudi Help on Oil Output," Wall Street Journal, 8 September 2000; "EU Executive Urges OPEC Production Hike," Reuters, 7 September 2000.
20. Vanessa Houlder, "Protests Over Fuel Price Rise Dismay Environmental Groups," Financial Times, 8 September 2000.
21. Peter Ford, "Gas Taxes Under Global Attack," Christian Science Monitor, 1 September 2000.
22. Richard W. Stevenson and Neela Banerjee, "Clinton Approves Releasing Some Oil from U.S. Reserve," New York Times, 23 September 2000.
23. Christopher Flavin, "The Real Price of Oil," International Herald Tribune, 28 September 2000.
24. Lester R. Brown, "OPEC Has World Over a Barrel Again," Worldwatch Issue Alert, 8 September 2000.
25. Banerjee, op. cit. note 18; idem, "OPEC Ratifies Oil Cutback; Iraq Remains a Puzzle," New York Times, 18 January 2001; "OPEC Prices Rebound

Sharply from OPEC Slide," Reuters, 19 January 2001.
26. Banerjee, op. cit. note 18.
27. MacKenzie, op. cit. note 6.
28. Peak estimates from ibid.; consumption increases from BP Amoco, op. cit. note 9.
29. Richard A. Kerr, "USGS Optimistic on World Oil Prospects," Science, 14 July 2000, p. 237.
30. Ibid.
31. Kofi Annan, "Who Suffers Most From High Oil Prices?" New Perspectives Quarterly, fall 2000, p. 64; Thalif Deen, "Poorer Nations Spend 60 Billion More on Oil Price Hike," InterPress News Service, 28 December 2000.
32. "IMF: Oil Prices Could Dampen World Growth," Associated Press, CNN on-line news service <www.cnn.com>, 12 October 2000; Alan Friedman, "Oil Prices Cutting Growth, World Bank Chief Warns," International Herald Tribune, 15 September 2000; Stephen Fidler and Alan Beattie, "High Oil Prices Will Hit Developing Nations," Financial Times, 21 September 2000.

COMMODITY PRICES WEAK (pages 122–23)

1. Commodity price index from International Monetary Fund (IMF), International Financial Statistics Yearbooks, 1979 and 2000 editions (Washington, DC: 1979 and 2000), and from idem, International Financial Statistics, February 2001 edition. The IMF price indices are on a current-dollar basis and were deflated using the World Bank's Manufacturing Unit Value (MUV) Index. This is a U.S.-dollar-based index of prices of manufactures exported from the leading industrial exporters (the United States, Japan, Germany, France, and the United Kingdom) weighted proportionately to these countries' exports to developing countries. The resulting values provide a measure of the real purchasing power of commodity prices on the world market. MUV Index values from Donald Mitchell, Development Prospects Group, World Bank, e-mail to author, 26 February 2001.
2. IMF, Yearbooks, op. cit. note 1; idem, February 2001, op. cit. note 1.
3. IMF, Yearbooks, op. cit. note 1; idem, February 2001, op. cit. note 1.
4. IMF, Yearbooks, op. cit. note 1; idem, February 2001, op. cit. note 1.
5. IMF, Yearbooks, op. cit. note 1; idem, February 2001, op. cit. note 1.
6. IMF, Yearbooks, op. cit. note 1; idem, February 2001, op. cit. note 1.

7. World Bank, *Global Economic Prospects and the Developing Countries 2001* (Washington, DC: 2000), p. 25. The World Bank also used the MUV Index to generate real commodity prices indexed to 1900 as equaling 100.

8. World Bank, op. cit. note 7.

9. Ibid.

10. Ibid., pp. 159–68.

11. David Malin Roodman, *The Natural Wealth of Nations* (New York: W.W. Norton & Company, 1998), pp. 54–57; Thomas Michael Power, *Lost Landscapes and Failed Economies* (Washington, DC: Island Press, 1996).

12. World Bank, *World Development Indicators 2000* (Washington, DC: 2000), Tables 4.2 and 4.5.

13. "Vulnerable Single-Commodity-Dependent Economies, 1996," in U.S. Central Intelligence Agency, *Handbook of International Economic Statistics 1998* (Washington, DC: February 1999).

14. Ibid.

15. Ibid.

16. IMF, *Yearbook 2000*, op. cit. note 1; World Bank, *Commodity Trade and Price Trends 1989–91* (Baltimore, MD: Johns Hopkins University Press, 1993).

17. Wheat and oil prices from IMF, *International Financial Statistics Yearbook* (Washington, DC: various years).

18. World Bank, "Change in Commodity Production and Trade," *Global Commodities Markets Online*, <www.worldbank.org/prospects/gcmonline/index.htm>, April 2000, p. 10.

19. Ibid.

20. Ibid.

21. Ibid. The 22 commodities included (in order of their production value) are: crude oil, coal, rice, wheat, maize, hardwood logs, soybeans, cotton, aluminum, sugar, iron ore, copper, bananas, gold, coffee, nitrogen fertilizer, palm oil, natural rubber, phosphate fertilizer, tea, cocoa, and potash fertilizer.

22. World Bank, op. cit. note 18.

23. Ibid.

24. Fileman Torres et al., "Agriculture in the Early XXI Century: Agrodiversity and Pluralism as a Contribution to Address Issues on Food Security, Poverty, and Natural Resource Conservation" (draft) (Rome: Global Forum on Agricultural Research, April 2000), p. 14.

25. The Commodity Futures Trading Commission provides data on the volume growth of U.S. and non-U.S. futures contracts; see <www.cftc.gov/annualreport00>, viewed 11 February 2001.

26. David Malin Roodman, *Still Waiting for the Jubilee: Pragmatic Solutions for the Third World Debt Crisis,* Worldwatch Paper 155 (Washington, DC: Worldwatch Institute, April 2001).

27. World Resources Institute, "Trouble Brewing: The Changing Face of Coffee Production," <www.igc.org/wri/trends/coffee.html>, viewed 14 February 2001.

URBAN RAIL SYSTEMS GATHER STEAM
(pages 126–27)

1. Types of urban rail from American Public Transit Association, "Public Transit Definitions," <www.apta.com>, viewed 29 January 2001.

2. Ibid.

3. Tony Pattison, ed., *Jane's Urban Transport Systems 2000–2001* (London: 2000), pp. 20–24.

4. Ibid.

5. Ibid.

6. Jan Scheurer et al., "Can Rail Pay?" Discussion Paper (Perth, Australia: Institute for Sustainability and Technology Policy (ISTP), Murdoch University, undated).

7. Ibid.

8. Seth Mydans, "Bangkok Opens Skytrain, But Will It Ease Car Traffic?" *New York Times*, 6 December 1999.

9. System length and size from Pattison, op. cit. note 3; riders from David Lamb, "A Heavenly Commute Above Bangkok's Crowded Streets," *Los Angeles Times*, 25 February 2000.

10. System size from Peter Reina, "Delayed Athens Subway Finally Begins Trial Operation," *Engineering News Record*, 20 December 2000; riders from Douglas Frantz, "Parthenon Next, Watch the Closing Doors," *New York Times*, 19 December 2000.

11. Christine Pirovolakis, "New Subway System to Cut Smog, Reduce Traffic Congestion in Capital," *International Environment Reporter*, 16 February 2000, pp. 169–70.

12. European Commission, *Transport in Figures*, <www.europa.eu.int>, viewed 8 December 2000.

13. American Public Transit Association (APTA), "Transit Ridership Report: Third Quarter 2000," 29 December 2000, <www.apta.com/stats/ridershp/index.htm>, viewed 29 January 2001.

14. Craig Savoye, "More Americans Trade Car Keys for Bus Passes," *Christian Science Monitor*, 17 May 2000; Aravind Adiga, "Americans' Love Affair With The Car May Be Starting to Fade," *Financial Times*, 15 August 2000; American Public Transportation Association (APTA), "Public Transportation Ridership Continues to Soar: U.S. Transit Ridership Shows 4.8 Percent Increase in

First Quarter," press release (Washington, DC: 17 July 2000); APTA, "Public Transportation Scored Another Record Year in 2000," press release (Washington, DC: 10 January 2001).

15. United Nations, *World Urbanization Prospects: The 1999 Revision*, Key Findings, <www.undp.org/popin/wdtrends/wdtrends.htm>, viewed 20 January 2001.

16. Estimates of farmland lost to suburban development from American Farmland Trust, *Farming on the Edge* (Washington, DC: March 1997), and from Liu Yinglang, "Legislation to Protect Arable Land," *China Daily*, 15 September 1998.

17. Vehicle contribution to air pollution from U.S. Environmental Protection Agency, *National Pollutant Emissions Trends, 1900–1998* (Research Triangle Park, NC: March 2000), pp. 3-9 to 3-11.

18. International Energy Agency, CO_2 *Emissions from Fuel Combustion* (Paris: Organisation for Economic Co-operation and Development, 1999).

19. Julian Wolinsky, "Light Rail: One Route to Livable Cities," *Railway Age*, July 1999, pp. 47–49.

20. Stacy C. Davis, ed., *Transportation Energy Data Book*, edition 20 (Oak Ridge, TN: Oak Ridge National Laboratory, U.S. Department of Energy, October 2000), p. 2-14.

21. Peter Newman and Jeffrey Kenworthy, *Sustainability and Cities: Overcoming Automobile Dependence* (Washington, DC: Island Press, 1999), pp. 123–24; Jeffrey R. Kenworthy et al., *An International Sourcebook of Automobile Dependence in Cities 1960–1990* (Boulder, CO: University Press of Colorado, 1999), pp. 619–20.

22. Jonas Rabinovitch and Josef Leitman, "Urban Planning in Curitiba," *Scientific American*, March 1996, pp. 26–33; Jonas Rabinovitch, "Innovative Land Use and Public Transport Policy," *Land Use Policy*, vol. 13, no. 1 (1996), pp. 51–67.

23. "World Bank Lending for Transport," <www.worldbank.org/html/fpd/transport/lending.htm>, viewed 7 June 2000. The remaining World Bank transportation lending was split between rural roads (12 percent), multi-modal and sector reform (5 percent), railways and highways (2 percent each), and other projects (1 percent).

24. Magda Stoczkiewicz, "The Conditions Attached to Western Money," *T&E Bulletin* (newsletter of the European Federation for Transport and Environment, Brussels), May 2000, Special Feature on Central and Eastern Europe, p. 2; idem, CEE Bankwatch Network, Brussels, discussion with author, 2 October 2000.

25. Kenworthy et al., op. cit. note 21, pp. 547–50.

26. Ibid.

27. Ibid.

28. "Bangkok's Train, Running on Empty," *The Economist*, 23 December 2000, p. 46.

GASOLINE TAXES VARY WIDELY
(pages 128–29)

1. "Oil Prices and Taxes in Year 2000: An IEA Statistical Fact Sheet," in International Energy Agency (IEA), *Energy Prices and Taxes: Quarterly Statistics, Second Quarter 2000* (Paris: Organisation for Economic Co-operation and Development (OECD), 2000), p. xiii.

2. U.S. Department of Energy (DOE), Energy Information Administration (EIA), "World Oil Supply, 1996–2000," <www.eia.doe.gov/emeu/ipsr/t22.txt>, viewed 20 January 2001. The members of the Organization of Petroleum-Exporting Countries are Algeria, Indonesia, Iran, Iraq, Kuwait, Libya, Nigeria, Qatar, Saudi Arabia, United Arab Emirates, and Venezuela.

3. DOE, op. cit. note 2.

4. DOE, "World Oil Demand, 1996–2000," <www.eia.doe.gov/emeu/ipsr/t24.txt>.

5. DOE, "Crude Oil Prices by Selected Type, 1970-2000," <www.eia.doe.gov/pub/energy.overview>. Prices in Figure 1, in nominal dollars, are for Saudi Arabian Light-34°API, which is one of several varieties of crude oil.

6. National average prices and taxes from IEA, *Monthly Price Statistics: End-User Oil Product Prices and Average Crude Oil Import Costs, October 2000*, <www.iea.org/statist/index.htm>, viwed 2 December 2000; capital city prices and 32¢ untaxed world average price from Dr. Gerhard Metschies, *GTZ Fuel Price Survey 2000* (Eschborn, Germany: Deutsch Gesellschaft für Technische Zusammenarbeit (GTZ), forthcoming), with preliminary data from idem, GTZ, e-mail to author, 28 December 2000.

7. Crude oil from DOE, op. cit. note 2, and from idem, op. cit. note 4; gasoline from idem, "World Apparent Consumption of Refined Petroleum Products, 1997," <www.eia.doe.gov/emeu/international/petroleu.html>, viewed 20 January 2001.

8. American Petroleum Institute, *How Much We Pay For Gasoline: 1999–April 2000 Review* (Washington, DC: May 2000).

9. Metschies, *GTZ Fuel Price Survey 2000*, op. cit. note 6.

10. Vehicle contribution to air pollution from U.S. Environmental Protection Agency, *National Pollu-*

Notes

tant *Emissions Trends, 1900–1998* (Research Triangle Park, NC: March 2000), pp. 3–9 to 3–11.

11. Vehicle contribution to carbon dioxide in IEA, *CO$_2$ Emissions from Fuel Combustion* (Paris: OECD, 1999).

12. "India Fuel Price Rise Seen Eroding Cost Margins," *Bridgenews Global Markets*, 30 September 2000.

13. "Vietnam Press: Hanoi Hikes Gasoline, Gas Oil Prices; Drops Oil Taxes," *Bridgenews Global Markets*, 21 September 2000.

14. Sean Yoong, "Malaysians Grow Anxious Over Imminent Gasoline Price Hike," *Associated Press*, 28 September 2000; Patvinder Singh, "Fuel Subsidy Too High," *New Straits Times-Management Times*, 26 September 2000.

15. "Indonesia Fuel Prices Rise 12 Percent; Minor Protests," *Associated Press*, 1 October 2000.

16. Crude oil prices from DOE, EIA, "International Crude Oil Price Data," <www.eia.doe.gov/emeu/international/petroleu.html#CrudePrices>, viewed 20 January 2001; weak European currency from G. Thomas Sims, "Euro-Zone Prices May Heat Up Soon: Higher Energy Costs, Euro's Weakness Could Spur Consumer-Level Inflation," *Wall Street Journal Europe*, 25 October 2000, and from "Euroshambles," *The Economist*, 4 September 2000.

17. Edmund L. Andrews, "Weiskirchen Journal: At $4 a Gallon, Finding Joy on the Road Not Taken," *New York Times*, 24 March 2000; Douglas Andrew, "Wrapup—More Countries Join European Fuel Price Protests," *Reuters*, 18 September 2000.

18. European Federation for Transport and the Environment, *Fuel Price Protests in the EU: A Commentary* (Brussels, Belgium: September 2000).

19. Netherlands from "Countries Make Concessions to End Protests Over Fuel Costs," *St. Louis Post-Dispatch*, 17 September 2000; Italy from Andrews, op. cit. note 17.

20. Charles Hutzler, "Higher Gas Prices in China Stir Concern," *Associated Press*, 30 June 2000.

21. "Indonesians Riot Over Fuel Prices," *Associated Press*, 3 October 2000; "Indonesian Students Release Hostages Held During Fuel Price Protest," *Bridgenews Global Markets*, 5 October 2000.

22. "Expected Impact of Rising Oil Prices on Asia (Part II)," *Bridgenews Global Markets*, 25 September 2000.

23. Gerhard P. Metschies, *Fuel Prices and Taxation: With Comparative Tables for 160 Countries* (Eschborn, Germany: GTZ, May 1999).

ANTIMICROBIAL RESISTANCE GROWING (pages 132–33)

1. U.S. General Accounting Office (GAO), *Antimicrobial Resistance: Data to Assess Public Health Threat from Bacteria Are Limited* (Washington, DC: April 1999), pp. 11–14; Chris Bright, "Super-bugs Arrive," *World Watch*, March/April 1999, p. 9.

2. Table 1 derived from the following: World Health Organization (WHO), "Global Strategy for Containment of Antimicrobial Resistance" (draft) (Geneva: 27 September 2000), pp. 23–24, 149–50, 153–54; idem, *Overcoming Antimicrobial Resistance* (Geneva: 2000), pp. 20, 22, 26, 28, 38–41, 45; Bright, op. cit. note 1; GAO, op. cit. note 1, p. 7; Daniel Boden et al., "HIV-1 Drug Resistance in Newly Infected Individuals," *Journal of the American Medical Association*, 22/29 September 1999, pp. 1135–41; WHO, *WHO Report on Infectious Diseases: Removing Obstacles to Healthy Development* (Geneva: 1999), pp. 46–49.

3. Jeffrey P. Koplan, Director of the Centers for Disease Control and Prevention, U.S. Department of Health and Human Services, Statement Before the Subcommittee on Labor, Health and Human Services, and Education, Committee on Appropriations, U.S. Senate, Washington, DC, 20 September 2000, p. 1; 1943 from Bright, op. cit. note 1.

4. Stuart B. Levy, "The Challenge of Antibiotic Resistance," *Scientific American*, March 1998.

5. Ibid.; Curtis J. Donskey et al., "Effect of Antibiotic Therapy on the Density of Vancomycin-Resistant Enterococci in the Stool of Colonized Patients," *New England Journal of Medicine*, 28 December 2000, pp. 1925–32.

6. Levy, op. cit. note 4.

7. Ibid.; Amanda Spake, "Losing the Battle of the Bugs," *U.S. News & World Report*, 10 May 1999.

8. Stuart B. Levy, "Antibiotic Resistance: An Ecological Imbalance," in D.J. Chadwick and J. Goode, eds., *Antibiotic Resistance: Origins, Evolutions, Selection and Spread*, Ciba Foundation Symposium 207 (Chichester, West Sussex, U.K.: Wiley, 1997), pp. 1–14.

9. GAO, op. cit. note 1, p. 15; 160 million from Richard P. Wenzel and Michael B. Edmond, "Managing Antibiotic Resistance," *New England Journal of Medicine*, 28 December 2000, p. 1962.

10. GAO, op. cit. note 1, p. 4.

11. Wenzel and Edmond, op. cit. note 9.

12. Jerry Avorn and Daniel H. Solomon, "Cultural and Economic Factors that (Mis)Shape Antibiotic Use: The Nonpharmacologic Basis of Therapeutics,"

Annals of Internal Medicine, 18 July 2000, pp. 128–35.

13. Ibid.

14. Cheapest and most effective from Paul Salopek, "Misuse of Antibiotics Giving Bugs a New Edge," *Chicago Tribune*, 11 January 2000; WHO, *WHO Report on Infectious Diseases*, op. cit. note 2.

15. Salopek, op. cit. note 14.

16. WHO, *Overcoming Antimicrobial Resistance*, op. cit. note 2, p. 42.

17. Estimate of 84 percent from Margaret Mellon, Charles Benbrook, and Karen Lutz Benbrook, *Hogging It: Estimates of Antimicrobial Abuse in Livestock* (Cambridge, MA: Union of Concerned Scientists, January 2001), p. xiii; Alliance for the Prudent Use of Antibiotics, "Why Should You Care About Antibiotic Resistance?" <www.health sci.tufts.edu/apua/Practitioners/RSMarticle.html>, viewed 6 December 2000.

18. Mellon, Benbrook, and Benbrook, op. cit. note 17, p. xii.

19. GAO, *Food Safety: The Agricultural Use of Antibiotics and Its Implications for Human Health* (Washington, DC: April 1999), p. 4; J. Raloff, "Waterways Carry Antibiotic Resistance," *Science News*, 5 June 1999, p. 356.

20. GAO, op. cit. note 1, p. 2.

21. Ibid., p. 4.

22. Laura M. McMurry, Margret Oethinger, and Stuart B. Levy, "Triclosan Targets Lipid Synthesis," *Nature*, 6 August 1998, pp. 531–32.

23. GAO, op. cit. note 1, pp. 9–10.

24. WHO, *Overcoming Antimicrobial Resistance*, op. cit. note 2, p. 42.

25. WHO, *WHO Report on Infectious Diseases*, op. cit. note 2.

26. Jean-François Trape et al., "Impact de la Résistance à la Chloroquine Sur la Mortalité Palustre," *Comptes Rendus de l'Académie des Sciences*, August 1998.

27. Eliot Marshall, "A Renewed Assault on an Old and Deadly Foe," *Science*, 20 October 2000, p. 429; John Rosamond and Aileen Allsop, "Harnessing the Power of the Genome in the Search for New Antibiotics," *Science*, 17 March 2000, pp. 1973–76.

28. "FDA Approves Synercid for Bloodstream Infections," 21 September 1999, and "FDA Approves Zyvox (Linezolid) for Gram-Positive Infections," 18 April 2000, both from *Doctor's Guide to the Internet*, at <www.docguide.com>.

29. Eliot Marshall, "Reinventing an Ancient Cure for Malaria," *Science*, 20 October 2000, pp. 437–38.

30. WHO, *Overcoming Antimicrobial Resistance*, op. cit. note 2, p. 22; Bright, op. cit. note 1, p. 11.

31. GAO, op. cit. note 1, p. 14.

32. WHO, *Overcoming Antimicrobial Resistance*, op. cit. note 2, p. 34.

33. The National Academies, "Better Surveillance and More Awareness Needed to Deal with Rise in Antibiotic Resistance," press release (Washington, DC: 14 May 1998).

34. Ibid.

35. Canada from Marc Kaufman, "Microbes Winning War," *Washington Post*, 13 June 2000; Iceland from David P. Fidler, "Legal Issues Associated with Antimicrobial Drug Resistance," *Emerging Infectious Diseases*, April-June 1998, p. 174.

36. Council of the European Union, "Council Regulation (EC) No 2821/98 of 17 December 1998 Amending, as Regards Withdrawal of the Authorisation of Certain Antibiotics, Directive 70/524/EEC Concerning Additives in Feedingstuffs," <www. europa.eu.int/eur-lex/en/lif/dat/1998/en_ 398R2821.html>, viewed 24 January 2001.

MALARIA'S LETHAL GRIP TIGHTENS
(pages 134–35)

1. World Health Organization (WHO), *The World Health Report 1999* (Geneva: 1999), p. 49.

2. B. Greenwood, "Malaria Mortality and Morbidity in Africa," *Bulletin of the World Health Organization*, August 1999, p. 617.

3. WHO, *WHO Expert Committee on Malaria, Twentieth Report*, Technical Report Series No. 892 (Geneva: 2000), p. 3.

4. UNICEF, "Malaria: Prevention and Treatment," *The Prescriber*, January 2000, pp. 3–5.

5. WHO, *Removing Obstacles to Healthy Development* (Geneva: 1999), p. 8.

6. WHO, op. cit. note 1, p. 50.

7. World Wildlife Fund, *Resolving the DDT Dilemma: Protecting Biodiversity and Human Health* (Washington, DC: June 1998), p. 1.

8. WHO, op. cit. note 1, p. 50.

9. Ibid.

10. David Nabarro, WHO Roll Back Malaria Cabinet Project, "The Roll Back Malaria Partnership and WHO's RBM Project: An Introduction," presentation at the Third Meeting of the Global Roll Back Malaria Partnership, Geneva, December 1999.

11. WHO, op. cit. note 1, p. 50.

12. Ibid.

13. "Malaria: Parasite's Drug-Resistance Threatens Africa," *UN Wire*, 23 March 1999.

14. WHO, "Malaria Endemic Countries," <mosquito. who.intl>, viewed 12 January 2001.

15. "Stowaway Mosquitoes Join International Jet-Set," *RBM News* (Roll Back Malaria Project, Geneva), September 2000, p. 3.

16. Peter B. Bloland, Mary Ettling, and Sylvia Meek, "Combination Therapy for Malaria in Africa: Hype or Hope?" *Bulletin of the World Health Organization*, December 2000, p. 1383.

17. "Preface," *Insecticide Treated Nets in the 21st Century*, Conference Report from the Second International Conference on Insecticide Treated Nets, held in Dar Es Salaam, Tanzania, 10–14 October 1999, <www.lshtm.ac.uk/itd/dcvbu/ malcon/itnpref.html>, viewed 15 January 2001.

18. Yeya Tiémoko Touré and Mario Coluzzi, "The Challenges of Doing More Against Malaria, Particularly in Africa," *Bulletin of the World Health Organization*, December 2000, p. 1376.

19. Ibid.

20. Bloland, Ettling, and Meek, op. cit. note 16, p. 1381.

21. Ibid.

22. Center for International Development (CID) at Harvard University and London School of Hygiene and Tropical Medicine (LSHTM), "Executive Summary for *Economics of Malaria* (forthcoming)," <mosquito.who.int/docs/abuja_sachs 2.doc>, viewed 12 January 2001; WHO, "Economic Costs of Malaria Are Many Times Higher Than Previously Estimated," press release (Geneva: 25 April 2000).

23. CID and LSHTM, op. cit. note 22.

24. Pim Martens and Lisbeth Hall, "Malaria on the Move: Human Population Movement and Malaria Transmission," *Emerging Infectious Diseases*, March-April 2000.

25. UNICEF, op. cit. note 4, p. 2.

26. Thomas C. Nchinda, "Malaria: A Reemerging Disease in Africa," *Emerging Infectious Diseases*, July-September 1998, pp. 398–403; M. A. Malakooti, K. Biomndo, and G. D. Shanks, "Reemergence of Epidemic Malaria in the Highlands of Western Kenya," *Emerging Infectious Diseases*, October-December 1998.

27. UNICEF, op. cit. note 4, p. 2.

28. Renato d'A. Gusmão, "The Control of Malaria in Brazil," paper presented at Contextual Determinants of Malaria, Lusanne, Switzerland, 10–14 May 2000.

29. Bloland, Ettling, and Meek, op. cit. note 16, p. 1379.

30. WHO, op. cit. note 5, p. 46.

31. Bloland, Ettling, and Meek, op. cit. note 16, p. 1380.

32. Ibid.

33. Henk Bouwman, "Malaria Control and the Paradox of DDT," *Africa: Environment & Wildlife*, May 2000, p. 56.

34. Ibid.

35. Ibid.

36. Ibid.

37. U.N. Environment Programme, "Governments Finalize Persistent Organic Pollutants," press release (Geneva: 10 December 2000).

38. "Chapter 3: Current Approaches," *Insecticide Treated Nets in the 21st Century*, op. cit. note. 17, p. 1.

39. "Malaria: Waiver by Uganda of Taxes and Tariffs on Insecticide-Treated Nets," *Weekly Epidemiological Record*, 21 July 2000, pp. 233–34.

40. WHO, op. cit. note 1, pp. 61–62.

41. Gusmão, op. cit. note 28.

BEING OVERWEIGHT NOW EPIDEMIC
(pages 136–37)

1. Worldwatch estimate based on U.N. Administrative Committee on Coordination, Subcommittee on Nutrition (UN ACC/SCN), *Fourth Report on the World Nutrition Situation* (Geneva: January 2000); on World Health Organization (WHO), *Obesity: Preventing and Managing the Global Epidemic* (Geneva: 1997), on K.M. Flegal et al., "Overweight and Obesity in the United States: Prevalence and Trends, 1960–1994," *International Journal of Obesity*, August 1994, pp. 41–43, and on Rafael Flores, Research Fellow, International Food Policy Research Institute (IFPRI), Washington, DC, e-mail to Brian Halweil, Worldwatch Institute, 5 November 1999, and discussion with Gary Gardner, 3 February 2000.

2. WHO, op. cit. note 1, p. xvi.

3. Body mass index is a person's weight in kilos divided by the square of height in meters.

4. Centers for Disease Control and Prevention (CDC), "Prevalence of Overweight and Obesity Among Adults: United States, 1999," <www.cdc. gov/nchs/products/pubs/pubd/hestats/obese/obse 99.htm>, viewed 21 December 2000.

5. Ibid.

6. National Center for Chronic Disease Prevention and Health Promotion, "Preventing Obesity Among Children," *Chronic Disease Notes & Reports*, winter 2000, p. 2.

7. Kumudini Mayur, "Obesity: A Growing Problem,"

The Futurist, October 1999, p. 14.

8. International Obesity Task Force, "Selected Obesity Rates Worldwide," <www.iotf.org>, viewed 23 February 2001.

9. Henri E. Cauvin, "The Fat Epidemic," *New York Times*, 19 December 2000.

10. WHO, op. cit. note 1, p. 30.

11. Catherine Geissler, "China: The Soya Pork Dilemma," *Proceedings of the Nutrition Society*, May 1999, p. 347; Barry M. Popkin et al., "Body Weight Patterns Among the Chinese: Results from the 1989 and 1991 China Health and Nutrition Surveys," *American Journal of Public Health*, May 1995, p. 692.

12. Rajen Anand, Introductory Presentation to Childhood Obesity: Causes and Prevention, symposium sponsored by the Center for Nutrition Policy and Promotion, U.S. Department of Agriculture (USDA), Washington DC, 27 October 1998.

13. Gina Kolata, "While Children Grow Fatter, Experts Search for Solutions," *New York Times*, 19 October 2000.

14. National Center for Chronic Disease Prevention and Health Promotion, op. cit. note 6, p. 1.

15. Adam Drewnowski and Barry M. Popkin, "The Nutrition Transition: New Trends in the Global Diet," *Nutrition Reviews*, February 1997, pp. 32–35.

16. Ibid.

17. Sugar from Katherine S. Tippett and Linda E. Cleveland, "How Current Diets Stack Up," in Elizabeth Frazao, ed., *America's Eating Habits: Changes and Consequences* (Washington, DC: USDA, Economic Research Service, April 1997), p. 65; fat from "Appendix Table 2: US Food Supply: Nutrients and Other Food Components per Capita per Day, 1970–1994," in ibid., p. 433, calculated by multiplying grams of fat by nine and dividing the resulting caloric equivalent by total calories.

18. Judy Putnam and Shirley Gerrior, "Trends in the U.S. Food Supply, 1970–1997," in Frazao, op. cit. note 17, p. 152.

19. National Center for Chronic Disease Prevention and Health Promotion, "Meeting the Challenge of the Obesity Epidemic Among Young People," *Chronic Disease Notes & Reports*, winter 2000, p. 5.

20. CDC, "Physical Activity and Health: A Report of the Surgeon General," <www.cdc.gov/nccdphp/sgr/summ.htm>, viewed 21 December 2000.

21. Peter G. Kopelman, "Obesity as a Medical Problem," *Nature*, 6 April 2000, p. 638.

22. Ibid.

23. WHO, *World Health Report 1998* (Geneva: 1998), p. 87.

24. Graham Colditz, "The Economic Costs of Obesity and Inactivity," Harvard School of Public Health, Cambridge, MA, unpublished manuscript, undated.

25. Cauvin, op. cit. note 9.

26. Denise Grady, "Diabetes Rises: Doctors Foresee a Harsh Impact," *New York Times*, 24 August 2000.

27. Ibid.

28. Ibid.

29. International Diabetes Federation, *Diabetes Around the World* (Brussels: 1998), p. 11.

30. WHO, *Diabetes Database*, <www.who.int/ncd/dia/databases0.htm>, viewed 19 January 2001.

31. John Anderson, Minister for Transport and Regional Services, Government of Commonwealth of Australia, "Launch of the Cycling Australia Strategy," speech at Hilton Hotel Adelaide, 19 February 1999.

32. Kelly D. Brownell, "Get Slim with Higher Taxes," *New York Times*, 15 December 1994.

33. CDC, op. cit. note 4.

HEALTH CARE SPENDING UNEVEN
(pages 138–39)

1. World Health Organization (WHO), *World Health Report 2000* (Geneva: 2000), p. 95; 9.2 percent from World Bank, *World Development Indicators 2000* (Washington, DC: 2000), p. 93.

2. WHO, op. cit. note 1, p. 6.

3. Ibid.

4. Ibid., p. 7.

5. WHO, *Investing in Health Research and Development*, Report of the Ad Hoc Committee on Health Research Relating to Future Intervention Options (Geneva: 1996), p. xxii.

6. Barry R. Bloom, "The Future of Public Health," *Nature*, 2 December 1999, p. C64.

7. WHO, op. cit. note 1, p. 7.

8. Ibid., p. 4.

9. World Bank, op. cit. note 1, p. 92; health care spending figure not weighted for gross domestic product.

10. WHO, op. cit. note 1, pp. 194–95.

11. World Bank, op. cit. note 1, p. 92.

12. Ibid.

13. Ibid.

14. Ibid.

15. WHO, *World Health Report 1999* (Geneva: 1999), pp. 5–7.

16. WHO, op. cit. note 5, p. iii.

17. WHO, *Health and Environment in Sustainable Development: Five Years After the Earth Summit* (Geneva: 1997), p. 173.

18. Ibid.

19. WHO, op. cit. note 1, p. 9.

20. Ibid., pp. 5–6; 1.2 billion from Christopher Flavin, "Rich Planet, Poor Planet," in Lester R. Brown et al., *State of the World 2001* (New York: W.W. Norton & Company, 2001), p. 7.

21. WHO, op. cit. note 5, p. 67.

22. WHO, op. cit. note 1, p. 79.

23. Norman Daniels et al., "Benchmarks of Fairness for Health Care Reform: A Policy Tool for Developing Countries," *Bulletin of the World Health Organization*, June 2000, p. 744.

24. Jeremy Hurst, "Challenges for Health Systems in Member Countries of the Organisation for Economic Co-operation and Development," *Bulletin of the World Health Organization*, June 2000, p. 754; 45 million from Fitzhugh Mullan, "Feeling O.K.? Just Wait," *New York Times*, 22 October 2000, with population data from U.S. Bureau of the Census, *International Data Base*, electronic database, Suitland, MD, updated 10 May 2000.

25. WHO, op. cit. note 1, pp. 6–7; Milt Freudenheim, "Insurers Push Rates Higher for Medicare Supplement," *New York Times*, 8 February 2001.

26. Anders Anell and Michael Willis, "International Comparison of Health Care Systems Using Resource Profiles," *Bulletin of the World Health Organization*, June 2000, p. 772.

27. "Morning Edition," *National Public Radio*, 15 February 2001.

28. World Bank, op. cit. note 1, p. 92.

29. Richard G.A. Feachem, "Health Systems: More Evidence, More Debate," *Bulletin of the World Health Organization*, June 2000, p. 715.

30. Ibid.

31. World Bank, op. cit. note 1, p. 92.

32. Organisation for Economic Co-operation and Development, "Public Expenditure on Health—% Total Expenditure on Health," *OECD Health Data 2000*, <www.oecd.org/els/health/software/fad13. htm>, viewed 1 February 2001.

33. Feachem, op. cit. note 29.

34. Daniels et al., op. cit. note 23, p. 744.

35. David U. Himmelstein et al., "Quality of Care in Investor-Owned vs Not-For-Profit HMOs," *Journal of the American Medical Association*, 14 July 1999, pp. 159–63.

36. WHO, op. cit. note 1, pp. 119–21.

MIGRANTS AND REFUGEES ON THE MOVE (pages 142–43)

1. Frances Williams, "150m Living in Foreign Countries," *Financial Times*, 2 November 2000.

2. International Organization for Migration (IOM), *World Migration Report 2000* (New York: IOM and United Nations, 2000).

3. Ibid.

4. Ibid.

5. Ibid.

6. Ibid.

7. John Gittings, "Population Not Taiwan 'Is China's Challenge,'" (London) *The Guardian*, 20 December 2000.

8. IOM, op. cit. note 2.

9. Ibid.

10. Ibid.

11. Ibid.

12. Ibid.

13. Ibid.

14. Thomas Homer-Dixon, *Environment, Scarcity, and Violence* (Princeton, NJ: Princeton University Press, 1999), p. 110.

15. Douglas Farah, "Refugee Tide Swells in West Africa," *Washington Post*, 13 February 2001.

16. Ibid.

17. IOM, op. cit. note 2.

18. U.N. High Commissioner for Refugees, "Refugees by Numbers 2000," <www.unhcr.ch/un&ref/ numbers/numb2000.pdf>, viewed 5 February 2001.

19. U.S. Committee for Refugees, *World Refugee Survey 2000* (Washington, DC: 2000).

20. IOM, op. cit. note 2.

21. Ibid.

22. Williams, op. cit. note 1.

23. Thalif Deen, "Trafficking in Humans Reprehensible, Says Annan," *IPS Terra Viva*, 14 December 2000.

24. Ibid.

25. IOM, op. cit. note 2.

26. Ibid.

24. World Bank cited in ibid.

WORLD'S MANY LANGUAGES DISAPPEARING (pages 144–45)

1. Michael Krauss, "The World's Languages in Crisis," *Language*, vol. 68, no. 1 (1992), pp. 4–10; David Crystal, *Language Death* (Cambridge, U.K.: Cambridge University Press, 2000).

2. Krauss, op. cit. note 1.

3. Daniel Nettle and Suzanne Romaine, *Vanishing Voices: The Extinction of the World's Languages* (New York: Oxford University Press, 2000), p. 2; Bernice Wuethrich, "Learning the World's

Languages—Before They Vanish," *Science*, 19 May 2000, pp. 1156–59; Jonathan Knight, "Lost for Words," *New Scientist*, 12 August 2000, pp. 16–17.

4. Krauss, op. cit. note 1, p. 7; Nettle and Romaine, op. cit. note 3, p. 29.

5. Summer Institute of Linguistics (SIL), Ethnologue Web site, <www.sil.org/ethnologue/top100.html>, updated February 1999. Figure 1 is based on first-language speakers only. Data points in Figure 1 for Arabic and German include regional variations of the languages.

6. SIL, op. cit. note 5. If all forms of Chinese are included, the total number rises to 1.2 billion.

7. SIL, op. cit. note 5; 4 percent from Barbara F. Grimes, ed., *Ethnologue: Languages of the World*, 14th ed., CD-ROM version (Dallas, TX: SIL, 2000).

8. First-language speakers from SIL, op. cit. note 5; English as a second language from Barbara Wallraff, "What Global Language?" *Atlantic Monthly*, November 2000, p. 56.

9. Krauss, op. cit. note 1; Nettle and Romaine, op. cit. note 3, p. 8.

10. Knight, op. cit. note 3.

11. Grimes, op. cit. note 7.

12. Ibid. Other estimates for India are considerably higher, on the order of 850–1,600 languages.

13. David Harmon, "Sameness and Silence: Language Extinction and the Dawning of a Biocultural Approach to Diversity," *Global Biodiversity*, winter 1998, pp. 7–8.

14. Grimes, op. cit. note 7.

15. Ibid.; Harmon, op. cit. note 13, pp. 7–8.

16. Knight, op. cit. note 3.

17. Nettle and Romaine, op. cit. note 3, p. 9; Krauss, op. cit. note 1, p. 5.

18. Krauss, op. cit. note 1, p. 5.

19. Nettle and Romaine, op. cit. note 3, p. 5.

20. Grimes, op. cit. note 7.

21. Nettle and Romaine, op. cit. note 3, p. 37.

22. Krauss, op. cit. note 1, p. 5; Nettle and Romaine, op. cit. note 3, p. 40.

23. Grimes, op. cit. note 7; "Cultural Losses Seen as Languages Fade," *New York Times*, 16 May 1999.

24. Nettle and Romaine, op. cit. note 3, p. 9.

25. Ibid., p. 40.

26. Grimes, op. cit. note 7.

27. Nettle and Romaine, op. cit. note 3, pp. 12–13; Grimes, op. cit. note 7.

28. Nettle and Romaine, op. cit. note 3, pp. 1–4.

29. Krauss, op. cit. note 1, p. 5.

30. Nettle and Romaine, op. cit. note 3, p. 39.

31. Ibid., pp. 126–49.

32. Rosemarie Ostler, "Disappearing Languages," *Whole Earth*, spring 2000; Grimes, op. cit. note 7; Nettle and Romaine, op. cit. note 3, p. 145.

33. Knight, op. cit. note 3.

34. Jared Diamond, *Guns, Germs and Steel* (New York: W.W. Norton & Company, 1997), pp. 324–29, 367–69.

35. Wuethrich, op. cit. note 3; Grimes, op. cit. note 7.

36. Wuethrich, op. cit. note 3; Knight, op. cit. note 3.

37. Nettle and Romaine, op. cit. note 3, p. 28; Jared Diamond, "Speaking With a Single Tongue," *Discover*, February 1993.

38. Nettle and Romaine, op. cit. note 3, p. 75.

39. Ibid., p. 60.

40. Robert Lee Holtz, "The Struggle To Save Dying Languages," *Los Angeles Times*, 25 January 2000.

41. Ostler, op. cit. note 32.

42. Knight, op. cit. note 3.

RELIGIOUS ENVIRONMENTALISM RISES
(pages 146–47)

1. Martin Palmer, Alliance of Religions and Conservation (ARC), e-mail to author, 9 February 2001.

2. Table 1 based on the following sources: World Wide Fund for Nature (WWF), "Progress Since Assisi: The Faiths' Commitment to the Environment," <www.panda.org/livingplanet/sacred_gifts/assisi.html>, viewed 13 October 2000; The Earth Charter Initiative, "About the Initiative," <www.earthcharter.org/welcome>, viewed 26 January 2001; "Bahá'í Involvement at the Earth Summit," <www.bahai.org/article-1-8-1-20.html>, viewed 24 January 2001; "Towards a Global Ethic (An Initial Declaration)," adopted at the 1993 Parliament of the World's Religions, 28 August–5 September 1993, Chicago, IL; ARC, "History of ARC," <www.icorec.f9.co.uk/history.htm>, viewed 23 January 2001; Bill Broadway, "A New Emphasis on the Nature of Religion," *Washington Post*, 24 October 1998; Harvard University Center for the Study of World Religions, <www.hds.harvard.edu/cswr/ecology>, viewed 26 January 2001; Forum on Religion and Ecology, "General Information," <environment.harvard.edu/religion/Information/home.html>, viewed 27 January 2001; Council for a Parliament of the World's Religions, "A Call to Our Guiding Institutions" (Chicago: 1999); Sushil Sharma, "Religious Leaders Vow to Conserve," *BBC News Online*, 15 November 2000; WWF and ARC, "Sacred Gifts for a Living Planet: Briefing for Journalists," press release (Gland, Switzerland: November 2000).

Notes

3. Todd Wilkinson, "Recruiting in Pews to Save Planet," *Christian Science Monitor*, 23 December 1999; Frances D'Emilio, "Pope Warns Farmers on Technology," *Associated Press*, 13 November 2000.
4. Robert Worth, "For Green Patriarch, Environmentalism Grows Out of Faith," *New York Times*, 14 November 2000.
5. WWF, "The Faiths," <www.panda.org/living planet/sacred_gifts/faiths.html>, viewed 22 January 2001; Marlise Simons, "Eastern Orthodox Leader Preaches Environment," *New York Times*, 6 December 1999.
6. WWF, "Journey to Kathmandu: Sacred Gifts for a Living Planet" (Gland, Switzerland: 2000), p. 2.
7. Ibid.
8. WWF and ARC, op. cit. note 2; U.N. Environment Programme (UNEP), "Global Ministerial Environment Forum Policy Issues: Emerging Policy Issues," discussion paper presented by the Executive Director to the Twenty-first Session of the UNEP Governing Council, Nairobi, 5–9 February 2001, pp. 34–35.
9. WWF and ARC, op. cit. note 2.
10. Devinder Sharma, "India's Disappearing Vultures Cause for Grave Concern," *Environment News Service*, 3 October 2000.
11. Investments from WWF and ARC, op. cit. note 2; Jon Tapper and Kathleen LaCamera, "United Methodist Church Chlorine-free Initiative," feature story (Gland, Switzerland: WWF, September 2000).
12. WWF and ARC, op. cit. note 2.
13. Ibid.
14. WWF, "World Religions Try to Break Deadlock on Climate Change," press release (Gland, Switzerland: 22 November 2000).
15. Germany from UNEP, op. cit. note 8, p. 35; convention from "Episcopal Church Vows to Use Green Power," *Environment News Service*, 19 May 2000.
16. Harvard University Center for the Study of World Religions, "Religions of the World and Ecology," brochure (Cambridge, MA: undated); Jane Lampman, "Earth's Alarm Calls for Deeper Values," *Christian Science Monitor*, 1 October 1998; Colin C. Campbell, "Art and Religion Can Speak With Authority, Too," *Christian Science Monitor*, 22 June 2000.
17. Simons, op. cit. note 5; ""Thou Shalt Not Covet the Earth," *The Economist*, 21 December 1996, pp. 108–09.
18. Wilkinson, op. cit. note 3.
19. WWF, op. cit. note 6.

20. Ibid.
21. Ibid., p. 4.
22. WWF, op. cit. note 5; idem, op. cit. note 6, p, 4.
23. "An Environmental Agenda for the World's Faiths," *New York Times*, 24 October 1998.
24. UNEP, op. cit. note 8; Broadway, op. cit. note 2.
25. UNEP, op. cit. note 8; Lampman, op. cit. note 16.
26. UNEP, op. cit. note 8.

EDUCATION STILL FALLING SHORT OF GOALS (pages 148–49)

1. Based on data in UNESCO, *Statistical Yearbook 1999 Database*, <unescostat.unesco.org/en/stats/stats0.htm>, viewed 26 February 2001.
2. For information on the World Conference on Education for All, see UNICEF, *The State of the World's Children 1999* (New York: 1999), p. 14; UNESCO database, op. cit. note 1.
3. UNESCO database, op. cit. note 1.
4. Ibid.
5. Ibid.
6. Ibid.
7. Ibid.
8. Ibid.
9. UNICEF, op. cit. note 2, p. 19.
10. UNESCO database, op. cit. note 1.
11. Kevin Watkins, *Education Now: Break the Cycle of Poverty*, Executive Summary (London: Oxfam International, 1999).
12. Ibid.
13. UNICEF, op. cit. note 2, p. 57.
14. Ibid., p. 14.
15. Ibid.
16. UNESCO, *Education for All Year 2000 Statistical Assessment, Statistical Document,* <unescostat. unesco.org/en/pub/pub_p/stat.html>, viewed 26 February 2001, p. 10.
17. Ibid., pp. 10–11.
18. UNESCO, *World Education Report 2000* (Paris: 2000), pp. 152–55.
19. "Literacy Up by 10 pc Over Last 6 Years: President," *The Times of India*, 9 September 1999.
20. UNICEF, op. cit. note 2, p. 15.
21. Ibid.
22. Ibid., p. 25.
23. "HIV/AIDS: 42 Million AIDS Orphans By 2010, UN Official Says," *UN Wire*, <www.unfoundation. org/unwire/archives/UNWIRE000609.cfm#>, viewed 26 February 2001.
24. Slide show, Joint United Nations Programme on HIV/AIDS (UNAIDS), <www.unaids.org/publications/documents/economics/agriculture/adf%5F

slides2.ppt>, viewed 25 February 2001.

25. "Education Can Help Save Young People from AIDS, UNAIDS Chief Says," press release (Geneva: UNAIDS, 26 April 2000).

26. Ibid.

27. Ibid.

28. UNICEF, op. cit. note 2, pp. 80–81.

29. Ibid., p. 81.

30. "Education in Free Fall: A Region in the Midst of Transition," in UNICEF, op. cit. note 2, pp. 16–17.

SOCIAL SECURITY FACING CHALLENGES
(pages 150–51)

1. Wouter van Ginneken, ed., *Social Security for the Informal Sector: Investigating the Feasibility of Pilot Projects in Benin, India, El Salvador, and Tanzania,* Issues in Social Protection, Discussion Paper No. 5 (Geneva: International Labour Organization (ILO), 1997).

2. Ibid.

3. Wouter van Ginneken, "Overcoming Social Exclusion," in *Social Security for the Excluded Majority* (Geneva: ILO, 1999), pp. 1, 33.

4. John Dixon, *Social Security in Global Perspective* (London: Praeger, 1999), p. 2.

5. Ibid., pp. 41–43.

6. Social Security Administration, "Guide to Reading the Country Summaries," in *Social Security Programs Around the World, 1999,* <www.ssa.gov/statistics/ssptw>, viewed 6 February 2001, p. 5.

7. Ibid., pp. 4–5.

8. Ibid., pp. vi–vii.

9. Ibid.

10. Ibid.

11. Dixon, op. cit. note 4, p. 207. Social security systems can be evaluated using several criteria, including performance (percentage of population covered, for example), efficiency (administrative cost per benefit dispersed), inputs (such as expenditures as a share of gross national product), or design. Design criteria probably provide the best evaluation, but they have their weaknesses: what is promised in the design is not always what is delivered. This is especially a problem in post-Soviet Europe and Asia, where economic difficulties have made fulfillment of government commitments difficult.

12. Dixon, op. cit. note 4, pp. 199–203.

13. Ibid., pp. 232–40.

14. Ibid., p. 221.

15. Ibid.

16. Van Ginneken, op. cit. note 3, p. 2.

17. Dixon, op. cit. note 4, p. 79.

18. Ibid., p. 110.

19. Worldwatch calculation based on data in ibid., pp. 106–10.

20. Ibid., p. 110.

21. United Nations, *World Population Prospects: The 1998 Revision* (New York: December 1998).

22. Ibid.

23. Ibid.

24. Ibid.

25. Denis Latulippe, *Effective Retirement Age and Duration of Retirement in the Industrial Countries Between 1950 and 1990,* Issues in Social Protection, Discussion Paper No. 2 (Geneva: ILO, July 2000).

26. Dixon, op. cit. note 4, p. 99.

27. Van Ginneken, op. cit. note 3, p. 3.

28. Ibid.

29. Van Ginneken, op. cit. note 1.

30. Maria Amparo Cruz-Saco Oyague, "Introduction: Context and Typology of Reform Models," in Maria Amparo Cruz-Saco and Carmelo Mesa-Lago, eds. *Do Options Exist? The Reform of Pension and Health Care Systems in Latin America* (Pittsburgh, PA: University of Pittsburgh Press, 1998), pp. 1–34.

31. Dixon, op. cit. note 4, p. 280.

32. Ibid., pp. 50, 51, 280.

33. Ibid.

THE VITAL SIGNS SERIES

Some topics are included each year in *Vital Signs*; others are covered only in certain years. The following is a list of topics covered in *Vital Signs* thus far, with the year or years they appeared indicated in parentheses. Those marked with a bullet (♦) appeared in Part One, which includes time series of data on each topic.

AGRICULTURE and FOOD

Agricultural Resources
- ♦ Fertilizer Use (1992–2001)
- ♦ Grain Area (1992–93, 1996–97, 1999–2000)
- ♦ Grain Yield (1994–95, 1998)
- ♦ Irrigation (1992, 1994, 1996–99)
- Livestock (2001)
- Organic Agriculture (1996, 2000)
- Pesticide Control (1996)
- ♦ Pesticide Trade (2000)
- Transgenic Crops (1999–2000)
- Urban Agriculture (1997)

Food Trends
- ♦ Aquaculture (1994, 1996, 1998)
- Biotech Crops (2001)
- ♦ Coffee (2001)
- ♦ Fish (1992–2000)
- ♦ Grain Production (1992–2001)
- ♦ Grain Stocks (1992–99)
- ♦ Grain Used for Feed (1993, 1995–96)
- ♦ Meat (1992–2000)
- ♦ Milk (2001)
- ♦ Soybeans (1992–2001)

THE ECONOMY

Resource Economics
- ♦ Aluminum (2001)
- Arms and Grain Trade (1992)

- Commodity Prices (2001)
- Fossil Fuel Subsidies (1998)
- ♦ Gold (1994, 2000)
- Metals Exploration (1998)
- ♦ Paper (1993, 1994, 1998–2000)
- Paper Recycling (1994, 1998, 2000)
- ♦ Roundwood (1994, 1997, 1999)
- Seafood Prices (1993)
- ♦ Steel (1993, 1996)
- Steel Recycling (1992, 1995)
- Subsidies for Environmental Harm (1997)
- Wheat/Oil Exchange Rate (1992–93, 2001)

World Economy and Finance
- ♦ Agricultural Trade (2001)
- Aid for Sustainable Development (1997)
- ♦ Developing-Country Debt (1992–95, 1999–2001)
- Environmental Taxes (1996, 1998, 2000)
- Food Aid (1997)
- ♦ Global Economy (1992–2001)
- Microcredit (2001)
- Private Finance in Third World (1996, 1998)
- R&D Expenditures (1997)
- Socially Responsible Investing (2001)
- Stock Markets (2001)
- ♦ Trade (1993–96, 1998–2000)
- Transnational Corporations (1999–2000)
- ♦ U.N. Finances (1998–99, 2001)

Other Economic Topics
- ♦ Advertising (1993, 1999)
  - Cigarette Taxes (1993, 1995, 1998)
  - Government Corruption (1999)
  - Health Care Spending (2001)
  - Pharmaceutical Industry (2001)
  - PVC Plastic (2001)
  - Satellite Monitoring (2000)
- ♦ Storm Damages (1996–2001)
- ♦ Television (1995)

ENERGY and ATMOSPHERE

Atmosphere
- ♦ Carbon Emissions (1992, 1994–2001)
- ♦ CFC Production (1992–96, 1998)
- ♦ Global Temperature (1992–2001)

Fossil Fuels
- ♦ Carbon Use (1993)
- ♦ Coal (1993–96, 1998)
- ♦ Fossil Fuels Combined (1997, 1999–2001)
- ♦ Natural Gas (1992, 1994–96, 1998)
- ♦ Oil (1992–96, 1998)

Renewables, Efficiency, Other Sources
- ♦ Compact Fluorescent Lamps (1993–96, 1998–2000)
- ♦ Efficiency (1992)
- ♦ Geothermal Power (1993, 1997)
- ♦ Hydroelectric Power (1993, 1998)
- ♦ Nuclear Power (1992–2001)
- ♦ Solar Cells (1992–2001)
- ♦ Wind Power (1992–2001)

THE ENVIRONMENT

Animals
- Amphibians (1995, 2000)
- Aquatic Species (1996)
- Birds (1992, 1994, 2001)
- Marine Mammals (1993)
- Primates (1997)
- Vertebrates (1998)

Natural Resource Status
- Coral Reefs (1994, 2001)
- Forests (1992, 1994–98)
- Groundwater Quality (2000)
- Ice Melting (2000)
- Ozone Layer (1997)
- Water Scarcity (1993, 2001)
- Water Tables (1995, 2000)
- Wetlands (2001)

Natural Resource Uses
- Biomass Energy (1999)
- Dams (1995)
- Ecosystem Conversion (1997)
- Energy Productivity (1994)
- Organic Waste Reuse (1998)
- Soil Erosion (1992, 1995)
- Tree Plantations (1998)

Pollution
- Acid Rain (1998)
- Algal Blooms (1999)
- Forest Damage from Air Pollution (1993)
- Lead in Gasoline (1995)
- Nuclear Waste (1992, ♦1995)
- Pesticide Resistance (♦1994, 1999)
- ♦ Sulfur and Nitrogen Emissions (1994–97)
- Urban Air Pollution (1999)

Other Environmental Topics
- Environmental Treaties (♦1995, 1996, 2000)
- Nitrogen Fixation (1998)
- Pollution Control Markets (1998)

THE MILITARY

- ♦ Armed Forces (1997)
  - Arms Production (1997)
- ♦ Arms Trade (1994)
  - Landmines (1996)
- ♦ Military Expenditures (1992, 1998)
- ♦ Nuclear Arsenal (1992–96, 1999, 2001)
  - Peacekeeping Expenditures (1993, ♦1994–2001)

♦ Wars (1995, 1998–2001)
  Small Arms (1998–99)

SOCIETY and HUMAN WELL-BEING

Health
  ♦ AIDS/HIV Incidence (1994–2001)
    Breast and Prostate Cancer (1995)
  ♦ Child Mortality (1993)
  ♦ Cigarettes (1992–2001)
    Drug Resistance (2001)
    Endocrine Disrupters (2000)
    Hunger (1995)
  ♦ Immunizations (1994)
  ♦ Infant Mortality (1992)
    Infectious Diseases (1996)
    Life Expectancy (1994, ♦1999)
    Malaria (2001)
    Malnutrition (1999)
    Noncommunicable Diseases (1997)
    Obesity (2001)
  ♦ Polio (1999)
    Safe Water Access (1995)
    Sanitation (1998)
    Traffic Accidents (1994)
    Tuberculosis (2000)

Reproduction and Women's Status
    Family Planning Access (1992)
    Female Education (1998)
    Fertility Rates (1993)
    Maternal Mortality (1992, 1997)
  ♦ Population Growth (1992–2001)
    Sperm Count (1999)
    Violence Against Women (1996)
    Women in Politics (1995, 2000)

Social Inequities
    Homelessness (1995)
    Income Distribution (1992, 1995, 1997)
    Language Extinction (1997, 2001)
    Literacy (1993, 2001)
    Prison Populations (2000)
    Social Security (2001)
    Unemployment (1999)

Other Social Topics
    Aging Populations (1997)
    Fast-Food Use (1999)
    Nongovernmental Organizations (1999)
    Refugees (♦1993–2000, 2001)
    Religious Environmentalism (2001)
  ♦ Urbanization (1995–96, 1998, 2000)
    Voter Turnouts (1996)
    Wind Energy Jobs (2000)

TRANSPORTATION and COMMUNICATION

  ♦ Air Travel (1993, 1999)
  ♦ Automobiles (1992–2001)
  ♦ Bicycles (1992–2001)
    Computer Production and Use (1995)
    Gas Prices (2001)
    Electric Cars (1997)
  ♦ Internet (1998–2000)
  ♦ Motorbikes (1998)
  ♦ Satellites (1998–99)
  ♦ Telephones (1998–2000)
  ♦ Tourism (2000)
    Urban Transportation (1999, 2001)